Learning Dart

Learn how to program applications with Dart 1.0,
a language specifically designed to produce
better-structured, high-performance applications

Ivo Balbaert

Dzenan Ridjanovic

PUBLISHING

BIRMINGHAM - MUMBAI

Learning Dart

First published: December 2013

Production Reference: 1191213

Published by Packt Publishing Ltd.
Livery Place
35 Livery Street
Birmingham B3 2PB, UK.

ISBN 978-1-84969-742-2

www.packtpub.com

Cover Image by Javier Barría C (jbarriac@yahoo.com)

Credits

Authors
Ivo Balbaert
Dzenan Ridjanovic

Reviewers
Sergey Akopkokhyants
Tom Alexander
Christophe Herreman
Yehor Lvivski
Christopher McGuire

Acquisition Editors
Saleem Ahmed
Rebecca Youe

Lead Technical Editor
Neeshma Ramakrishnan

Technical Editors
Venu Manthena
Amit Singh
Hardik B. Soni
Gaurav Thingalaya

Copy Editors
Roshni Banerjee
Brandt D'Mello
Tanvi Gaitonde
Shambhavi Pai
Lavina Pereira
Adithi Shetty
Laxmi Subramanian

Project Coordinators
Apeksha Chitnis
Wendell Palmer

Proofreader
Clyde Jenkins

Indexer
Monica Ajmera Mehta

Graphics
Ronak Dhruv
Disha Haria

Production Coordinator
Pooja Chiplunkar

Cover Work
Pooja Chiplunkar

About the Authors

Ivo Balbaert is currently a lecturer for (Web) Programming and Databases at CVO Antwerpen (www.cvoantwerpen.be), a community college in Belgium. He received a Ph.D. in Applied Physics from University of Antwerp in 1986. He worked for 20 years in the software industry as a developer and consultant in several companies, and for 10 years as a project manager at the University Hospital of Antwerp. From 2000 onward, he switched to partly teaching and partly developing software (KHM Mechelen, CVO Antwerp). He also wrote an introductory book in Dutch about developing in Ruby and Rails: *Programmeren met Ruby en Rails, Van Duuren Media*, ISBN: 978-90-5940-365-9, 2009, 420 p. In 2012, he authored a book on the Go programming language: *The Way To Go, IUniverse*, ISBN: 978-1-4697-6917-2, 600 p.

Dzenan Ridjanovic is a university professor who is planning his early retirement to focus on the development of web applications with Dart, HTML5, web components, and NoSQL databases. For more than 10 years, he was a Director of Research and Development in the Silverrun team (http://www.silverrun.com/), which created several commercial tools for analysis, design, and development of data-driven applications. He was a principal developer of Modelibra (http://www.modelibra.org/) tools and frameworks for model-driven development in Java. Recently, he has been developing the Dartling framework for design and code generation of Dart models. His projects are at GitHub (https://github.com/dzenanr), where he is considered a Dart expert (http://osrc.dfm.io/dzenanr). He writes about his projects at *On Dart* blog (http://dzenanr.github.io/). His courses are available at *On Dart Education* (http://ondart.me/). He markets his Dart efforts at On Dart G+ Page (https://plus.google.com/+OndartMe). Dzenan Ridjanovic wrote a book in 2009, under the *Creative Commons License*, entitled *Spiral Development of Dynamic Web Applications: Using Modelibra and Wicket* (http://www.modelibra.org/).

I want to thank my spouse Amra for her constant care and support, the Dart team for creating a missing web language, and Ivo Balbaert for his productive writing.

About the Reviewers

Sergey Akopkokhyants is a Java certified technical architect with more than 19 years of experience in designing and developing client and server-side applications. For the last five years, Sergey has been responsible for customizing and producing web-oriented applications for wholesale business management solutions projects for several worldwide mobile communications companies. Sergey is passionate about web designing and development, and believes that an investment in bleeding edge technologies will always give a return to both the individual and the organization. He is also the author and owner of several open source projects on GitHub, including the Dart Web Toolkit (DWT). Sergey likes sharing knowledge and experience with others, and helping them to increase their skills and productivity.

Tom Alexander graduated with a Computer Science degree from Rensselaer Polytechnic Institute. He currently works for TripAdvisor as a software engineer, where he works on the mobile version of the website.

Christophe Herreman is a versatile and passionate software architect with more than 10 years of professional experience. He is also a Certified Scrum Master and has general knowledge of many tools and platforms. For the last few years, Christophe has mainly worked on web-based applications in a variety of domains, such as healthcare, education, traffic control, and electronics. His main tasks have been: architecture and development of the client software using Flex, ActionScript and Adobe AIR, HTML, JavaScript, and client-server integrations with Java, .NET, and PHP; automating the build process with tools such as Maven, Ant, Batch, Jenkins/ Hudson; setting up unit, integration and functional tests; reviewing, auditing, and improving existing codebases; coaching and mentoring teams. Christophe is also a regular speaker at conferences and user groups, as well as an active open source contributor. He's the founder of the Spring ActionScript framework and the AS3Commons project and a committer on the Apache Flex project. In the past, he has lectured on software and web development at the University College of West-Flanders, Belgium. Together with his partner, he runs the Belgium-based software consultancy firm Stack & Heap (www.stackandheap.com).

Yehor Lvivski thinks that it's never too late to learn and always tries to know the current trends of the web and predict the future ones. He has always wanted to be a designer, but later found an area where he can combine both his design and engineering skills. For the last six years, Yehor was involved in game development, added a nice interactive UI for a search engine, created his own CSS animations library, and several open source projects. He really likes to create a great visual experience. Yehor now works for SpatialKey, and is involved in changing the future of data analysis. Not only does he like to create things, but he's also an active speaker at different local and global conferences. He believes that knowledge sharing is the key point to evolution.

Christopher McGuire is an application developer currently working in Glasgow, Scotland. He graduated from the University of Strathclyde in 2011 with a B.Sc (Hons) in Computer Science and currently works for an investment bank. Chris has experience in developing Enterprise Standard Server applications, primarily using Java and other object oriented-languages, while also developing web/mobile front-end applications using native Android/iOS and HTML5. From this, he has multiple applications published on the Google Play market. In addition to this, Chris has developed multiple web applications and has a strong interest in new and emerging technologies, which have led him to become part of the Dart community and develop several more applications using this language.

www.PacktPub.com

Support files, eBooks, discount offers and more

You might want to visit www.PacktPub.com for support files and downloads related to your book.

Did you know that Packt offers eBook versions of every book published, with PDF and ePub files available? You can upgrade to the eBook version at www.PacktPub.com and as a print book customer, you are entitled to a discount on the eBook copy. Get in touch with us at service@packtpub.com for more details.

At www.PacktPub.com, you can also read a collection of free technical articles, sign up for a range of free newsletters and receive exclusive discounts and offers on Packt books and eBooks.

http://PacktLib.PacktPub.com

Do you need instant solutions to your IT questions? PacktLib is Packt's online digital book library. Here, you can access, read and search across Packt's entire library of books.

Why Subscribe?

- Fully searchable across every book published by Packt
- Copy and paste, print and bookmark content
- On demand and accessible via web browser

Free Access for Packt account holders

If you have an account with Packt at www.PacktPub.com, you can use this to access PacktLib today and view nine entirely free books. Simply use your login credentials for immediate access.

Table of Contents

Preface

Developing a web application or software in general, is still a challenging task. There is a client/browser side and a server side with databases. There are many different technologies to master in order to feel comfortable with a full client/server stack. There are different frameworks with different objectives. There are also different programming languages that a developer must learn each one more suitable either for the server or the client side.

Learning Dart will help a developer to become more focused by using Dart both for clients and servers. Using the same language will ensure that a developer will lose neither performance nor flexibility. Dart can be used within its virtual machine, or its code may be compiled to JavaScript. In both cases, the performance benchmarks show promising scores (`https://www.dartlang.org/performance/`). Dart is both an object-oriented and a functional language. With Dart, a mix of both approaches is possible, providing great professional freedom and a programming background flexibility. In addition, Dart provides many libraries and tools (`http://pub.dartlang.org/`) that allow a developer to focus on the task at hand and not be concerned with all the aspects of software development.

With `Polymer.dart` (`https://www.dartlang.org/polymer-dart/`), a new approach towards developing web applications with web components will be discovered, allowing a developer to divide a web page into sections and re-use an already developed and tested web component for each section. In the near future, different catalogs of web components will appear, enabling an engineering approach to software development after waiting for many years. A web component may be composed from other web components. It may pass data to its components. A web component may also inherit its behavior from another web component. It may access an already instantiated web component.

Spiral approach

The spiral approach to software learning and development, which preserves a project history as a series of code snapshots or spirals, is used in this book.

The following three points are important in the spiral approach:

- The history of development is preserved
- Simple solutions are provided first; later on, these solutions may be replaced by more advanced solutions
- Only concepts used in a spiral are explained

All of these three points are important in teaching and learning technologies.

Learning new software concepts and technologies is a challenging task. Learning in spirals, from simple to more advanced concepts but with concrete software applications, helps readers get a reasonable confidence level early on, and motivates them to learn by providing more useful applications. With each new spiral, the project grows and new concepts are introduced. A new spiral is explained with respect to the previous one. The difference between two consecutive spirals is that the next spiral has the new code introduced and the old code modified or deleted. This is named learning by anchoring to what we already understand. With a new spiral, we can come back to what we did previously and improve it. In this way, learning in spirals can touch the same topic several times, but each time with more details in a better version.

What this book covers

Learning Dart has 12 chapters. It begins with basic elements of Dart and it ends with a client/server application that uses MongoDB (http://www.mongodb.org/) for data persistence on the server side.

Chapter 1, Dart – A Modern Web Programming Language, helps you understand what Dart is all about. Dart is presented as a major step forward in the web programming arena.

Chapter 2, Getting to Work with Dart, lets you get a firm grasp on how to program in Dart. The code and data structures in Dart, and its functional principles, are explained by exploring practical examples.

Chapter 3, Structuring Code with Classes and Libraries, lets you understand how to use Dart classes to organize code. Dart libraries are introduced to show how complex software may be packaged.

Chapter 4, Modeling Web Applications with Model Concepts and Dartlero, enables you to design a small model graphically in the Model Concepts tool, which is developed in Dart. A model is then represented in Dart as several classes that inherit some data and operations from classes of the Dartlero model framework, also developed in Dart.

Chapter 5, Handling the DOM in a New Way, helps you to learn how to access HTML elements in Dart. Some elements will even be created in Dart and placed properly in the Document Object Model (DOM) of a web page. Dart will also handle user events, such as a click on a button. Finally, you will be able to create a simple game in Dart.

Chapter 6, Combining HTML Forms with Dart, lets you enter data in a form that will be validated by HTML5 and Dart. Then, the valid data will be saved in the local storage of a browser.

Chapter 7, Building Games with HTML5 and Dart, lets you create, step-by-step, a well-known memory game based on what you have learned already. Each step will be a new spiral represented as a complete project in Dart Editor. The first spiral will draw only a rectangle, while the last spiral will be a game that you may show to your friends.

Chapter 8, Developing Business Applications with Polymer Web Components, helps you to create several web components by using `Polymer.dart`. Those web components will be used in different sections of a single-page application. Three different projects with web components will be presented in this chapter.

Chapter 9, Modeling More Complex Applications with Dartling, explains how a graphical model can be transformed into a JSON document and then used to generate a complete model in Dart, by using the Dartling domain model framework together with its tools. Dartling follows the Model View Controller (MVC) pattern to separate a model from its views.

Chapter 10, MVC Web and UI Frameworks in Dart – An Overview, introduces you to different frameworks already developed in Dart. Because Dart is a brand new language, those frameworks are at early stages of their useful life.

Chapter 11, Local Data and Client-Server Communication, explains how you can store application data in a local database named IndexedDB, which will then be sent as a JSON document to a Dart server. Asynchronous programming with futures will also be covered in this chapter.

Chapter 12, Data-driven Web Applications with MySQL and MongoDB, explains how you can use database drivers to save (and load) data to (and from) a relational database and a NoSQL database. Data sent from a browser as a JSON document will easily be saved in MongoDB in the same JSON form. Two clients will exchange data with the server so that both of them will be up-to-date.

What you need for this book

In order to benefit from this book, you need to have some basic experience in programming. It is also useful to have some understanding of HTML and CSS. What you really need to bring is your enthusiasm to learn how to become a web developer of the future. All the software used in the book are freely available on the Web:

- `https://www.dartlang.org/`

- `https://github.com/Ivo-Balbaert/learning_dart`

- `https://github.com/dzenanr`

- `http://www.mysql.com/`

- `http://www.mongodb.org/`

One of the authors has already taught three times an introductory course to programming with some material from this book. The book also has its own website at `http://www.learningdart.org/`. Other educational resources for Dart can be found at `http://ondart.me/`.

Who this book is for

The book is intended for web application programmers, game developers, and other software engineers. Because of its dual focus (Dart and HTML5), the book can appeal to both web developers who want to learn a modern way of developing web applications, and to developers who seek guidance on how to use HTML5. The audience would include mainstream programmers coming with an object-oriented background (Java, .NET, C++, and so on) as well as web programmers using JavaScript, who seek a more structured and tooled way of developing. Both groups would leverage their existing knowledge and expertise: the first, by offering them a way of developing modern web applications using techniques they already know, and the second, by giving them a more productive and engineered way of developing (business) web applications. The article at the following link describes well what Dart has to offer for the web developers of the future: `http://news.cnet.com/8301-1023_3-57613760-93/mixbook-sees-perfect-storm-for-googles-dart-language-q-a/`.

Conventions

In this book, you will find a number of styles of text that distinguish among different kinds of information. Here are some examples of these styles, and an explanation of their meaning.

Code words in text, database table names, folder names, filenames, file extensions, pathnames, dummy URLs, user input, and Twitter handles are shown as follows: "The `calculateRabbits` function calculates and returns an integer value; this is indicated by the word `int` preceding the function name."

A block of code is set as follows:

```
void main() {
  print("The number of rabbits increases as:\n");
  for (int years = 0; years <= NO_YEARS; years++) {
    rabbitCount = calculateRabbits(years);
    print("After $years years:\t $rabbitCount animals");
}
```

When we wish to draw your attention to a particular part of a code block, the relevant lines or items are set in bold:

```
void main() {
  print("The number of rabbits increases as:\n");
  for (int years = 0; years <= NO_YEARS; years++) {
    rabbitCount = calculateRabbits(years);
    print("After $years years:\t $rabbitCount animals");
}
```

Any command-line input or output is written as follows:

```
git clone git://github.com/dzenanr/collision_clones.git
```

New terms and **important words** are shown in bold. Words that you see on the screen, in menus or dialog boxes for example, appear in the text like this: "You can change this behavior by navigating to **Tools** | **Preferences** | **Run and Debug**, and change the **Break on Exceptions** to **None**."

 Warnings or important notes appear in a box like this.

 Tips and tricks appear like this.

Reader feedback

Feedback from our readers is always welcome. Let us know what you think about this book—what you liked or may have disliked. Reader feedback is important for us to develop titles that you really get the most out of.

To send us general feedback, simply send an e-mail to feedback@packtpub.com, and mention the book title via the subject of your message.

If there is a topic that you have expertise in and you are interested in either writing or contributing to a book, see our author guide on www.packtpub.com/authors.

Customer support

Now that you are the proud owner of a Packt book, we have a number of things to help you to get the most from your purchase.

Downloading the example code

You can download the example code files for all Packt books you have purchased from your account at http://www.packtpub.com. If you purchased this book elsewhere, you can visit http://www.packtpub.com/support and register to have the files e-mailed directly to you.

Errata

Although we have taken every care to ensure the accuracy of our content, mistakes do happen. If you find a mistake in one of our books—maybe a mistake in the text or the code—we would be grateful if you would report this to us. By doing so, you can save other readers from frustration and help us improve subsequent versions of this book. If you find any errata, please report them by visiting http://www.packtpub.com/submit-errata, selecting your book, clicking on the **errata submission form** link, and entering the details of your errata. Once your errata are verified, your submission will be accepted and the errata will be uploaded on our website, or added to any list of existing errata, under the Errata section of that title. Any existing errata can be viewed by selecting your title from http://www.packtpub.com/support.

Piracy

Piracy of copyright material on the Internet is an ongoing problem across all media. At Packt, we take the protection of our copyright and licenses very seriously. If you come across any illegal copies of our works, in any form, on the Internet, please provide us with the location address or website name immediately so that we can pursue a remedy.

Please contact us at copyright@packtpub.com with a link to the suspected pirated material.

We appreciate your help in protecting our authors, and our ability to bring you valuable content.

Questions

You can contact us at questions@packtpub.com if you are having a problem with any aspect of the book, and we will do our best to address it.

1
Dart – A Modern Web Programming Language

In this chapter we will investigate:

- What Dart is all about
- Why it is a major step forward in the web programming language arena

We will get started with the Dart platform and have a look at its tools. Soon enough we will be programming and taking a dive in a simple functional todo list program, so that you realize how familiar it all is.

What is Dart?

Dart is a new general and open source programming language with a vibrant community developed by Google Inc. and its official website is `https://www.dartlang.org`. It was first announced as a public preview on October 10, 2011. Dart v1.0, the first production release, came out on November 14, 2013, guaranteeing a stable platform upon which production-ready apps can be built. World class language designers and developers are involved in this project, namely, *Lars Bak* and *Kasper Lund* (best known from their V8 JavaScript engine embedded in the Chrome browser, which revolutionized performance in the JavaScript world) and *Gilad Bracha* (a language theorist known from the development of the Strongtalk and Newspeak languages and from the Java specification). Judged by the huge amount of resources and the number of teams working on it, it is clear that Google is very serious about making Dart a success.

 Take your time to familiarize yourself with the site `dartlang.org`. It contains a wealth of information, code examples, presentations, and so on to supplement this book, and we will often reference it.

Dart looks instantly familiar to the majority of today's programmers coming from a Java, C#, or JavaScript/ActionScript background; you will feel at ease with Dart. However, this does not mean it is only a copy of what already exists; it takes the best features of the statically typed "Java-C#" world and combines these with features more commonly found in dynamic languages such as JavaScript, Python, and Ruby. On the nimble, dynamic side Dart allows rapid prototyping, evolving into a more structured development familiar to business app developers when application requirements become more complex.

Its main emphasis lies on building complex (if necessary), high-performance, and scalable-rich client apps for the modern web. By modern web we mean it can execute in any browser on any kind of (client) device, including tablets and smart phones, taking advantage of all the features of HTML5, and is ported to the ARM-architecture and the Android platform. Dart is designed with performance in mind, by the people who developed V8. Because the Dart team at Google believes web components will be the foundation for the next evolution of web development, Dart comes out of the box with a **web component** library (web components are pieces of web code containing HTML and Dart or JavaScript that you can re-use in different pages and projects, in other words it is a reliable infrastructure of widgets).

But Dart can also run independently on servers. Because Dart clients and servers can communicate through web sockets (a persistent connection that allows both parties to start sending data at any time), it is in fact an end-to-end solution. It is perfect on the frontend for developing web components with all the necessary application logic, nicely integrated with HTML5 and the browser document model (DOM). On the backend server side, it can be used to develop web services, for example, to access databases, or cloud solutions in Google App Engine or other cloud infrastructures.

Moreover, it is ready to be used in the multicore world (remember, even your cell phone is multicore nowadays) because a Dart program can divide its work amongst any number of separate processes, called **isolates**, an actor-based concurrency model as in Erlang.

Dart is a perfect fit for HTML5

To appreciate this fully we have to take a look at the history of client-side web development.

A very short history of web programming

A web application is always a dialog between the client's browser requesting a page and the server responding with processing and delivering the page and its resources (such as pictures and other media). In the technology of the early dynamic web (the 90s of the previous century, extending even until today), the server performed most of the work: compiling a page, executing the code, fetching data from a data store, inserting the data in the page templates, and in the end producing a stream of HTML and JavaScript that was delivered to the browser. The client digested this stream, rendering the HTML into a browser screen while executing some JavaScript, so processing on the client side was minimal. The whole range of applications using Perl, Python, Ruby, PHP, JSP (Java Server Pages), and ASP.NET follows this principle. It is obvious that the heavy server loads impact negatively the number of clients that could be served, as well as the response time in these applications. This mismatch is even clearer when we realize that the power of the client platforms (with their multicore processors and large memories) is heavily underutilized in this model.

The plugin model, in which the browser started specialized software (such as the Adobe Flash Player) for handling all kinds of media and other resources, partly tipped the balance to the client side. Following this trend, a whole range of technologies for developing **Rich Internet applications (RIA)** were developed that executed application code in the browser at the client side instead, ranging from Java applets around 1995 and Microsoft Active X Objects, culminating in the Adobe Flex and Microsoft Silverlight frameworks. While they have their merits, it is clear that they are more like a parasite in the browser; for example, a virtual machine that executes code, such as ActionScript or C#, that is alien to the browser environment.

Dart empowers the web client

Empowering the client is the way to go, but this should better be done with software technology intimately linked to the browser itself: HTML and JavaScript. In order to eliminate the need for alien plugins, the power of HTML needs to be enlarged, and this is precisely what is achieved with **HTML5**, for example, with its `<audio>` and `<video>` tags. **JavaScript** is the ubiquitous language of the Web and it can, as with Dart, request/send data from/to the server without blocking the user experience through technologies such as Ajax. But flexible and dynamic as JavaScript may be, today it is also often called the assembly language for the web.

JavaScript is not the way to go for complex apps

Why is this? JavaScript was from the beginning not designed to be a robust programming language, despite its name that suggests an affiliation with Java. It was designed to be a simple interpreted language that could be used by nonprofessional programmers and that would be complemented by Java for more serious work. But Java went away to prosper on the server, and JavaScript (JS for short) invaded the browser space. Today JS is being used to develop big and complex web applications, with server components such as Node.js, far beyond the original purpose of this language. Most people who have worked on a large client-side web application written entirely in JS will sooner or later come to the conclusion that its use in these applications is overstretched and the language was not meant to build that kind of software.

Understanding program structure is crucial in large, complex applications: this makes code maintenance, navigating in code, debugging, and refactoring easier. But unfortunately JS code is hard to reason about because there is almost no declarative syntax and it is very hard to detect dependencies between different scripts that can appear in one web page. JavaScript is also very permissive: almost anything (spelling mistakes, wrong types, and so on) is tolerated, making it hard to find errors and unpredictable results. Furthermore, JS allows you to change the way built-in core objects function, a practice often called monkey patching (for a reason!). Would you trust a language in which the following statement is true in its entirety and all of its comparisons?

```
10.0 == '10' == new Boolean(true) == '1'
```

Because of this sometimes undefined nature of JS, its performance is often very unpredictable, so building high-performance web apps in it is tricky.

Google, GWT, and Dart

Google is the web firm par excellence: its revenue model is entirely based on its massive web applications, such as Gmail (some half a million lines of JS), Google Docs, Google Maps, and Google Search. So it is no wonder that these teams encountered the difficulties of building a large JS application and strived for a better platform. Due to the fundamental flaws of JS and its slow evolution, something better was needed. A first attempt was **Google Web Toolkit (GWT)** where development was done in Java, which was then compiled to JS. Although reasonably successful because it enabled a structured and tooled approach to application building, again it was clear that the use of Java is somewhat awkward in a web environment. Thus arose the idea for Dart: a kind of hybrid platform between the dynamic nature of JS and the structured and toolable languages such as Java and C#. In order for Dart to run in all modern web browsers, as for GWT, it must be compiled to JS. Google has provided a special build of Chromium, called Dartium, that provides a **Dart virtual machine (VM)** to execute Dart code on-the-fly without any compilation step (this VM will soon be incorporated into Chrome; for the time being Chrome can be used to test the JS version of your Dart app).

Advantages of Dart

That way Dart can get a better performance profile than JS (remember that the same experts who developed the V8 JS VM are forging Dart, see https://www.dartlang.org/performance/), and at the same time maintain the simple and rapid development process of JS in the browser: the edit code, save, and refresh browser cycle to view the latest version, rather than having to stop, recompile, and run for every little change. Dart delivers high performance on all modern web browsers and environments ranging from small handheld devices to server-side execution. When it runs on its own VM, Dart is faster than JS (in Dart v1.0 around two times the performance of JS). Moreover, through **snapshotting** (a mechanism inherited from Smalltalk) a Dart app has a fast application startup time, in contrast to js where all the source code has to be interpreted or compiled from source.

Dart can execute in the browser, either in its own Dart VM (only in Chrome for the moment) or compiled to JS, so Dart runs everywhere JS does. The Dart VM can also run standalone on a client or server.

Another big advantage compared with GWT is that Dart is much better integrated with the web page and like JS can directly manipulate the page elements and the document structure, that is, the **Document Object Model (DOM)**. Like JS, it has intimate access to the new HTML5 APIs, for example, drawing with the canvas, playing audio and video clips, or using the new local storage possibilities. Following the RIA model mentioned earlier, Dart executes the full application code in the browser, requesting data from the server and rebuilding the page user interface when needed. Because Dart wants to be part of the web, not just sit on top, the team has also built a Dart to JavaScript interop layer, to call JavaScript from Dart and the other way around. Together with its out-of-browser and server capabilities, Dart is also conceived for building complex, large-scale web applications. This can be clearly seen from its object-oriented nature, and Dart code is built with code clarity and structure (using libraries and packages) in mind.

To summarize:

* Dart compiles to JavaScript
* When run on its VM, Dart is faster than JavaScript
* Dart is better suited for large-scale applications

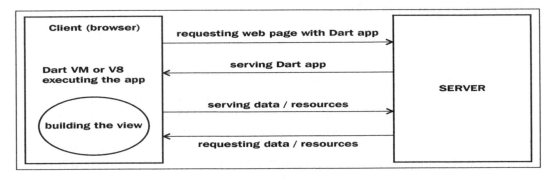

The Dart web model

Getting started with Dart

The Dart project team wants us to get an optimal development experience, so they provide a full but lightweight IDE: the **Dart Editor**, a light version of the well-known Eclipse environment. Installing this is the easiest way to get started, because it comprises the full Dart environment.

Installing the Dart Editor

Because Eclipse is written in Java, we need a Java Runtime Environment or JRE (Version 6 or greater) on our system (this is not needed for Dart itself, only for the Dart Editor). To check if this is already the case, go to `http://www.java.com/en/download/installed.jsp`.

If it is not the case, head for `http://www.oracle.com/technetwork/java/javase/downloads/index.html`, and click on the **JRE DOWNLOAD** button, choose the JRE for your platform and then click on **Run** to start the installation.

Then go to `https://www.dartlang.org/` and click on the appropriate **Download Dart** button and under "Everything you need" choose the appropriate button (according to whether your installed OS is 32 bit or 64 bit) to download the editor.

 This is also the page where you can download the SDK separately, or the Dartium browser (a version of Chrome to test your Dart apps) or download the Dart source code.

You are prompted to save a file named `darteditor-os-xnn.zip`, where `os` can be `win32`, `linux`, or `macos`, and `nn` is `32` or `64`. Extracting the content of this file will create a folder named `dart` containing everything you need: `dart-sdk`, `dartium`, and `DartEditor`. This procedure should go smooth but if you encounter a problem, please review `https://www.dartlang.org/tools/editor/troubleshoot.html`.

 In case you get the following error message: **Failed to load the JNI shared library C:\Program Files(x86)\Java\jre6\\bin\client\jvm.dll**, do not worry. This happens when JRE and Dart Editor do not have the same bit width. More precisely, this happens when you go to `www.java.com` to download JRE. In order to be sure what JRE to select, it is safer to go to `http://www.oracle.com/technetwork/java/javase/downloads/index.html`, click on the **JRE DOWNLOAD** button and choose the appropriate version. If possible, use a 64-bit versions of JRE and Dart Editor.

Your first Dart program

Double-click on DartEditor.exe to open the editor. Navigate to **File** | **New Application** or click on the first button below the menu (**Create a new Dart Application...**). Fill in an application name (for example, dart1) and choose the folder where you want the code file to be created (make a folder such as dart_apps to provide some structure; you can do this while using the **Browse** button). Select **Command-line application**.

With these names a folder dart1 is made as a subfolder of dart_apps, and a source-file dart1.dart is created in dart1\bin with the following code (we'll explain the pubspec.yaml and the packages folder in one of the following examples):

```
void main() {
  print("Hello, World!");
}
```

Downloading the example code

You can download the example code files for all Packt books you have purchased from your account at http://www.packtpub.com. If you purchased this book elsewhere, you can visit http://www.packtpub.com/support and register to have the files e-mailed directly to you.

Here we see immediately that Dart is a C-syntax style language, using { } to surround code and ; to terminate statements. Every app also has a unique main() function, which is the starting point of the application.

This is probably the shortest app possible, but it can be even shorter! The keyword void indicates (as in Java or C#) that the method does not explicitly return an object (indeed a print only produces output to the console), but return types can be left out. Furthermore, when a function has only one single expression, we can shorten this further to the following elegant shorthand syntax:

```
main() => print("Hello, World!");
```

Now, change the printed string to "Becoming a Dart Ninja!" and click on the green arrow button (or press *Ctrl + R*) to run the application. You should see something like the following screenshot (where the **Files**, **Apps**, and **Outline** items from the **Tools** menu were selected):

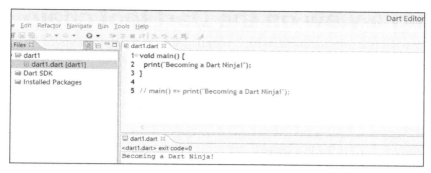

The Dart Editor

You have successfully executed your first Dart program!

Near the bottom of the screen we see our string printed out, together with the message `exit code=0` meaning all went well.

The **Files** tab is useful for browsing through your applications, and for creating, copying, moving, renaming, and deleting files. The **Outline** tab (available via **Tools | Outline**) now only shows `main()`, but this tool will quickly become very useful because it provides an overview of the code in the active file.

Because this was a command-line application, we could just as easily have opened a console in our folder `dart1` and executed the command: `dart dart1.dart` to produce the same output as shown in the following screenshot:

A Dart console application

To let this work, you must first let the OS know where to find the dart VM; so, for example, in Windows you change the `PATH` environment variable to include `C:\dart\dart-sdk\bin`, if your Dart installation lives in `C:\dart`.

Getting a view on the Dart tool chain

Dart comes with *batteries included*, which means that a complete stack of tools is provided by Google to write Dart apps, compile, test, document, and publish them. Moreover, these tools are platform independent (being made for 32- and 64-bit Linux, OS X, and Windows) and they are integrated in the Dart Editor IDE. The Dart Editor contains everything a seasoned developer needs to work with confidence on his app:

- Syntax coloring for keywords
- Autocompletion for class members (by typing . after a name you get a list of available properties and methods)
- Folding/unfolding code blocks
- Tools for navigating the code (a handy overview of the code with the Outline, find callers of a method, and so on)
- Full debugging capabilities of both browser and server applications
- Choose your preferred editor style by navigating to **Tools** | **Preferences** | **Visual Theme**
- Quick fixes for common errors
- Refactoring capabilities
- Direct access to the online API documentation by navigating to **Help** | **API Reference**

The code you make is analyzed while you type, indicating warning (yellow triangles) or errors (red underscores or stop signs). To get more acquainted and experiment with these possibilities, go and read the documentation at https://www.dartlang.org/tools/editor/ and play with one of the samples such as Sunflower or Pop, Pop, Win! (you can find the samples by navigating to **Tools** | **Welcome Page**). From now on use the editor in conjunction with the code examples of the book, so that you can try them out and test changes.

The Dart execution model

How a Dart app executes is sketched in the following diagram:

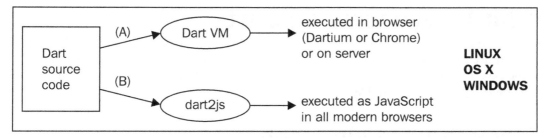

Dart execution model

The Dart code produced in the Dart Editor (or in a plugin for Eclipse or IntelliJ) can:

- Execute in the **Dart VM**, hosted in Dartium or Chrome (Dartium is an experimental version of Chrome to test out Dart) or directly in the operating system (the browser VM knows about HTML, the server VM does not, but can use, for example, IO and sockets, so they are not completely equivalent)

- Be compiled to JS with the dart2js compiler, so that it can run in all recent browsers

Code libraries in Dart are called packages and the core **Dart SDK** contains the basic types and functionalities for working with collection, math, html, uri, json, and so on. They can be recognized by the syntax dart:prefix, for example, dart:html. If you want to use a functionality from a library in a code file, you must import it by using the following as the first statement(s) in your code (dart:core is imported by default):

```
import 'dart:html';
```

The Dart code can be tested with the **unit test** package, and for documentation you can use the **dartdoc** tool (which you can find by navigating to **Tools | Generate Dartdoc** in Dart Editor), which generates a local website structured like the official API documentation on the Web. The **pub** tool is the Dart package manager: if your app needs other packages besides the SDK, pub can install them for you (from the **Tools** menu item in Dart Editor, select **Pub Get** or **Pub Upgrade**) and you can also publish your apps with it in the web repository http://pub.dartlang.org/.

We will see all of these tools in action in *Chapter 2, Getting to Work with Dart*.

A bird's eye view on Dart

It's time to get our feet wet by working on a couple of examples. All code will be thoroughly explained step by step; along the way we will give you a lot of tips and in the next chapter we will go into more detail on the different possibilities, thus gaining deeper insight into Dart's design principles.

Example 1 – raising rabbits

Our first real program will calculate the procreation rate of rabbits, which is not only phenomenal but indeed exponential. A female rabbit can have seven litters a year with an average of four baby rabbits each time. So starting with two rabbits, at the end of the year you have 2 + 28 = 30 rabbits. If none of the rabbits die and all are fertile, the growth rate follows the following formula, where *n* is the number of rabbits after the years specified:

$$n(\text{years}) = 2 \times e^{(k \times \text{years})}$$

Here the growth factor k = ln(30/2) = ln15. Let us calculate the number after each year for the first 10 years.

Go to **File | New Application** as before, select **Command-line application** and type the following code, or simply open the script from chapter_1 in the provided code listings. (Don't worry about the file pubspec.yaml; we'll discuss it in the web version.)

The calculation is done in the following Dart script prorabbits_v1.dart:

```
import 'dart:math'                                        (1)

void main() {
  var n = 0; // number of rabbits                         (2)

  print("The number of rabbits increases as:\n");         (3)
  for (int years = 0; years <= 10; years++) {             (4)
    n = (2 * pow(E, log(15) * years)).round().toInt();    (5)
    print("After $years years:\t $n animals");            (6)
  }
}
```

Our program produces the following output:

```
The number of rabbits increases as:

After  0 years:     2 animals
After  1 years:     30 animals
After  2 years:     450 animals
After  3 years:     6750 animals
After  4 years:     101250 animals
After  5 years:     1518750 animals
After  6 years:     22781250 animals
After  7 years:     341718750 animals
After  8 years:     5125781250 animals
After  9 years:     76886718750 animals
After 10 years:  1153300781250 animals
```

So if developing programs doesn't make you rich, breeding rabbits will. Because we need some mathematical formulas such as natural logarithms log and power pow, we imported dart:math in line (1). Our number of livestock n is declared in line (2); you can see that we precede its name with var. Here, we don't have to indicate the type of n as int or num (so called *type annotations*), as Dart uses *optional typing*.

 Local variables are commonly declared untyped as var.

We could have declared it to be of type num (number) or int, because we know that n is a whole number. But this is not necessary as Dart will derive that from the context in which n is used. The other num type is called double, used for decimal numbers. Also the initialization part (= 0) could have been left out. With no initialization var n; or even int n; gives n the value null, because every variable in Dart is an object. The keyword null simply indicates that the object has no value yet (meaning it is not yet allocated in heap memory). It will come as no surprise that // indicates the beginning of a comment, and /* and */ can be used to make a multi-line comment.

 Comment a section of code by selecting it and then click on **Toggle comment** in the **Edit** menu.

In lines (3) and (6) we see that within a quoted string we can use escape characters such as \n and \t to format our output. Line (4) uses the well-known for-loop that is also present in Dart. In order to have the count of animals as a whole number we needed to apply the round function. The pow function produces a double and because 6750.0 animals doesn't look so good, we have to convert the double to an int with the toInt() function. In line (6), the elegant string substitution mechanism (also called string interpolation) is used: print takes a string as argument (a string variable: any expression enclosed within " " or ' ') and in any such quoted string expression you can substitute the value of variable n by writing $n. If you want the value of an expression within a string, such as a + b, you have to enclose the expression with braces, for example, ${a + b}.

> You don't have to write the ${n} when displaying a variable n; just use $n. You can also simply use print(n).

It is important to realize that we did not have to make any class in our program. Dart is no class junkie like Java or C#. A lot can be done only with functions; but if you want to represent real objects in your programs, classes is the way to go (see the *Example 2 – banking section*).

Extracting a function

This version of our program is not yet very modular; we would like to extract the calculation in a separate method calculateRabbits(years) that takes the number of years as a parameter. This is shown in the following code (version 2 line (4) of prorabbits_v2.dart) with exactly the same output as version 1:

```dart
import 'dart:math';

int rabbitCount = 0;                                        (1)
const int NO_YEARS = 10;                                    (2)
const int GROWTH_FACTOR = 15;                               (3)

void main() {
  print("The number of rabbits increases as:\n");
  for (int years = 0; years <= NO_YEARS; years++) {
    rabbitCount = calculateRabbits(years);                  (4)
    print("After $years years:\t $rabbitCount animals");
  }
}

int calculateRabbits(int years) {                           (5)
  return (2 * pow(E, log(GROWTH_FACTOR) *
    years)).round().toInt();
}
```

We could have written this new function ourselves, but Dart has a built-in refactoring called Extract Method. Highlight the line:

```
n = (2 * pow(E, log(15) * years)).round().toInt();
```

> Right-click and select **Extract Method**. Dart will do the bulk of the work for you, but we can still simplify the proposed code by omitting the parameter n.

The `calculateRabbits` function calculates and returns an integer value; this is indicated by the word `int` preceding the function name. We give the function a type here because it is top level, but the program would have run without the function-type indication.

This new function is called by `main()`. This is the way a Dart program works: all lines in `main()` are executed in sequence, calling functions as needed, and the execution (and with it the Dart VM) stops when the ending } of `main()` is reached. We rename the variable n to `rabbitCount`, so we need no more comments.

> Renaming a variable is also a built-in refactoring. Select the variable (all occurrences are then indicated), right-click, and select **Rename**.

A good programmer doesn't like hardcoded values such as 10 and 15 in a program; what if they have to be changed? We replace them with constant variables, indicated with keyword `const` in Dart, whose name is, by convention, typed in capital letters and parts separated by _, see lines (2) and (3).

> Take care of your top-level variables, constants, and functions because they will probably be visible outside your program (sometimes called the interface or API of your program); type them and name them well.

And now for some practice:

1. Examine this second version by going to **Tools | Outline**.
2. Set a breakpoint on the line `rabbitCount = calculateRabbits(years);` by double-clicking in the margin in front.
3. Run the program and learn how to use the features of the Debugger tool (Press *F5* to step line by line, *F6* or *F7* to step over or out of a function, and *F8* to resume execution until the next breakpoint is hit).

4. Watch the values of the `years` and `rabbitCount` variables.

The output should resemble the following screenshot:

Debugging prorabbits_v2.dart

A web version

As a final version for now, let us build an app that uses an HTML screen where we can input the number of years of rabbit elevation and output the resulting number of animals. Go to **File** | **New Application**, but this time select **Web application**. Now a lot more code is generated that needs explaining. The app now contains a subfolder `web`; this will be the home for all of the app's resources, but for now it contains a stylesheet (`.css` file), a hosting web page (`.html`), and a startup code file (in our case `prorabbits_v3.dart`). The first line in this file makes HTML functionality available to our code:

```
import 'dart:html';
```

We remove the rest of the example code so only an empty `main()` function remains. Look at the source of the HTML page, right before the `</body>` tag; it contains the following code:

```
<script type="application/dart" src="prorabbits_v3.dart"></script>
<script src="packages/browser/dart.js"></script>
```

The first line is evident: our Dart script must be started. But wait, how do we know that there is a Dart VM available in this browser? This will be checked in the second JavaScript file, `dart.js`; the first few lines of code in this file are:

```
if (navigator.webkitStartDart) {
  // Dart VM is available, start it!
} else {
  // Fall back to compiled JavaScript
}
```

The Dart VM exists for the moment only in Dartium (soon in Chrome). For other browsers we must supply the Dart-to-JS compiled scripts; this compilation can be done in the Editor by navigating to **Tools | Generate Javascript**. The output size is minimal: *dead* js code that is not used is eliminated in a process called tree shaking. But where does this mysterious script `dart.js` come from? `src="packages/browser/dart.js"` means that it is a package available in the Dart repository `http://pub.dartlang.org/`.

External packages that your app depends on need to be specified in the section, `dependencies`, in the file `pubspec.yaml`. In our app this section contains the following parameters:

```
name: prorabbits_v3
description: Raising rabbits the web way
dependencies:
  browser: any
```

We see that our app depends on the browser package; any version of it is OK. The package is added to your app when you right-click on the selected `pubspec.yaml` and select **Pub Get**: a folder `packages` is added to your app, and per package a subfolder is added containing the downloaded code, in our case `dart.js`. (In *Chapter 2, Getting to Work with Dart*, we will explore pub in greater depth.)

For this program we replace the HTML `<p id="sample_text_id"></p>` as shown in the following code:

```
<input type="number" id="years" value="5" min="1" max="30">
<input type="button" id="submit" value="Calculate"/>
<br/>Number of rabbits: <label id="output"></label>
```

The input field with type number (new in HTML5) gives us a NumericUpDown control with a default value 5 and limited to the range 1 to 30. In our Dart code, we now have to handle the click-event on the button with id as submit. We do this in our main() function with the following line of code:

```
query Selector ("#submit").onClick.listen( (e) => calcRabbits() );
```

query Selector ("#submit") gives us a reference in the code to the button, listen redirects to an anonymous function (see *Chapter 2, Getting to Work with Dart*) to handle this event e, which calls the function calcRabbits() shown in the following code:

```
calcRabbits() {
  // binding variables to html elements:
  InputElement yearsInput  = querySelector("#years");      (1)
  LabelElement output = querySelector("#output");          (2)
  // getting input
  String yearsString = yearsInput.value;
  int years = int.parse(yearsString);
  // calculating and setting output:
  output.innerHtml = "${calculateRabbits(years)}";
}
```

Here in lines (1) and (2), the input field and the output label are bound to the variables in_years and output. This is always done in the same way: the query Selector() function takes as its argument a CSS-selector, in this case the ID of the input field (an ID is preceded by a # sign). We typed in_years as an InputElement (because it is bound to an input field), that way we can access its value, which is always a string. We then convert this string to an int type with the function int. parse(), because calculateRabbits needs an int parameter. The result is shown as HTML in the output label via string substitution, see the following screenshot:

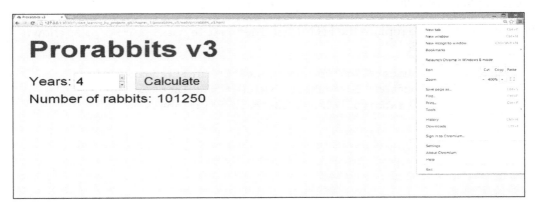

The screen of prorabbits_v3

All objects in Dart code that are bound to HTML elements are instances of the class `Element`. Notice how you can change the Dart and HTML code; save and hit refresh in Dartium (Chrome) to get the latest version of your app.

Example 2 – banking

All variables (strings, numbers, and also functions) in Dart are objects, so they are also instances of a class. The class concept is very important in modeling entities in real-world applications, making our code modular and reusable. We will now demonstrate how to make and use a simple class in Dart modeling a bank account. The most obvious properties of such an object are the owner of the account, the bank account number, and the balance (the amount of money it contains). We want to be able to deposit an amount of money in it that increases the balance, or withdrawing an amount so as to decrease the balance. This can be coded in a familiar and compact way in Dart as shown in the following code:

```dart
class BankAccount {
  String owner, number;
  double balance;
  // constructor:
  BankAccount(this.owner, this.number, this.balance);      (1)
  // methods:
  deposit(double amount) => balance += amount;             (2)
  withdraw(double amount) => balance -= amount;
}
```

Notice the elegant constructor syntax in line (1) where the incoming parameter values are automatically assigned to the object fields via `this`. The methods (line (2)) can also use the shorthand `=>` function syntax because the body contains only one expression. If you prefer the `{ }` syntax, they will be written as follows:

```dart
deposit(double amount) {
  balance += amount;
}
```

The code in `main()` makes a `BankAccount` object `ba` and exercises its methods (see program `banking_v1.dart`):

```dart
main() {
  var ba = new BankAccount("John Gates",
    "075-0623456-72", 1000.0);
  print("Initial balance:\t\t ${ba.balance} \$");
  ba.deposit(250.0);
  print("Balance after deposit:\t\t ${ba.balance} \$");
  ba.withdraw(100.0);
  print("Balance after withdrawal:\t ${ba.balance} \$");
}
```

The preceding code produces the following output:

```
Initial balance:              1000.0 $
Balance after deposit:        1250.0 $
Balance after withdrawal:     1150.0 $
```

Notice how when you type `ba.` in the editor, the list of `BankAccount` class members appears to autocomplete your code. By convention, variables (objects) and functions (or methods) start with a lower case letter and follow the camelCase notation (`http://en.wikipedia.org/wiki/CamelCase`), while class names start with a capital letter, as well as the word-parts in the name. Remember Dart is case sensitive!

Making a todo list with Dart

Since this has become the "Hello World" for web programmers, let's make a simple todo list and start a new web application `todo_v1`. To record our tasks we need an input field corresponding with `InputElement` in Dart:

```
<input id="task" type="text" placeholder=
  "What do you want to do?"/>
```

The HTML5 placeholder attribute lets you specify default text that appears in the field.

We specify a list tag (`UListElement`) that we will fill up in our code:

```
<ul id="list"/>
```

The following is the code from `todo_v1.dart`:

```
import 'dart:html';

InputElement task;
UListElement list;

main() {
  task = querySelector('#task');                      (1)
  list = querySelector('#list');                      (2)
  task.onChange.listen( (e) => addItem() );           (3)
}

void addItem() {
  var newTask = new LIElement();                      (4)
  newTask.text = task.value;                          (5)
  task.value = '';                                    (6)
  list.children.add(newTask);                         (7)
}
```

We bind our HTML elements to the Dart objects task and list in lines (1) and (2). In line (3) we attach an event-handler addItem to the onChange event of the textfield task: this fires when the user enters something in the field and then leaves it (either by pressing *Tab* or *Enter*). UListElement is in fact a collection of LIElements (these are its children); so for each new task we make a LIElement (4), assign the task's value to it (5), clear the input field (6), and add the new LIElement to the list in (7). In the following screenshot you can see some tasks to be performed:

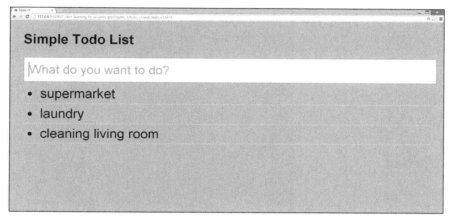

A simple todo list

Of course this version isn't very useful (unless you want to make a print of your screen); our tasks aren't recorded and we can't indicate which tasks are finished. Don't worry; we will enhance this app in the future versions.

Summary

We covered a lot of ground in this introductory chapter, but by now you know the case for Dart in the context of web applications, where Dart apps can live and how they are executed, and the various tools to work with Dart, in particular the Dart Editor.

You also got acquainted with some simple command line and web Dart apps and got a feeling for the Dart syntax. In the next chapter, we explore the various code and data structures of Dart more systematically and any obscurities that are still there in your mind will surely disappear. More coming soon to a Dart center near you...

2

Getting to Work with Dart

In this chapter you will get a firm grasp on how to program in Dart. The code and data structures in Dart and its functional principles are explained by exploring practical examples. We will look at the following topics:

- Variables – if, how, and when to type them
- What are the basic types that you can use?
- Documenting your programs
- How to influence the order of execution of a program
- Using functions in Dart
- How to recognize and catch errors and exceptions?

You will see plenty of examples, also revisiting the code from *Chapter 1, Dart – A Modern Web Programming Language*. Because most of this will be familiar to you, we will discuss these topics succinctly and emphasize only that which is new or different. You can refer to http://www.dartlang.org/docs/dart-up-and-running/contents/ch02.html if you need more detailed explanations. We encourage you to play with the code examples, the best way to become familiar with Dart. The full API reference documentation is available at http://api.dartlang.org. Experiment in the Dart Editor to find out if in doubt!

Variables – to type or not to type

In our first example (Raising rabbits) in *Chapter 1, Dart – A Modern Web Programming Language*, we started by declaring a variable rabbitCount dynamically with var, and then in the second version we gave it a static type int (refer to the file prorabbits_v1.dart and prorabbits_v2.dart in *Chapter 1, Dart – A Modern Web Programming Language*) and concluded that *typing is optional* in Dart. This seems confusing and has provoked a lot of discussion: "is Dart a dynamic language like Ruby or JavaScript, or a static language like Java or C#?" After all, some of us were raised in the (static) belief that typed variables are absolutely necessary to check if a program is correct, a task mainly performed by the compiler (but the Dart VM has no separate compiler step, and dart2js, the Dart to JS compiler, doesn't check types because JS is fully dynamic).

It turns out that no mainstream language actually has a perfect type system (static types don't guarantee program correctness) and that not letting a program run because of an obscure type error blocks the programmer's creativity; however, it is true that static type checks can prevent bugs. On the other hand, the dynamic belief states that typing variables hinders the programmer's fantasy (and wears out the fingers). In their world, grave errors due to wrong types occur only when the program is running; to avoid such calamities, they have to rely on a rigorous unit testing discipline.

Dart takes a pragmatic middle stand: web programming is already accustomed to dynamically typed languages that are more flexible, and Dart honors that and adheres to a system of optional or loose typing. You can start out writing your code without types while you're still experimenting and doing quick prototyping. In a more advanced stage, you can annotate (some of) the code with types. This will enhance the readability of your code for your fellow developers and as such it is additional documentation. Furthermore, it allows the Dart analyzer tools to check the code for the types used and report possible errors, so it makes more useful developer tools possible.

As the app becomes larger and more stable, types can be added to aid debugging and impose structure where desired, making the code more robust, documented, and more maintainable. Dart code can evolve from a simple, untyped experimental prototype to a complex, modular application with types. Moreover, as you will experience while working in the Dart Editor, with types the IDE (Integrated Development Environment) can suggest better autocompletion for the properties and methods of any code object. The two extremes (no typing or everything typed) are not encouraged.

In general, give everything in your code that can be seen publicly a type (in the sense that it is visible in and can be used from outside code, sometimes called the interface), such as top-level variables and functions including their arguments. That way, other apps can use your code with increased safety.

Using `var` (or `final` or `const`) for an object leaves it untyped, but in fact Dart internally considers this object to be of type `dynamic`, the unknown type. The keyword `dynamic` is very rarely used in code.

To cope with this dilemma, Dart has two runtime modes (ways of executing programs):

- **Checked mode**: This is typically used when you develop, debug, and test. The IDE will warn you when you misuse variables in a typed context (a tool called the dart-analyzer continuously checks your code, while saving and even while you type). The types are checked when executing assignments, when passing arguments to a function, and when returning a result from a function. By default your program is also run in this mode, breaking the execution when a (typing) error occurs (you can change this behavior by navigating to **Run | Manage Launches | VM settings** and unchecking the **Run in checked mode** checkbox).

- **Production mode**: This is when your program runs for real, that is, it used by customers. Then Dart runs as a fully dynamic language and ignores type information, giving a performance boost because the checks don't need to be performed.

Errors (indicated in the Editor by a white x in a red circle) prevent you from running the program. For example, delete an ending `;` or `}` from some source code and see what happens.

Warnings (a black ! in a yellow triangle) indicate that the code might not work. For example, in the following code snippet (from `chapter_2\checked_mode.dart`), a warning is indicated in line `(1)`:

```
int age = 'Dart';               (1)
print('$age');
```

The warning sign is shown in front of the line and the string `Dart` is yellow underlined. If you hover the cursor over one of these, you see the message: **A value of type 'String' is not assignable to 'int'**. If you try to run this example in the default checked mode in Dart Editor, you'll get the following output:

```
Unhandled exception:
type 'String' is not a subtype of type 'int' of 'age'.
#0  main (file:///E:/dart/Book/code/chapter_2/checked_mode/bin/
checked_mode.dart:2:14)
```

But if you uncheck and let it run in production mode, it runs and the normal output `Dart` appears in the console. Dart expects the developer to have thoroughly checked and tested the program:

 Warnings do not prevent you from running a program in production mode in most cases.

A variable is just a nickname for an object, the same object can have multiple variables referring to it, and a variable name can also switch from one object to another, such as in the following code:

```
var name = 'John';
name = 'Lucy';      // name now refers to another String object
```

But sometimes you don't want this to happen; you want a variable to always point at the same object (such as immutable variables in functional languages or in other words a read-only variable). This is possible in Dart using the keyword `final`, such as in the following code (refer to `final.dart`):

```
final name = 'John';
name = 'Lucy';           //   (1)  warning!
```

Now, line (1) generates a warning: **Final variables cannot be assigned a value**, but the execution is even stopped in production mode! The keywords `var` and `final` used as such both refer to a dynamic untyped variable, but `final` can be used together with a type, as shown in the following code:

```
final String name = 'John';
```

The `const` keyword (that we used already in `prorabbits_v2.dart` in *Chapter 1, Dart – A Modern Web Programming Language*) like `final` also refers to something whose value cannot change, but it is more restricted. It must be a literal value (such as `100` or `Dart` or another `const`) or a calculation with known numbers, a so-called compile-time constant. For example, see the following code:

```
const NO_SECINMIN = 60;
const NO_SECINDAY = NO_SECINMIN * 60 * 24;
```

The following is an example that shows the difference:

```
int daysInWeek = 7;
final fdaysInYear = daysInWeek * 52;
const DAYSINYEAR =  daysInWeek * 52;  //  (2) error!
```

Now, line (2) gives an error:

```
'const' variables must be constant value.
```

In summary, types are not used for performance optimization and they don't change program behavior, but they can help you write and maintain your code; a little typing goes a long way. A combination of tool support, static analysis, checked mode assertions, and unit tests can make you feel just as safe in Dart as in any statically typed language, yet more productive.

Built-in types and their methods

Like Ruby, Dart is a purely object-oriented (OO) language, so every variable in Dart points to an object and there are no primitive types as in Java or C#. Every variable is an instance of a class (that inherits from the base class `Object`) and has a type, and when uninitialized has the value `null`. But for ease-of-use Dart has built-in types for numbers, Booleans, and strings defined in `dart:core`, that look and behave like primitive types; that is, they can be made with literal values and have the basic operations you expect (to make it clear, we will use full typing in `builtin_types. dart`, but we could have used `var` as well).

A **String** (notice the capital) is a sequence of Unicode (UTF-16) characters, for example:

```
String country = "Egypt";
String chineseForWorld = '世界';
```

They can be indicated by paired ' or " (use "" when the string contains ' and vice versa). Adjacent string literals are concatenated. If you need multiline strings, use triple quotes ''' or """ (handy for defining chunks of HTML!).

Escape characters are not interpreted when the string is prefixed by r, a so-called raw string, invaluable when defining regular expressions. The empty string '' or "" is not the same as `null`. The following are all legal strings:

```
String q = "What's up?";
String s1 = 'abc'
            "def";
  print(s1); // abcdef
  String multiLine = '''
    <h1> Beautiful page </h1>
    <div class="start"> This is a story about the landing
       on the moon </div>
    <hr>
  ''';
  print(multiLine);
  String rawStr = r"Why don't you \t learn Dart!";
  // output: Why don't you \t learn Dart!
  print(rawStr);
  var emptyStr = ''; // empty string
```

The numeric types are `num` (number), `int` (integer), and `double`; the last two are subtypes of `num`:

```
int n = 42;
double pi = 3.14;
```

Integers can use hexadecimal notation preceding with `0x`, as shown in the following code:

```
int hex = 0xDEADBEEF;
```

And they can be of arbitrary precision, as shown in the following code:

```
int hugePrimeNumber = 4776913109852041418248056622882488319;
```

 You cannot use this feature if you rely on compilation to JS, because here we are restricted to JS integers!

Doubles are of a 64-bit precision and can use scientific notation:

```
double d1 = 12345e-4;
```

The `num` type has the usual `abs()`, `ceil()`, and `floor()` methods as well as `round()` for rounding. Use either `int` or `num`, but `double` only in the specific case you need a decimal number that cannot be an integer.

Booleans can only have the value `true` or `false`:

```
bool selected = false;
```

In contrast to JS where any variable can be evaluated as true or false, Dart does not permit these strange behaviors in checked mode; in production mode every value different from `true` is treated as `false`.

Conversions

To use numbers as strings use the `toString()` method and to convert a `String` to an `int` use `int.parse()`:

```
String lucky = 7.toString();
int seven = int.parse('7');
```

Likewise, converting a `String` to a `double` is done with `double.parse()`:

```
double pi2 = double.parse('3.1415');
```

If you want to retain only a certain amount of decimal numbers from a `double`, use
`toStringAsFixed()`:

```
String pi2Str = pi2.toStringAsFixed(3);
  //  3.142 (notice rounding occurs)
```

To convert between num types use `toDouble()` for int to double and `toInt()` for
double to int (truncation occurs!).

Operators

All operators in Dart follow the normal priority rules; when in doubt or for clarity,
use () around expressions that must be executed first.

We have our familiar number operators (+, -, *, /, and %) in Dart, and assignments
with these can be shortened as +=. Use ~/ to get an integer result from a division.
Likewise, we have pre- and postfix ++ and -- to add or subtract 1 to or from a
number, and <, <=, >, and >= to check the order of numbers or Strings.

> Strings a and b can be concatenated with + as a + b,
> but string interpolation such as '$a $b' executes
> faster, so prefer this.

Numbers have also bitwise and shift operators for manipulating individual bits.

To see if two variables have the same content use == or != for different content.
These expressions result in Boolean values, such as b1 and b2 in this snippet
(brackets are only used for clarity):

```
var i = 100;
var j = 1000;
var b1 = (i == j);
var b2 = (i != j);
print('$b1'); // false
print('$b2'); // true
```

For numbers and strings == is true when both variables have the same value.

> == is an operator and can be redefined for any type;
> generally it will check whether both arguments have the
> same value. Use the `identical(a,b)` function to check
> whether variables a and b refer to the same object.

For Strings both hold true; the same String is only one object in memory, and if the string variable gets a new value, it references another address in memory. Strings are immutable.

```
var s = "strings are immutable";
var t = "strings are immutable";
print(s == t); // true, they contain the same characters
print(identical(s, t)); // true, they are the
  // same object in memory
```

Boolean values or expressions can be combined with an AND operator (&&) or an OR operator (||), or negated with a NOT operator (!).

Because we will be working a lot with objects and types in Dart code, it is important to be able to test if an object is or is! (not) of a certain type (class):

```
var b3 = (7 is num); // () are not necessary
print('$b3');         // true
var b4 = (7 is! double);
print('$b4');         // true, it's an int
```

A very useful built-in function that can be used for micro unit testing is assert. Its parameter is a Boolean expression. When this is true, nothing happens at runtime; but when it is false, the program stops with an AssertionError. You can sprinkle them around in your code to test certain conditions that must be true; in the production mode, assert statements are ignored. So for the last example we could have written:

```
assert(b4 == true) or shorter assert(b4)
```

We will use these throughout the example code, but will not print them in the text for brevity.

The [] indexing operator is used to obtain an element from a collection (a group of variables) at a certain index, the first element has index 0.

To convert or cast a variable v to a certain type T, use the as operator: v as T

If v is indeed of that type, all is well and you can access all methods of T, but if this fails an error is generated.

Some useful String methods

Strings are all pervasive and Dart provides handy methods to work with them, for details refer to the documentation at the following link:

`http://api.dartlang.org/docs/releases/latest/dart_core/String.html`

We show some examples in `string_methods.dart`:

- You can test that the owner of a bank account (a `String`) is not filled in with `owner.isEmpty`, which returns a Boolean value:

```
assert("".isEmpty);
```

- `length()` returns the number of UTF-16 characters:

```
assert('Google'.length == 6);
```

- Use `trim()` to remove the leading and trailing whitespace:

```
assert('\thello  '.trim() == 'hello');
```

- Use `startswith()`, `endswith()`, and `contains()` to detect the presence of subwords:

```
var fullName = 'Larry Page';
assert(fullName.startsWith('La'));
assert(fullName.endsWith('age'));
assert(fullName.contains('y P'));
```

- Use `replaceAll()` to replace a substring; notice that the original string was not changed (strings are immutable!):

```
var composer = 'Johann Sebastian Bach';
var s = composer.replaceAll('a', '-');
print(s); // Joh-nn Seb-sti-n B-ch
assert(s != composer); // composer didn't change
```

- Use the `[]` operator to get the character at index `i` in the string:

```
var lang = "Dart";
assert(lang[0] == "D");
```

- Find the location of a substring inside a string with `indexOf()`:

```
assert(lang.indexOf("ar") == 1);
```

- Extract a part of a string with `substring()`:

```
assert("20000 rabbits".substring(9, 13) == 'bits');
```

When printing any object the `toString()` method, which returns a String, is automatically called. If no particular version of this method was provided, the `toString()` method from class `Object` is called, which prints the type of the object, as shown in the following code:

```
print('$ba');        //       produces Instance of 'BankAccount'
```

 If you need a readable representation of an object, give its class a `toString()` method.

In `banking_v2.dart` we provide the following method:

```
String toString() => 'Bank account from $owner with
    number $number and balance $balance';
```

Now `print('$ba');` produces the following output:

```
Bank account from John Gates with number 075-0623456-72
    and balance 1000.0
```

If you need many operations in building your strings, instead of creating new strings at each operation and thus using more memory, consider using a `StringBuffer` object for better efficiency. A `StringBuffer` doesn't generate a new `String` object until `toString()` is called. An example is given in the following code:

```
var sb = new StringBuffer();
sb.write("Use a StringBuffer ");
sb.writeAll(["for ", "efficient ", "string ", "creation "]);
sb.write("if you are ");
sb.write("building lots of strings.");
var fullString = sb.toString();
print('$fullString');
sb.clear();  // sb is empty again
assert(sb.toString() == '');
```

Dates and times

Almost every app needs time info, so how can we do this in Dart? The `dart:core` package has a class `DateTime` for this. In our banking app we could add the attributes `dateCreated` and `dateModified` to our class `BankAccount`. In the constructor, `dateCreated` is initialized to the moment at which the account is created; in our `deposit` and `withdraw` methods we update `dateModified`. This is shown in the following code (refer to `banking_v2.dart`):

```
class BankAccount {
  String owner, number;
  double balance;
  DateTime dateCreated, dateModified;

  BankAccount(this.owner, this.number, this.balance)  {
    dateCreated = new DateTime.now();
  }

  deposit(double amount) {
    balance += amount;
    dateModified = new DateTime.now();
  }
  // other code
}
```

We can print this out with the following command:

```
print('Bank account created at: ${ba.dateCreated}');
```

The output produced is as follows:

```
Bank account created at: 2013-02-10  10:42:45.387
```

The method `DateTime.parse(dateString)` produces a `DateTime` object from a String in one of the suitable formats: `20130227 13:27:00` or `2010-01-17`. All weekdays and month names are defined as `const int`, such as `MON` and `JAN`. You can extract all date parts as an int with methods such as `second`, `day`, `month`, `year`, as shown in the following code:

```
ba.dateModified.weekday
```

A time span is represented by a `Duration` object, `difference()` gives the duration between two `DateTime` objects, and you can `add` and `subtract` a duration from a `DateTime`.

Lists

This is the basic collection type for making an ordered group of objects, it can be of fixed size (called an array in other languages) or it can grow dynamically. Again `length` returns the number of elements in the List; the last element has index `length` − 1. An empty List with `length` equal to `0` and property `isEmpty` equal to `true` can be created in two ways: literal or with a constructor (refer to `lists.dart`):

```
var empty = [];
var empty2 = new List(); // equivalent
assert(empty.isEmpty && empty2.isEmpty && empty.length == 0);
```

We can either define and populate a List with a literal by using `[]` as in the following code:

```
var langs = ["Java","Python","Ruby", "Dart"];
```

Or we can define a List with a constructor and an `add()` method:

```
var langs2 = new List();
langs2.add("C");
langs2.add("C#");
langs2.add("D");
print(langs2); // [C, C#, D]
```

A read-only List with constant elements resulting in better performance can be defined as shown in the following code:

```
var readOnlyList = const ["Java","Python","Ruby", "Dart"];
```

The `[]` operator can be used to fetch and set List elements:

```
var langBest = langs[3];
assert(langBest=="Dart");
langs2[2] = "JavaScript";
```

But using an index greater than or equal to the List length provokes a `RangeError` in runtime (with no compile-time check!):

```
langs[4] = "F#";   // RangeError !
```

To check if a List contains a certain item, use the method with that name:

```
print('${langs.contains("Dart")}'); // true
```

When you know the type of the list elements, the list itself can be typed; for example, `langs` and `langs2` are both of type `List<String>`.

A String can be `split` over a certain character or pattern (which could be a space `" "` or even `""`) producing a `List<String>`, which can then be further analyzed, as shown in the following code:

```
var number = "075-0623456-72";
var parts = number.split('-');
print('$parts'); // produces [075, 0623456, 72]
```

In simple scenarios data records are written line after line in text files, each line containing the data of one object. In each line the data fields are separated by a certain character, such as a `;`. We could read in and split each line of the file, and obtain a List of fields for each object to be shown on a screen or processed further. Conversely a List can be joined by concatenating all its elements in one String (here with a separator `'-'`):

```
var str = parts.join('-');
assert(number==str);
```

A list with N elements is used mostly to support an efficient search of the whole list, or a large number of the list's elements. The time it takes to search a list grows linearly with N; it is of order O(N).

In summary, a List is an ordered collection of items that can be retrieved or changed by index (0-based, working via index is fast), and that can contain duplicates. You can find more useful functions in the API, but we will come back to List again in the *The collection hierarchy and its functional nature* section in *Chapter 3, Structuring Code with Classes and Libraries.* (For API docs, see the documentation at `http://api.dartlang.org/docs/releases/latest/dart_core/List.html`.)

Maps

Another very useful and built-in type is a Map, basically a dictionary of (`key:value`) pairs where the value is associated with the key. The number of pairs is the length of the Map. Keys must be unique, they may not be null, and the lookup of the value from the key is fast; remember, however, that the order of the pairs is not guaranteed! Similar to a List, a Map can be created literally with `{}` as shown in the following code:

```
Map webLinks = {  'Dart': 'http://www.dartlang.org/',
    'HTML5': 'http://www.html5rocks.com/' };
```

The keys must be of type `String` for a literal Map.

Or it can be created with a constructor (refer to `maps.dart`):

```
Map webLinks2 = new Map();
webLinks2['Dart'] = 'http://www.dartlang.org/';        (1)
webLinks2['HTML5'] = 'http://www.html5rocks.com/';
```

The empty Map created with `var map = {}` or `var map = new Map()` has `length` as 0; the length of a Map is not fixed. You can fetch the value corresponding to a certain key with:

```
var link = webLinks2['Dart']; // 'http://www.dartlang.org/'
```

If the key is not in the Map, you get `null` (it is not an error):

```
var link2 = webLinks2['C'];  // null
```

To check if your Map contains a certain key, use the `containsKey()` method:

```
if (webLinks2.containsKey('C'))
  print("The map webLinks2 contains key 'C'");
else
  print("The map webLinks2 does not contain key 'C'");
// prints: The map webLinks2 does not contain key 'C'
```

To obtain a List of the keys or values, use the methods with the same name:

```
var keys = webLinks2.keys.toList();
print('$keys'); // [Dart, HTML5, ASP.NET]
// getting the values:
var values = webLinks2.values.toList();
print('$values');
// printed output:
// [http://www.learningdart.org/, http://www.html5rocks.com/,
// http://www.asp.net/]
```

Setting a value is done with the syntax shown in line (1); this applies both to inserting a new key-value pair in the map, or changing the value for an existing key:

```
webLinks2['Dart'] = 'http://www.learningdart.org/';  // change
webLinks2['ASP.NET'] = 'http://www.asp.net/';  // new key
```

A very handy method is `putIfAbsent`, which makes your code a lot cleaner. It takes two parameters: a key and a function that returns a value. The method tests if the key already exists; if not, the function is evaluated and the resulting key-value pair is inserted in the map (for example, we use a very simple function that directly returns a value, but this could be a calculation or a database-lookup operation):

```
webLinks2.putIfAbsent('F#', () => 'www.fsharp.net');
assert(webLinks2['F#']=="www.fsharp.net");
```

Again for performance reasons, use `const` maps when the keys and values are literals or constants:

```
var cities =  const {'1':'London','2':'Tokyo','3':'Madrid'};
```

A Map can also be explicitly typed, for example, a Map with integer keys and String values:

```
Map<int, String>
```

A Map with N elements is used mostly to support an efficient direct access to a single element of the map based on its key. This will always execute in the same time regardless of the size of the input dataset; the algorithm is of order O(1).

For the API docs for Map see the documentation at the following link:
`https://api.dartlang.org/docs/channels/stable/`
`latest/dart_core/Map.html`

Documenting your programs

Documenting an application is of utmost importance in software engineering and Dart makes this very easy. The single-line (`//`) and multiline comments (`/* */`) are useful (for example, to comment out code or mark lines with `//` TODO), and they have counterparts `///` and `/** */` called documentation comments. In these comments (to be placed on the previous line), you can include references to all kinds of objects in your code (classes, methods, fields, and so on) and the **Dartdoc** tool (in Dart Editor go to **Tools** | **Generate Dartdoc**) will generate HTML documentation where these references become links. To demonstrate we will add docs to our banking example (refer to `banking_v2doc.dart`):

```
/**
 * A bank account has an [owner], is identified by a [number]
 * and has an amount of money called [balance].
 * The balance is changed through methods [deposit] and [withdraw].
 */
class BankAccount {
  String owner, number;
  double balance;
  DateTime dateCreated, dateModified;

  BankAccount(this.owner, this.number, this.balance)  {
    dateCreated = new DateTime.now();
  }

  /// An amount of money is added to the balance.
  deposit(double amount) {
```

```
  }

  /// An amount of money is subtracted from the balance.
  withdraw(double amount) {

  }
}
```

This results in the following documentation when viewing `banking_v2doc\docs\`
`index.html` in a browser:

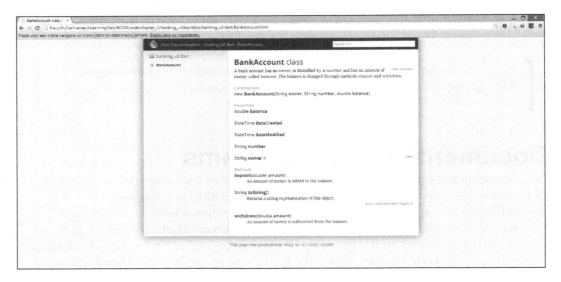

Changing the execution flow of a program

Dart has the usual control structures with no surprises here (refer to `control.dart`).

An `if...else` statement (with an optional `else`) is as follows:

```
var n = 25;
if (n < 10) {
  print('1 digit number: $n');
} else if (n >=  10 && n < 100){
  print('2+ digit number: $n'); // 2+ digit number: 25
} else {
  print('3 or more digit number: $n');
}
```

Single-line statements without { } are allowed, but don't mix the two. A simple and short if...else statement can be replaced by a *ternary operator*, as shown in the following example code:

```
num rabbitCount = 16758;
(rabbitCount > 20000) ? print('enough for this year!') :
  print('breed on!');   // breed on!
```

If the expression before ? is true, the first statement is executed, else the statement after : is executed. To test if a variable v refers to a real object, use: if (v != null) { ... }.

Testing if an object v is of type T is done with an if statement: if (v is T).

In that case we can safely cast v to type T and access all members of T:

```
if (v is T) {
  (v as T).methodOfT()
}
```

For example, if we don't know for sure that ba2 is a BankAccount, the code in line (1) in the following code will generate an error; we can avoid this with an if test in line (2):

```
var ba1, ba2;
ba1 = new BankAccount("Jeff", "5768-346-89", 758.0);
if (ba1 is BankAccount) ba1.deposit(42.0);
print('${ba1.balance}'); // 800.0
(ba2 as BankAccount).deposit(100.0); <-- NoSuchMethodError   (1)
if (ba2 is BankAccount) {                                    (2)
  (ba2 as BankAccount).deposit(100.0);
  print('deposited 100 on ba2'); // statement not reached
} else {
  print('ba2 is not a BankAccount'); // ba2 is not a BankAccount
}
```

We can replace multiple if...else if with a switch case statement; switch tests the value of an integer or string variable in () against different constant values in case clauses:

```
switch(ba1.owner) {
  case 'Jeff':
    print('Jeff is the bank account owner'); // this is printed
    break;
  case 'Mary':
    print('Mary is the bank account owner');
    break;
```

```
    default:
      print('The bank account owner is not Jeff, nor Mary');
}
```

Each case must end with a `break` or a `continue` with a label; use `default` when no other case matches; multiple cases can be combined.

Repetition can be coded with a `for` loop if the number of repetitions is known or with a `while` or `do...while` loop if the looping depends on a condition:

```
var langs = ["Java","Python","Ruby", "Dart"];
for (int i = 0; i < langs.length; i++) {
  print('${langs[i]}');
}
```

Notice that the condition `i` value should be less than the length of the List.

If you don't need the index `i`, the `for...in` loop provides a simpler alternative:

```
var s = '';
var numbers = [0, 1, 2, 3, 4, 5, 6, 7];
for (var n in numbers) {
  s = '$s$n ';
}
print(s);  // 0 1 2 3 4 5 6 7
```

In each loop the variable `n` takes the value of the next collection element.

Conditions without counters are best tested in a `while` loop:

```
while (rabbitCount <= 20000) {
  print('keep breeding');
  rabbitCount += 4;
}
```

Don't get involved in an infinite loop by forgetting a statement that changes the condition! You can always break out from a loop with a `break`:

```
while (true) {
  if (rabbitCount > 20000) break;
  rabbitCount += 4;
}
```

Likewise, skip the execution of the body of the loop with a `continue`:

```
s = '';
for (var n in numbers) {
  if (n % 2 == 0) continue; // skip even numbers
```

```
    s = '$s$n ';
  }
  print('$s');  // 1 3 5 7
```

Using functions in Dart

Functions are another tool for changing the control flow; a certain task is delegated to a function by calling it and providing some arguments. A function does the requested task and returns a value; the control flow returns where the function was called. In Java and C#, classes are indispensable and they are the most important structuring concept.

But Dart is both functional and object oriented. Functions are first-class objects themselves (they are of type **Function**) and can exist outside of a class as **top-level functions** (inside a class they are called **methods**). In prorabbits_v2.dart of *Chapter 1, Dart – A Modern Web Programming Language*, calculateRabbits is an example of a top-level function; and deposit, withdraw, and toString from banking_v2.dart of this chapter are methods, to be called on as an object of the class. Don't create a static class only as a container for helper functions!

Return types

A function can do either of the following:

*   Do something, wherein the return type, if indicated, is void, for example, the display function in return_types.dart. In fact, such a function does return an object, namely null (see the print in line (1) of the following code).

*   Return an expression exp resulting in an object different from null, explicitly indicated by a return exp, as in displayStr (line (2)).

The { return exp; } syntax can be shortened to => exp; as shown in display and displayStrShort; we'll use this *function expression* syntax wherever possible. exp is an expression, but it cannot be a statement like if. A function can be an argument to another function, as display in print, line (1), or in line (4) where the function isOdd is passed to the function where:

```
main() {
  print(display('Hello')); // Message: Hello.    null    (1)
  print(displayStr('Hello')); // Message: Hello.         (2)
  print(displayStrShort('Hello')); // Message: Hello.
  print(display(display("What's up?")));                 (3)
  [1,2,3,4,5].where(isOdd).toList();      // [1, 3, 5]   (4)
```

```
}

display(message) => print('Message: $message.');

displayStr(message) {
  return 'Message: $message.';
}

displayStrShort(message) => 'Message: $message.';
isOdd(n) => n % 2 == 1;


}
```

By omitting the parameter type, the `display` function is more general; its argument can be a String, num, Boolean, List, and so on.

Parameters

As all parameter variables are objects, all parameters are passed by reference; that means that the underlying object can be changed from within the function. Two types of parameters exist: the required (they come first in the parameter list), and the optional parameters. Optional parameters that depend on their position in the list are indicated between `[]` in the definition of the function. All parameters we have seen so far in examples were required, but usage of only optional parameter(s) is also possible, as shown in the following code (refer to `parameters.dart`):

```
webLanguage([name]) =>  'The best web language is: $name';
```

When called as shown in the following code, it produces the output shown as comments:

```
print(webLanguage());  // The best web language is: null
print(webLanguage('JavaScript')); // The best web language is:
  // JavaScript
```

An optional parameter can have a default value as shown in the following code:

```
webLanguage2([name='Dart']) =>  'The best web language is: $name';
```

If this function is called without argument, the optional value is substituted instead, but when called with an argument, this takes precedence:

```
print(webLanguage2());  // The best web language is: Dart
print(webLanguage2('JavaScript')); // The best web language is:
  // JavaScript
```

An example with required and optional parameters, with or without default values
(name=value), is as follows:

```
String hi(String msg, [String from, String to])
                => '$msg from $from to $to';
String hi2(String msg, [String from='me', String to='you'])

                => '$msg from $from to $to';
```

Here msg always gets the first parameter value, from and to get a value when there
are more parameters in that order (for that reason they are called positional):

```
print(hi('hi'));                 // hi from null to null
print(hi('hi', 'me'));           // hi from me to null
print(hi('hi', 'me', 'you'));    // hi from me to you
print(hi2('hi'));                // hi from me to you
print(hi2('hi', 'him'));         // hi from him to you
print(hi2('hi', 'him', 'her'));  // hi from him to her
```

When calling a function with optional parameters it is often not clear what the code
is doing. This can be improved by using named optional parameters. These are
indicated by { } in the parameter list, such as in hi3:

```
String hi3(String msg, {String from, String to}) =>
  '$msg from $from to $to';
```

They are called with name:value and because of the name the position does not
matter:

```
print(hi3('hi', to:'you', from:'me')); // hi from me to you
```

Named parameters can also have default values (name:value):

```
String hi4(String msg, {String from:'me', String to:'you'}) =>
  '$msg from $from to $to';
```

It is called as follows:

```
print(hi4('hi', from:'you')); // hi from you to you
```

The following list summarizes the parameters:

- Optional positional parameters: [param]
- Optional positional parameters with default values: [param=value]
- Optional named parameters: {param}
- Optional named parameters with default values: {param:value}

First class functions

A function can contain other functions, as calcRabbits contains calc(years) in prorabbits_v4.dart:

```
String calculateRabbits(int years) {
  calc(years) => (2 * pow(E, log(GROWTH_FACTOR) *
    years)).round().toInt();
  var out = "After $years years:\t ${calc(years)} animals";
  return out;
}
```

This can be useful if the inner function needs to be called several times within the outer function, but it cannot be called from outside this outer function. A slight variation is to store the function in a variable calc that has type Function, as in prorabbits_v5.dart:

```
String calculateRabbits(int years) {
  var calc = (years) => (2 * pow(E, log(GROWTH_FACTOR) *
    years)).round().toInt();                              (1)
  assert(calc is Function);
  var out = "After $years years:\t ${calc(years)} animals";
  return out;
}
```

The right-hand side of line (1) is an anonymous function or *lambda* that takes parameter years and returns the expression after => (the lambda operator). It could also have been written as follows:

```
var calc2 = (years) {
  return (2 * pow(E, log(GROWTH_FACTOR) *
    years)).round().toInt();
};
```

In prorabbits_v6.dart, the function calc is made top-level and is passed in the function lineOut as a parameter named fun:

```
void main() {
  print("The number of rabbits increases as:\n");
  for (int years = 0; years <= NO_YEARS; years++) {
    lineOut(years, calc(years));
  }
}

calc(years) => // code omitted, same as line(1)
  //in the preceding code
```

```
lineOut(yrs, fun) {
    print("After $yrs years:\t ${fun} animals");
}
```

As a variation to the previous code, `prorabbits_v7.dart` has the inner function `calc`, which has no parameter and yet it can use the variable `years` that exists in the surrounding scope. For that reason `calc` is called a **closure**; it closes over the surrounding variables, retaining their values.

```
String calculateRabbits(int years) {
    calc() => (2 * pow(E, log(GROWTH_FACTOR) *
        years)).round().toInt();

    var out = "After $years years:\t ${calc()} animals";
    return out;
}
```

Closures can also be defined as top-level functions, as `closure.dart` shows. The function `multiply` returns a function (that itself takes a parameter `i`). So `mult2` in the following code is a function that needs to be called with a parameter, for example, `mult2(3)`:

```
// short version:  multiply(num n) => (num i) => n * i;
// long version:
Function multiply(num n) {
    return (num i) => n * i;
}

main() {
    var two = 2;
    var mult2 = multiply(two); // this is called partial application
    assert(mult2 is Function);
    print('${mult2(3)}'); // 6
}
```

This closure behavior (true lexical scoping) is most clearly seen in `closure2.dart`, where three anonymous functions (each of which retains the value of `i`) are added to a List `lstFun`. When calling them (the call is made with the `()` operator after the list element `lstFun[i]`), they know their value of `i`; this is a great improvement over JavaScript.

```
main() {
    var lstFun = [];
    for(var i in [10, 20, 30]) {
        lstFun.add( () => print(i) );
    }
```

```
print(1stFun[0]());  //  10  null
print(1stFun[1]());  //  20  null
print(1stFun[2]());  //  30  null
}
```

While all these code variations might now perhaps seem as just a esthetical, they can make your code clearer in more complex examples and we'll make good use of them in the forthcoming apps. The definition of a function comprises its name, parameters, and return type and is also called its *signature*. If you find this signature occurring often in your code, you can define it as a function type with typedef, as shown in the following code:

```
typedef int addInts(int a, b);
```

Then you can use addInts as the type of a function that takes two values of int and returns an int.

Both in functional and OO programming it is essential to break a large problem into smaller ones. In functional programming, the decomposition in functions is used to support a divide-and-conquer approach to problem solving. A last remark: Dart does *not* have *overloading of functions* (or methods or constructors) because typing the arguments is not a requirement, Dart can't make the distinction. Every function must have a unique name, and there can be only one constructor named after the class, but a class can have other constructors as well.

Recognizing and catching errors and exceptions

As a good programmer, you test your app in all possible conditions. Dart defines a number of errors for those things that you should remedy in your code, such as CastError when a cast fails, or NoSuchMethodError when the class of the object on which the method is called does not have this method, and neither do any of its parent classes. All these are subclasses of the Error class, and you should code so that they do not occur. But when something unexpected occurs while running the app, and the code cannot cope with it, an Unhandled Exception occurs. Especially input values that are read in from the keyboard, a file, or a network connection can be dangerous. Suppose input is such a value that is supposed to be an integer (refer to exceptions.dart); we try to convert it to an int type in line (1):

```
var input = "47B9"; // value read from input,
   should be an integer
int inp = int.parse(input);                    (1)
```

While running the program on the console with the command `dart exceptions.dart`, our program terminates with an exception:

```
Unhandled exception:
FormatException: 47B9
#0      int.parse (dart:core-patch:1586:41)
#1      main (file:///E:/dart/code/chapter_2/
  exceptions/bin/exceptions.dart:4:22)
```

When running in Dart Editor the default behavior is that the debugger kicks in so that you can examine the exception and the values of all variables (you can change this behavior by navigating to **Tools | Preferences | Run and Debug**, and change the **Break on Exceptions** to **None**). The generated `FormatException` is clear, the input was in the wrong format. A lot of other exceptions exist such as `IntegerDivisionByZeroException`, `IOException` (failure to read or write a file), and `HttpException` (when requesting a page from a web server); they are all subclasses from the `Exception` class. When they are generated they are objects that contain information about the exception. How can we handle this exception so that our program does not crash? For this Dart follows the familiar `try...on/catch...finally` pattern:

- `try`: To try the dangerous statement(s)
- `on/catch`: To catch the exception (a specific one that you know can occur or a general exception) and stop it from propagating
- `finally`: It contains code (perhaps to clean up, or close files or connections) that will be executed, whether or not an exception occurs, but it is optional

A minimal exception handler could be as shown in the following code:

```
try {
  int inp = int.parse(input);
} on FormatException {
  print ('ERROR: You must input an integer!');
}
```

This prints out the text in the `on` part. Use `catch` if you want to examine the exception object. The last clause in the `try` statement should be an `on Exception catch(e)` or better even a simple `catch(e)` to stop any type of error or exception. So the most general exception handler is:

```
try {
  int inp = int.parse(input);
} on FormatException { // or any other specific exception
  print ('ERROR: You must input an integer!');
} on Exception catch(e) { // Any other exception
```

```
    print('Unknown exception: $e');
  } catch(e) {   // No specified type, handles all
    print('Something really unknown: $e');
  } finally {
    print('OK, I have cleaned up the mess');
  }
```

If you comment out the on FormatException part, you'll see that $e contains FormatException: 47B9

Should an abnormal condition occur, you can generate or throw an exception in your code yourself with throw. An example is given in the following code:

```
var radius = 8;
var area = PI * pow(radius, 2);
if (area > 200) {           // area is 201.06192982974676
  throw 'This area is too big for me.';
}
```

You can also throw a real Exception object with throw new Exception("…").The keyword throw produces an expression, so it can be used after a => operator like this:

```
clearBalance() => throw const UnimplementedError();
```

This is handy to remind yourself while testing that this method hasn't yet been implemented! The bottom line is to test your code exhaustively and provide exception handling for unforeseeable events that your app cannot process in a normal way.

Debugging exercise

The following little program (debuggingex.dart) results in a RangeError. Use the debugger from the beginning to see where it goes wrong and correct it. In Dart Editor, double-click on a narrow column to the left of for (var i=0; i<=lst. length; i++) { in order to create a breakpoint (a blue circle). Run the program and use step over to get a new value of the i variable. Correct the program to avoid the range error. However, don't use try...catch to handle the error because this is a programmer's mistake!

```
// calculate and print the squares of the list items:
var lst = [1, 2, 3, 4, 5];

void main() {
  for (var i=0; i<=lst.length; i++) {
    print(lst[i] * lst[i]);
  }
}
```

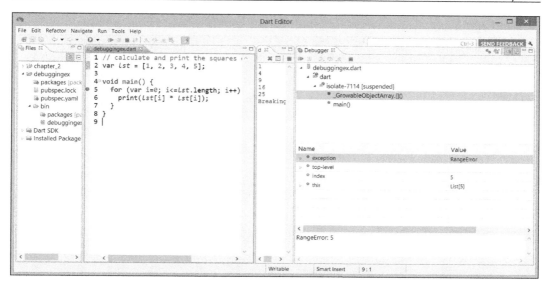

Summary

By now you have acquired a lot of technical skills and gained insights into how Dart works. The main ideas to take away from this chapter are:

- The relevance of typing variables in Dart and when to apply them: type the public API of your app in order to enhance tooling and documentation, which is produced with the built-in tool Dartdoc

- Dart's constructs are very familiar but the approach is quite refreshing, leading to elegant code

- In particular, Dart incorporates quite a few functional ways of coding: functions are quite powerful and working with collections uses this intensively

In the next chapter we will see that Dart is a familiar object-oriented language using classes. Generic types are also available, and we show how to use libraries to structure your growing code. Using external libraries is easy with the pub tool, and tests can be integrated with the unit testing library.

3

Structuring Code with Classes and Libraries

In this chapter we will look at the object-oriented nature of Dart. If you have prior knowledge of an OO language, most of this chapter will feel familiar. Nonetheless, coding classes in Dart is more succinct when introducing some nice new features such as factory constructors and generalizing the use of interfaces. If you come from the JavaScript world, you will start to realize that classes can really structure your application.

Data mostly comes in collections. Dart has some neat classes to work with collections, and they can be used for any type of collections. That's why they are called generic. As soon as you get a few code files in your project, structuring them by making libraries becomes essential for code maintainability. Also, your code will probably use existing libraries written by other developers; to make it easy, Dart has its own package manager called pub. Automating the testing of code on a functional level is done with a built-in unit test library.

We will look at the following topics:

- Using classes and objects
- Collection types and generic classes
- Structuring your code using libraries
- Managing library dependencies with pub
- Unit testing in Dart

We will wrap it all up in a small but useful project to calculate word frequencies in an extract of text.

A touch of class – how to use classes and objects

We saw in *Chapter 1, Dart – A Modern Web Programming Language,* how a class contains members such as properties, a constructor, and methods (refer to `banking_v2.dart`). For those familiar with classes in Java or C#, it's nothing special and we can see already certain simplifications:

- The short constructor notation lets the parameter values flow directly into the properties:

```
BankAccount(this.owner, this.number, this.balance) { … }
```

- The keyword `this` is necessary here and refers to the actual object (being constructed), but it is rarely used elsewhere (only when there is a name conflict). Initialization of instance variables can also be done in the so-called **initializer list**, in this shorter version of the constructor:

```
BankAccount(this.owner, this.number, this.balance):
  dateCreated = new DateTime.now();
```

- The variables are initialized after the colon (`:`) and are separated by a comma. You cannot use the keyword `this` in the initializer expression. If nothing else needs to be done, the constructor body can be left out.

- The properties have automatic getters to read the value (as in `ba.balance`) and, when they are not `final` or `constant`, they also have a setter method to change the value (as in `balance += amount`).

You can start out by using dynamic typing (`var`) for properties, especially when you haven't decided what type a property will become. As development progresses, though, you should aim to change dynamic types into strong types that give more meaning to your code and can be validated by the tools.

Properties that are Boolean values are commonly named with `is` at the beginning, for example, `isOdd`.

A class has a default constructor when there are no other constructors defined. Objects (instances of the class) are made with the keyword `new`, and an object `is` of the type of the class. We can test this with the is operator, for example if object `ba` is of type `BankAccount`, then the following is true: `ba is BankAccount`. Single inheritance between classes is defined by the `extends` keyword, the base class of all classes being `Object`.

Member access uses the dot (.) notation, as in ba.balance or ba.withdraw(100.0). A class can contain objects that are instances of other classes: a feature known as **composition** (aggregation). For example, we could decide at a later stage that the String owner in the BankAccount class should really be an object of a Person class, with many other properties and methods.

A neat feature to simplify code is the **cascade operator** (..); with it, you can set a number of properties and execute methods on the same object, for example, on the ba object in the following code (it's not chaining operations!):

```
ba
  ..balance = 5000.0
  ..withdraw(100.0)
  ..deposit(250.0);
```

We'll focus on what makes Dart different and more powerful than common OO languages.

Visibility – getters and setters

What about the visibility or access of class members? They are public by default, but if you name them to begin with an underscore (_), they become private. However, private in Dart does not mean only visible in its class; a private field (property)—for example, _owner—is visible in the entire library in which it is defined but not in the client code that uses the library.

For the moment, this means that it is accessible in the code file where it is declared because a code file defines an implicit library. The entire picture will become clear in the coming section on libraries. A good feature that enhances productivity is that you can begin with public properties, as in project_v1.dart. A Project object has a name and a description and we use the default constructor:

```
main() {
  var p1 = new Project();
  p1.name = 'Breeding';
  p1.description = 'Managing the breeding of animals';
  print('$p1');
  // prints: Project name: Breeding - Managing
     the breeding of animals
}

class Project {
  String name, description;
  toString() => 'Project name: $name - $description';
}
```

Suppose now that new requirements arrive; the length of a project name must be less than 20 characters and, when printed, the name must be in capital letters. We want the Project class to be responsible for these changes, so we create a private property, _name, and the get and set methods to implement the requirements (refer to project_v2.dart):

```
class Project {
  String _name; // private variable
  String description;

    String get name => _name == null ? "" :_name.toUpperCase();
  set name(String prName) {
    if (prName.length > 20)
      throw 'Only 20 characters or less in project name';
    _name = prName;
  }

  toString() => 'Project name: $name - $description';
}
```

The get method makes sure that, in case _name is not yet filled in, an empty string is returned.

The code that already existed in main (or in general, the client code that uses this property) does not need to change; it now prints Project name: BREEDING - Managing the breeding of animals and, if a project name that is too long is given, the code generates an exception.

 Start your class code with public properties and, later, change some of them to private if necessary with getters and/or setters without breaking client code!

A getter (and a setter) can also be used without a corresponding property instead of a method, again simplifying the code, such as the getters for area, perimeter, and diagonal in the class Square (square_v1.dart):

```
import 'dart:math';

void main() {
  var s1 = new Square(2);
  print('${s1.perimeter}'); // 8
  print('${s1.area}');       // 4
  print('${s1.diagonal}');   // 2.8284271247461903
}
```

```dart
class Square {
  num length;
  Square(this.length);

  num get perimeter => 4 * length;
  num get area => length * length;
  num get diagonal => length * SQRT2;
}
```

SQRT2 is defined in `dart:math`.

The new properties (derived from other properties) cannot be changed because they are getters. Dart doesn't do function overloading because of optional typing, but does allow **operator overloading**, redefining a number of operators (such as ==, >=, >, <=, and < — all arithmetic operators — as well as [] and [] =). For example, examine the operator > in `square_v1.dart`:

```dart
bool operator >(Square other) => length > other.length
    ? true : false;
```

If s1 and s2 are `Square` objects, we can now write code like this:
if (s2 > s1) { … }.

> Use overloading of operators sparingly and only when it seems a good fit and that it would be unsurprising to fellow developers.

Types of constructors

All OO languages have class constructors, but Dart has some special kinds of constructors covered in the following sections.

Named constructors

Because there is no function overloading, there can be only one constructor with the class name (the so-called **main constructor**). So if we want more, we must use named constructors, which take the form `ClassName.constructorName`. If the main constructor does not have any parameters, it is called a **default constructor**. If the default constructor does not have a body of statements such as `BankAccount();`, it can be omitted. If you don't declare a constructor, a default constructor is provided for you. Suppose we want to to create a new bank account for a person by copying data from another of his/her bank accounts, for example, the owner's name. We could do this with the named constructor `BankAccount.sameOwner` (refer to `banking_v3.dart`):

```
BankAccount.sameOwner(BankAccount acc)  {
  owner = acc.owner;
}
```

We could also do this with the initializer version:

```
BankAccount.sameOwner(BankAccount acc): owner = acc.owner;
```

When we make an object via this constructor and print it out, we get:

```
Bank account from John Gates with number null and balance null
```

A constructor can also redirect to the main constructor by using the `this` keyword like so:

```
BankAccount.sameOwner2(BankAccount acc): this(acc.owner, "000-0000000-
00", 0.0);
```

We initialize the number and balance to dummy values, because `this()` has to provide three arguments for the three parameters of the main constructor.

factory constructors

Sometimes we don't want a constructor to always make a new object of the class; perhaps we want to return an object from a cache or create an object from a subtype instead. The `factory` constructor provides this flexibility and is extensively used in the Dart SDK. In `factory_singleton.dart`, we use this ability to implement the singleton pattern, in which there can be only one instance of the class:

```
class SearchEngine {
  static SearchEngine theOne;                              (1)
  String name;
```

```
    factory SearchEngine(name) {                              (2)
      if (theOne == null) {
        theOne = new SearchEngine._internal(name);
      }
      return theOne;
    }
// private, named constructor
  SearchEngine._internal(this.name);                          (3)
// static method:
    static nameSearchEngine () => theOne.name;                (4)
  }


main() {
  //substitute your favorite search-engine for se1:
  var se1 = new SearchEngine('Google');                       (5)
  var se2 = new SearchEngine('Bing');                         (6)
  print(se1.name);                         // 'Google'
  print(se2.name);                         // 'Google'
  print(SearchEngine.theOne.name);         // 'Google'        (7)
  print(SearchEngine.nameSearchEngine());  // 'Google'        (8)
  assert(identical(se1, se2));                                (9)
}
```

In line (1), the static variable theOne (here of type SearchEngine itself, but it could also be of a simple type, such as num or String) is declared: such a variable is the same for all instances of the class. It is invoked on the class name itself, as in line (7); that's why it is also called a class variable. Likewise, you can have static methods (or class methods) such as nameSearchEngine (line (4)) called in the same way (line (8)).

 Static methods can be useful, but don't create a class containing static methods only to provide common or widely used utilities and functionality; use top-level functions instead.

In lines (5) and (6), two SearchEngine objects se1 and se2 are created through the factory constructor in line (2). This checks whether our static variable theOne already refers to an object or not. If not, a SearchEngine object is created through the named constructor SearchEngine._internal from line (3); if it had already been created, nothing is done and the object theOne is returned in both cases. The two SearchEngine objects se1 and se2 are in fact the same object, as is proven in line (9). Note that the named constructor SearchEngine._internal is private; a factory invoking a private constructor is also a common pattern.

const constructors

Two squares created with the same length are different objects in memory. If you want to make a class where each object cannot change, provide it with `const` constructors and make sure that every property is `const` or `final`, for example, class `ImmutableSquare` in `square_v1.dart`:

```
class ImmutableSquare {
  final num length;
  static final ImmutableSquare ONE = const ImmutableSquare(1);
  const ImmutableSquare(this.length);
}
```

Objects are created with `const` instead of `new`, using the `const` constructor in the last line of the class to give `length` its value:

```
var s4 = const ImmutableSquare(4);
var s5 = const ImmutableSquare(4);
assert(identical(s4,s5));
```

Inheritance

Inheritance in Dart comes with no surprises if you know the concept from Java or .NET. Its main use is to reduce the codebase by factoring common code (properties, methods, and so on) into a common parent class. In `square_v2.dart`, the class `Square` inherits from the `Rectangle` class, indicated with the `extends` keyword (line (4)). A `Square` object inherits the properties from its parent class (see line (1)), and you can refer to constructors or methods from the parent class with the keyword `super` (as in line (5)):

```
main() {
  var s1 = new Square(2);
  print(s1.width);                              (1)
  print(s1.height);
  print('${s1.area()}'); // 4
  assert(s1 is Rectangle);                       (2)
}

class Rectangle {
  num width, height;
  Rectangle(this.width, this.height);
  num area() => width * height;                  (3)
}
```

```
class Square extends Rectangle {              (4)
  num length;
  Square(length): super(length, length) {     (5)
    this.length = length;
  }
  num area() => length * length;              (6)
}
```

Methods from the parent class can be overridden in the derived class without special annotations, for example, method `area()` (lines `(3)` and `(6)`). An object of a child class is also of the type of the parent class (see line `(2)`) and thus can be used whenever a parent class object is needed. This is the basis of what is called the polymorphic behavior of objects. All classes inherit from the class `Object`, but a class can have only one direct parent class (single inheritance) and constructors are not inherited. Does author mean an object, the class of this object, its parent class, and so on (until `Object`); they are all searched for the method that is called on. A class can have many derived classes, so an application is typically structured as a class hierarchy tree.

In OO programming, the class decomposition (with properties representing components/objects of other classes) and inheritance are used to support a divide-and-conquer approach to problem solving. Class A inherits from class B only when A is a subset of B, for example, a Square is a Rectangle, a Manager is an Employee; basically when class B is more generic and less specific than class A. It is recommended that inheritance be used with caution because an inheritance hierarchy is more rigid in the maintenance of programs than decomposition.

Abstract classes and methods

Looking for parent classes is an abstraction process, and this can go so far that the parent class we have decided to work with can no longer be fully implemented; that is, it contains methods that we cannot code at this point, so-called **abstract methods**. Extending the previous example to `square_v3.dart`, we could easily abstract out a parent class, `Shape`. This could contain methods for calculating the area and the perimeter, but they would be empty because we can't calculate them without knowing the exact shape. Other classes such as `Rectangle` and `Square` could inherit from `Shape` and provide the implementation for these methods.

```
main() {
  var s1 = new Square(2);
  print('${s1.area()}');        // 4
  print('${s1.perimeter()}');   // 8
  var r1 = new Rectangle(2, 3);
```

```
  print('${r1.area()}');        // 6
  print('${r1.perimeter()}');   // 10
  assert(s1 is Shape);
  assert(r1 is Shape);
  // warning + exception in checked mode: Cannot instantiate
  // abstract class Shape
  // var f = new Shape();
}

abstract class Shape {
  num perimeter();
  num area();
}

class Rectangle extends Shape {
  num width, height;
  Rectangle(this.width, this.height);
  num perimeter() => 2 * (height + width);
  num area() => height * width;
}

class Square extends Shape {
  num length;
  Square(this.length);
  num perimeter() => 4 * length;
  num area() => length * length;
}
```

Also, making instances of Shape isn't very useful, so it is rightfully an abstract class. An abstract class can also have properties and implemented methods, but you cannot make objects from an abstract class unless it contains a factory constructor that creates an object from another class. This can be useful as a default object creator for that abstract class. A simple example can be seen in factory_abstract.dart:

```
void main() {
  Animal an1 = new Animal();            (1)
  print('${an1.makeNoise()}'); // Miauw
}

abstract class Animal {
  String makeNoise();
  factory Animal() => new Cat();         (2)
}

class Cat implements Animal {
  String makeNoise() => "Miauw";
}
```

Animal is an abstract class; because we most need cats in our app, we decide to give it a factory constructor to make a cat (line (2)). Now we can construct an object from the Animal class (line (1)) and it will behave like a cat. Note that we must use the keyword implements here to make the relationship between the class and the abstract class (this is also an interface, as we discuss in the next section). Many of the core types in the Dart SDK are abstract classes (or interfaces), such as num, int, String, List, and Map. They often have factory constructors that redirect to a specific implementation class for making an object.

The interface of a class – implementing interfaces

In Java and .NET, an abstract class without any implementation in its methods is called an **interface** — a description of a collection of fields and methods — and classes can implement interfaces. In Dart, this concept is greatly enhanced and there is no need for an explicit interface concept. Here, every class implicitly defines its own interface (also called API) containing all the public instance members of the class (and of any interfaces it implements). The abstract classes of the previous section are also interfaces in Dart. Interface is not a keyword in the Dart syntax, but both words are used as synonyms. Class B can implement any other class C by providing code for C's public methods. In fact, the previous example, square_v3.dart, continues to work when we change the keyword extends to implements:

```
class Rectangle implements Shape {
  num width, height;
  Rectangle(this.width, this.height);
  num perimeter() => 2 * (height + width);
  num area() => height * width;
}
```

This has the additional benefit that class Rectangle could now inherit from another class if necessary. Every class that implements an interface is also of that type as is proven by the following line of code (when r1 is an object of class Rectangle):

```
assert(r1 is Shape);
```

extends is much less used than implements, but it also clearly has a different meaning. The inheritance chain is searched for a called method, not the implemented interfaces.

Implementing an interface is not restricted to one interface. A class can implement many different interfaces, for example, `class Cat implements Mammal, Pet { ... }`. In this new vision, where every class defines its own interface, abstract classes (that could be called explicit interfaces) are of much less importance (in fact, the keyword `abstract` is optional; leaving it off only gives a warning of unimplemented members). This interface concept is more flexible than in most OO languages and doesn't force us to define our interfaces right from the start of a project. The `dynamic` type, which we discussed briefly in the beginning of this chapter, is in fact the base interface that every other class (also `Object`) implements. However, it is an interface without properties or methods and cannot be extended.

In summary, interfaces are used to describe functionality that is shared (implemented) by a number of classes. The implementing classes must fulfill the interface requirements. Coding against interfaces is an excellent way to provide more coherence and structure in your class hierarchy.

Polymorphism and the dynamic nature of Dart

Because Dart fully implements all OO principles, we can write polymorphic code, in which an object can be used wherever something of its type, the type of its parent classes, or the type of any of the interfaces it implements is needed. We see this in action in `polymorphic.dart`:

```
main() {
  var duck1 = new Duck();
  var duck2 = new Duck('blue');
  var duck3 = new Duck.yellow();
  polytest (new Duck()); // Quack   I'm gone, quack!      (1)
  polytest (new Person());
    // human_quack  I am a person swimming                (2)
}

polytest(Duck duck) {                                     (3)
  print('${duck.sayQuack()}');
  print('${duck.swimAway()}');
}

abstract class Quackable {
  String sayQuack();
}
```

```
class Duck implements Quackable {
  var color;
  Duck([this.color='red']);
  Duck.yellow() { this.color = 'yellow';}

  String sayQuack() => 'Quack';
  String swimAway() => "I'm gone, quack!";
}

class Person implements Duck {                      (4)
  sayQuack() => 'human_quack';
  swimAway() => 'I am a person swimming';           (5)

  noSuchMethod(Invocation invocation) {             (6)
    if (invocation.memberName == new Symbol("swimAway"))
      print("I'm not really a duck!");
  }
}
```

The top-level function `polytest` in line (3) takes anything that is a `Duck` as argument. In this case, this is not only a real duck, but also a person because class `Person` also implements `Duck` (line (4)). This is polymorphism. This property of a language permits us to write code that is generic in nature; using objects of interface types, our code can be valid for all classes that implement the interface used.

Another property shows that Dart also resembles dynamic languages such as Ruby and Python; when a method is called on an object, its class, parent class, the parent class of the parent class, and so on (until the class `Object`), are searched for the method called. If it is found nowhere, Dart searches the class tree from the class to `Object` again for a method called `noSuchMethod()`.

`Object` has this method, and its effect is to throw a `noSuchMethodError`. We can use this to our advantage by implementing this method in our class itself; see line (6) in class `Person` (the argument mirror is of type `Invocation`, its property `memberName` is the name of the method called, and its property `namedArguments` supplies a Map with the method's arguments). If we now remove line (5) so that `Person` no longer implements the method `swimAway()`, the Editor gives us a warning:

```
Concrete class Person has unimplemented members from
  Duck: String swimAway().
```

But if we now execute the code, the message `I'm not really a duck!` is printed when `print('${duck.swimAway()}')` is called for the `Person` object. Because `swimAway()` didn't exist for class `Person` or any of its parent classes, `noSuchMethod` is then searched, found in the class itself, and then executed. `noSuchMethod` can be used to do what is generally called **metaprogramming** in the dynamic languages arena, giving our applications greater flexibility to efficiently handle new situations.

Collection types and generics

In the *Built-in types and their methods* section in *Chapter 2, Getting to Work with Dart*, we saw that very powerful data structures such as List and Map are core to Dart and not something added afterwards in a separate library as in Java or .NET.

Typing collections and generics

How can we check the type of the items in a List or Map? A List created either as a literal or with the default constructor can contain items of any type, as the following code shows (refer to `generics.dart`):

```
var date = new DateTime.now();
// untyped List (or a List of type dynamic):
var lst1 = [7, "lucky number", 56.2, date];
print('$lst1'); // [7, lucky number, 56.2,
  // 2013-02-22 10:08:20.074]
var lst2 = new List();
lst2.add(7);
lst2.add("lucky number");
lst2.add(56.2);
lst2.add(date);
print('$lst2'); // [7, lucky number, 56.2,
  // 2013-02-22 10:08:20.074]
```

While this makes for very versatile Lists most of the time, you know that the items will be of a certain type, such as `int` or `String` or `BankAccount` or even `List`, themselves. In this case, you can indicate type `E` between `<` and `>` in this way: `<E>`. An example is shown in the following code:

```
var langs = <String>["Python","Ruby", "Dart"];
var langs2 = new List<String>();                        (1)
langs2.add("Python");
langs2.add("Ruby");
langs2.add("Dart");
var lstOfString = new List<List<String>>();             (2)
```

(Don't forget the `()` at the end of lines `(1)` and `(2)` because this calls the constructor!

With this, Dart can control the items for us; `langs2.add(42);` gives us a warning and a `TypeErrorImplementation` exception when run in checked mode:

```
type 'int' is not a subtype of type 'String' of 'value'
```

Here, `value` means 42. However, when we run in production mode, this code runs just fine. Again, indicating the type helps us to prevent possible errors and at the same time documents your code.

Why is the special notation `<>` also used as `List<E>` in the API documents for List? This is because all of the properties and methods of List work for any type `E`. That's why the `List<E>` type is called generic (or parameterized). The formal type parameter `E` stands for any possible type.

The same goes for Maps; a Map is in fact a generic type `Map<K, V>`, where `K` and `V` are formal type parameters for the types of the keys and values respectively, giving us the same benefits as the following code demonstrates:

```
var map = new Map<int, String>();
map[1] = 'Dart';
map[2] = 'JavaScript';
map[3] = 'Java';
map[4] = 'C#';
print('$map'); // {1: Dart, 2: JavaScript, 3: Java, 4: C#}
map['five'] = 'Perl'; // String is not assignable to int   (3)
```

Again, line (3) gives us a `TypeError` exception in checked mode, not in production mode. We can test the generic types like this:

```
print('${langs2 is List}'); // true
print('${langs2 is List<String>}'); // true            (4)
print('${langs2 is List<double>}'); // false           (5)
```

We see that, in line (5), the type of the List is checked; this check works even in production mode! (Uncheck the **Run in Checked Mode** checkbox in **Run | Manage Launches** and click on **Apply** to see this in action.) This is because generic types in Dart (unlike in Java) are **reified**; their type info is preserved at runtime, so you can test the type of a collection even in production mode. Note, however, that this is the type of the collection only. When adding the statement `langs2.add(42);` (which executes fine in production mode), the check in line (4) still gives us the value `true`. If you want to check the types of all the elements in a collection in production mode, you have to do this for each element individually, as shown in the following code:

```
for (var s in langs2) {
  if (s is String) print('$s is a String');
  else             print ('$s is not a String!');
}
// output:
//  Python is a String
//  Ruby is a String
//  Dart is a String
//  42 is not a String!
```

Checking the types of generic Lists gives mostly expected results:

```
print(new List
<String>() is List<Object>);    // true   (1)
print(new List<Object>() is List<String>);   // false (2)
print(new List<String>() is List<int>);      // false (3)
print(new List<String>() is List);           // true  (4)
print(new List() is List<String>);           // true  (5)
```

Line (1) is true because Strings (as everything) are Objects. (2) is false because not every Object is a String. (3) is false because Strings are not of type int (4) is true because Strings are also of the general type `dynamic`. Line (5) can be a surprise: `dynamic` is `String`. This is because generic types without type parameters are considered substitutable (subtypes of) for any other version of that generic type.

The collection hierarchy and its functional nature

Apart from `List` and `Map`, there are other important collection classes, such as `Queue` and `Set`, among others specified in the `dart:collection` library; most of them are generic. We can't review them all here but the most important ones have the following relations (an arrow is UML notation for "is a subclass of" (`extends` in Dart):

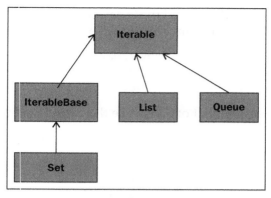

The collection hierarchy

`List` and `Queue` are classes that inherit from `Iterable`, and `Set` inherits from `IterableBase`; all these are abstract classes. The `Map` class is also abstract and forms on its own the root of a whole series of classes that implement containers of values associated with keys, sometimes also called dictionaries. Put simply, the `Iterable` interface allows you to enumerate (or iterate, that is, read but not change) all items of a collection one-by-one using what is called an **Iterator**. As an example, you can make a collection of the numbers 0 to 9 by making an Iterator with:

```
var digits = new Iterable.generate(10, (i) => i);
```

The iteration can be performed with the `for` (*item* in *collection*) statement:

```
for (var no in digits) {
  print(no);
} // prints 0 1 2 3 4 5 6 7 8 9 on successive lines
```

This prints all the numbers from 0 to 9 successively. Members such as `isEmpty`, `length`, and `contains()`, which we saw in action with List (refer to `lists.dart`) are already defined at this level, but there is a lot more. `Iterable` also defines very useful methods for filtering, searching, transforming, reducing, chaining, and so on. This shows that Dart has a lot of the characteristics of a functional language: we see lots of functions taking functions as parameters or returning functions. Let us look at some examples applied to a list by applying `toList()` to our `Iterable` object digits:

```
var digList = digits.toList();
```

An even shorter and more functional version than `for...in` is `forEach`, which takes as parameter a function that is applied to every item `i` of the collection in turn. In the following example, an anonymous function that simply prints the item is shown:

```
digList.forEach((i) => print('$i'));
```

Use `forEach` whenever you don't need the index of the item in the loop. This also works for Maps, for example, to print out all the keys in the following map:

```
Map webLinks =    {  'Dart': 'http://www.dartlang.org/',
   'HTML5': 'http://www.html5rocks.com/' };
webLinks.forEach((k,v) => print('$k')); // prints: Dart    HTML5
```

If we want the first or last element of a List, use the corresponding functions.

If you want to skip the first *n* items use `skip(n)`, or skip by testing on a condition with `skipWhile(condition)`:

```
var skipL1 = digList.skip(4).toList();
print('$skipL1'); // [4, 5, 6, 7, 8, 9]
var skipL2 = digList.skipWhile((i) => i <= 6).toList();
print('$skipL2'); // [7, 8, 9]
```

The functions `take` and `takeWhile` do the opposite; they take the given number of items or the items that fulfill the condition:

```
var takeL1 = digList.take(4).toList();
print('$takeL1'); // [0, 1, 2, 3]
var takeL2 = digList.takeWhile((i) => i <= 6).toList();
print('$takeL2'); // [0, 1, 2, 3, 4, 5, 6]
```

If you want to test whether any of the items fulfill a condition, use `any`; to test whether all of the items do so, use `every`:

```
var test = digList.any((i) => i > 10);
print('$test');   // false
var test2 = digList.every((i) => i < 10);
print('$test2');   // true
```

Suppose you have a List and you want to filter out only these items that fulfill a certain condition (this is a function that returns a Boolean, called a **predicate**), in our case the even digits; here is how it's done:

```
var even = (i) => i.isEven;                          (1)
var evens = digList.where(even).toList();            (2)
print('$evens'); // [0, 2, 4, 6, 8]                  (3)
evens = digList.where((i) => i.isEven).toList();     (4)
print('$evens'); // [0, 2, 4, 6, 8]
```

We use the `isEven` property of `int` to construct an anonymous function in line (1). It takes the parameter `i` to test its evenness, and we assign the anonymous function to a function variable called `even`. We pass this function as a parameter to `where`, and we make a list of the result in line (2). The output in line (3) is what we expect.

It is important to note that `where` takes a function that for each item tests a certain condition and thus returns `true` or `false`. In line `(4)`, we write it more tersely in one line, appropriate and elegant for short predicate functions. Why do we need the call `toList()` in this and the previous functions? Because `where` (and the other `Iterable` methods) return a so-called lazy `Iterable`. Calling `where` alone does nothing; it is `toList()` that actually performs the iteration and stuffs the results in a List (try it out: if you leave out `toList()`, in line (4), then the right-hand side is an instance of `WhereIterable`).

If you want to apply a function to every item and form a new List with the results, you can use the `map` function; in the following example, we triple each number:

```
var triples = digList.map((i) => 3 * i).toList();
print('$triples'); // [0, 3, 6, 9, 12, 15, 18, 21, 24, 27]
```

Another useful utility is to apply a given operation with each item in succession, combined with a previously calculated value. Concretely, say we want to sum all elements of our List. We can of course do this in a `for` loop, accumulating the sum in a temporary variable:

```
var sum = 0;
for (var i in digList) {
  sum += i;
}
print('$sum'); // 45
```

Dart provides a more succinct and functional way to do this kind of manipulation with the `reduce` function (eliminating the need for a temporary variable):

```
var sum2 = digList.reduce((prev, i) => prev + i);
print('$sum2'); // 45
```

We can apply `reduce` to obtain the minimum and maximum of a numeric List as follows:

```
var min = digList.reduce(Math.min);
print('minimum: $min'); // 0
var max = digList.reduce(Math.max);
print('maximum: $max'); // 9
```

For this to work, we need to import the math library:

```
import 'dart:math' as Math;
```

We could do this because min and max are defined for numbers, but what about other types? For this, we need to be able to compare two List items: i1 and i2. If i2 is greater than i1, we know the min and max of the two and we can sort them. Dart has this intrinsically defined for the basic types int, num, String, Duration, and Date. So in our example, with types int we can simply write:

```
var lst = [17, 3, -7, 42, 1000, 90];
lst.sort();
print('$lst'); // [-7, 3, 17, 42, 90, 1000]
```

If you look up the definition of sort(), you will see that it takes as optional argument a function of type int, compare(E a, E b), belonging to the Comparable interface. Generally, this is implemented as follows:

- if a < b return -1

- if a > b return 1

- if a == b return 0

In the following code, we use the preceding logic to obtain the minimum and maximum of a List of Strings:

```
var lstS = ['heg', 'wyf', 'abc'];
var minS = lstS.reduce((s1,s2) =>
  s1.compareTo(s2) < 0 ? s1 : s2);
print('Minimum String: $minS'); // abc
```

In a general case, we need to implement compareTo ourselves for the element type of the list, and it turns out that the preceding code lines can then be used to obtain the minimum and maximum of a List of a general type! To illustrate this, we will construct a List of persons; these are objects of a very simple Person class:

```
class Person {
  String name;
  Person(this.name);
}
```

We make a List of four Person objects and try to sort it as shown in the following code:

```
var p1 = new Person('Peeters Kris');
var p2 = new Person('Obama Barak');
var p3 = new Person('Poetin Vladimir');
var p4 = new Person('Lincoln Abraham');
var pList = [p1, p2, p3, p4];
pList.sort();
```

We then get the following exception:

```
type 'Person' is not a subtype of type 'Comparable'.
```

This means that class Person must implement the Comparable interface by providing code for the method compareTo. Because String already implements this interface, we can use the compareTo method for the person's names:

```
lass Person implements Comparable{
  String name;
  Person(this.name);
  // many other properties and methods
  compareTo(Person p) => name.compareTo(p.name);
}
```

Then we can get the minimum and maximum and sort our Person List in place simply by:

```
var minP = pList.reduce((s1,s2) => s1.compareTo(s2)
  < 0 ? s1 : s2);
print('Minimum Person: ${minP.name}'); // Lincoln Abraham
var maxP = pList.reduce((s1,s2) => s1.compareTo(s2)
  < 0 ? s2 : s1);
print('Maximum Person: ${maxP.name}'); // Poetin Vladimir

pList.sort();
pList.forEach((p) => print('${p.name}'));
```

The preceding code prints the following output (on successive lines):

```
Lincoln Abraham    Obama Barak    Peeters Kris    Poetin Vladimir
```

For using Queue, your code must import the collection library by using import 'dart:collection'; because that's the library this class is defined in. It is another collection type, differing from a List in that the first (head) or the last item (tail) are important here. You can add an item to the head with addFirst or to the tail with add or addLast; or you can remove an item with removeFirst or removeLast:

```
var langsQ = new Queue();
langsQ.addFirst('Dart');
langsQ.addFirst('JavaScript');
print('${langsQ.elementAt(1)}'); // Dart
var lng = langsQ.removeFirst();
assert(lng=='JavaScript');
langsQ.addLast('C#');
langsQ.removeLast();
print('$langsQ'); // {Dart}
```

You have access to the items in a Queue by index with `elementAt(index)`, and `forEach` is also available. For this reason, Queues are ideal when you need a **first-in first-out** data structure (**FIFO**), or a **last-in first-out** data structure (**LIFO**, called a **stack** in most languages).

Lists and Queues allow duplicate items. If you don't need ordering and your requirement is to only have unique items in a collection, use a `Set` type:

```
var langsS = new Set();
langsS.add('Java');
langsS.add('Dart');
langsS.add('Java');
langsS.length == 2;
print('$langsS'); // {Dart, Java}
```

Again, Sets allow for the same methods as List and Queue from their place in the collection hierarchy (see the *The collection hierarchy figure*). They also have the specific intersection method that returns the common elements between a Set and another collection.

Here is a handy flowchart to decide which data structure to use:

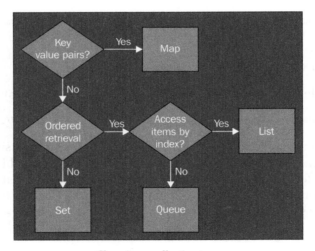

Choosing a collection type

 Maps have unique keys (but not values) and Sets have unique items, while Lists and Queues do not. Lists are ideal for arbitrary access to items anywhere in the collection (by index), but changing their size can be costly. Queues are the type to use if you mainly want to operate on the head or tail of the collection.

Structuring your code using libraries

Using classes, extending them, and implementing interfaces are the way to go to structure your Dart code. But how do we group together a number of classes, interfaces, and top-level functions that are coupled together? To package an application or to create a shareable code base, we use a **library**. The Dart SDK already provides us with some 30 utility libraries, such as dart:core, dart:math, and dart:io. You can look them up in your Editor by going to **Help | API Reference** or via the URL http://api.dartlang.org. All built-in libraries have the dart: prefix. We have seen them in use a few times and know that we have to import them in our code as import 'dart:math'; in prorabbits_v7.dart. Web applications will always import dart:html (dart:core is the most fundamental library and so is imported automatically).

Likewise, we can create our own libraries and let other apps import them to use their functionality. To illustrate this, let us do so for our rabbit-breeding application (perhaps there is a market for this app after all). For an app this simple, this is not needed, of course. However, every Dart app that contains a main() function is also a library even when not indicated. We make a new app called breeding that could contain all kinds of breeding calculations. We group together all the constants that we will need in a file called constants.dart, and we move the function that calculates the rabbit breeding to a file named rabbits.dart in a subfolder called rabbits. All files now have to declare how they are part of the library. There is one code file (the library file in the bin subfolder; its file icon in the Editor is shown in bold) that contains the library keyword; in our example, this is breeding.dart in line (1):

```
library breeding;                              (1)

import 'dart:math';                            (2)

part 'constants.dart';                          (3)
part 'rabbits/rabbits.dart';

void main() {                                  (4)
  print("The number of rabbits increases as:\n");
  for (int years = 0; years <= NO_YEARS; years++) {
    print("${calculateRabbits(years)}");
  }
}
```

A library needs a name; here it is `breeding` (all lowercase, and not in quotes); other apps can import our library through this name. This file also contains all necessary `import` statements (line (2)) and then sums up (in no particular order) all source files that together constitute the library. This is done with the `part` keyword, followed by the quoted (relative) pathname to the source file. For example, when `rabbits.dart` resides in a subfolder called `rabbits`, this will be written as:

```
part 'rabbits/rabbits.dart';
```

But everything is simpler if all files of a library reside in one folder. So, the library file presents an overview of all the part files in which it is split; if needed, we can structure our library with subfolders, but Dart sees all this code as a single file. Furthermore, all library source files need to indicate that they are part of the library (we show only `rabbits.dart` here); again, the library name is not quoted (line (1)):

```
part of breeding;                                       (1)

String calculateRabbits(int years) {
  calc() => (2 * pow(E, log(GROWTH_FACTOR) *
    years)).round().toInt();

  var out = "After $years years:\t ${calc()} rabbits";
  return out;
}
```

 GROWTH_FACTOR is defined in the file `constants.dart`.

All these statements (`library`, `import`, `part`, and `part of`) need to appear at the top before any other code. The Dart compiler will import a specific source file only once even when it is mentioned several times. If there is a main entry function in our library, it must be in the library file (line (4)); start the app to verify that we obtain the same breeding results as in our previous versions. A library that contains `main()` is also a runnable app in itself but, in general, a library does not need to contain a `main()` function. The `part of` annotation enforces that a file can only be part of one library. Is this a restriction? No, because it strengthens the principle that code must not be duplicated. If you have a collection of business classes in an app, group them in their own library and import them into your app; that way, these classes are reusable.

 You can start coding your app (library) in a single file. Gradually, you begin to discover units of functionality of classes and/or functions that belong together;, then you can move these into part files, with the library file structuring the whole.

Using a library in an app

To show how we can use our newly made library in another app, create a new application app_breeding; in its startup file (app_breeding.dart), we can call our library as shown in the following code:

```
import '../../breeding/bin/breeding.dart';          (1)

int years;

void main() {
  years = 5;
  print("The number of rabbits has attained:");
  print("${calculateRabbits(years)}");
}
// Output:
//The number of rabbits has attained:
//After 5 years:    1518750 rabbits
```

The import statement in line (1) points to the main file of our library, relative in the file system to the .dart file we are in (two folder levels up with two periods (..) and then into subfolder bin of breeding). As long as your libraries retain the same relative position to your client app (while deploying it in production), this works. You can also import a library from a (remote) website using a URL in this manner:

```
import 'http://www.breeding.org/breeding.dart';
```

Absolute file paths in import are not recommended because they break too easily when deploying. In the next section, we discuss the best way of importing a library by using the package manager called pub.

Resolving name conflicts

If you only want one or a few items (variables, functions, or classes) from a library, you have the option of only importing these by enumerating them after show:

```
import 'library1.dart' show var1, func1, Class1;
```

The inverse can also be done; if you want to import everything from the library excluding these items, use hide:

```
import 'library1.dart' hide var1, func1, Class1;
```

We know that everything in a Dart app must have a unique name; or, to put it another way, there can be no name conflicts in the app's namespace. What if we have to import into our app two libraries that have the same names for some of their objects? If you only need one of them, you can use show and/or hide. But what if you need both? In such a case, you can give one of the libraries an alias and differentiate between both by using this alias as a prefix. Suppose library1 and library2 both have an object A; you can use this as follows:

```
import 'library1.dart';          // contains class A
import 'library2.dart' as libr2; // contains class A

var obj1 = new A();              // Use A from library1.
var obj2 = new libr2.A();        // Use A from library2.
```

Use this feature only when you really have to, for example, to solve name conflicts or aid in readability. Finally, the export command (possibly combined with show or hide) gives you the ability to combine (parts of) libraries. Refer to the app export.

Suppose liba.dart contains the following code:

```
library liba;
abc() => 'abc from liba';
xyz() => 'xyz from liba';
```

Additionally, suppose libb.dart contains the following code:

```
library libb;
import 'liba.dart';
export 'liba.dart' show abc;
```

Then, if export.dart imports libb, it knows method abc but not method xyz:

```
import 'libb.dart';
void main() {
  print('${abc()}'); // abc from liba
  // xyz();  // cannot resolve method 'xyz'
}
```

Visibility of objects outside a library

In the *A touch of class – how to use classes and objects* section, we mentioned that starting a name with _ makes it private at library level (so it is only known in the library itself not outside of it). This is the case for all objects: variables, functions, classes, methods, and so on. Now we will illustrate this in our breeding library.

Suppose `breeding.dart` now contains two top-level variables:

```
String s1 = 'the breeding of cats';          (1)
var _s2  = 'the breeding of dogs';           (2)
```

We can use them both in `main()` but also anywhere else in the library, for example, in `rabbits.dart`:

```
String calculateRabbits(int years) {
  print('$s1 and $_s2');
  //...
  return out;
}
```

But if we try to use them in the app `breeding.dart`, which imports `breeding`, we get a warning in line (3) of the following code in the Editor; it says **cannot resolve _s2; s1 is visible but _s2 is not**.

```
void main() {
  years = 5;
  // ...
  print('$s1 and $_s2');                     (3)
}
```

An exception occurs when the code is run (both in checked and production mode). Note that, in lines (1) and (2), we typed the public variable `s1` as `String`, while the private variable `_s2` was left untyped. This is a general rule: give the publicly visible area of your library strong types and signatures. Privacy is an enhancement for developers used to JavaScript but people coming from the OO arena will certainly ask why there is no class privacy. There are probably a number of reasons: classes are not as primordial in Dart as in OO languages, Dart has to compile to JavaScript, and so on. Class privacy is not needed to the extent usually imagined, and if you really want to have it in Dart you can do it. Let the library only contain the class that has some private variables; these are visible only in this class because other classes or functions are outside this library.

Managing library dependencies with pub

Often your app depends on libraries (put in a package) that are installed in the cloud (in the pub repository, or the GitHub repository, and so on). In this section, we discuss how to install such packages and make them available to your code.

In the web version of our rabbits program (prorabbits_v3.dart) in *Chapter 1, Dart – A Modern Web Programming Language*, we discussed the use of the pubspec. yaml file. This file is present in every Dart project and contains the dependencies of our app on external packages. The **pub** tool takes care of installing (or updating) the necessary packages: right-click on the selected pubspec.yaml file and choose **Pub Get** (or **Upgrade**, in case you need a more recent version of the packages). Alternatively, you can double-click on the pubspec.yaml ; then, a screen called **Pubspec Details** appears that lets you change the contents of the file itself. This screen contains a section called **Pub Actions** where you will find a link to **Run Pub Get**). It even automatically installs so-called transitive dependencies: if the package to install needs other packages, they will also be installed.

Let's prepare for the next section on unit testing by installing the unittest package with the pub tool. Create a new command-line application and call it unittest_v1. When you open the pubspec screen, you see no dependencies; however, at the bottom there is a tab called **Source** to go to the text file itself. This shows us:

```
name: unittest_v1
description: A sample command-line application
#dependencies:
#   unittest: any
```

The lines preceded with # are commented out in a .yaml file; remove these to make our app dependent on the unittest package. If we now run **Pub Get**, we see that a folder called packages appears, containing in a folder called unittest the complete source of the requested package. The same subfolders appear under the bin folder. If needed, the command pub get can also be run outside the Editor from the command line. The unittest package belongs to the Dart SDK. In the Dart Editor installation, you can find it at D:\dart\dart-sdk\pkg (substitute D:\dart with the name of the folder where your Dart installation resides). However pub installs it from its central repository pub.dartlang.org, as you can see in the following screenshot. Another file pubspec.lock is also created (or updated); this file is used by the pub tool and contains the version info of the installed packages (don't change anything in here). In our example, this contains:

```
# Generated by pub. See: http://pub.dartlang.org/doc/glossary.
html#lockfile
        packages:
      dartlero:
        description:
          ref: null
          resolved-ref: c1c36b4c5e7267e2e77067375e2a69405f9b59ce
          url: "https://github.com/dzenanr/dartlero"
        source: git
        version: "1.0.2"
```

```
path:
    description: path
    source: hosted
    version: "0.9.0"
stack_trace:
    description: stack_trace
    source: hosted
    version: "0.9.0"
unittest:
    description: unittest
    source: hosted
    version:
```

The following screenshot shows the configuration information for `pubspec.yaml`:

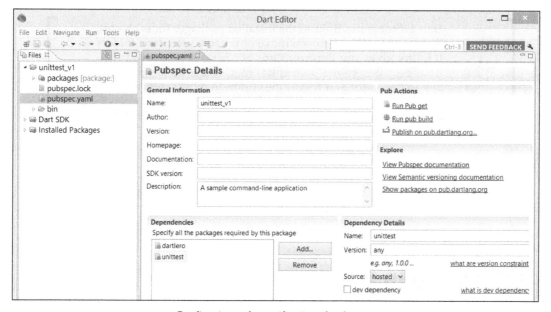

Configuring pub specifications for the app

The pubspec screen, as you can see in the preceding screenshot, also gives you the ability to change or fill in complementary app info, such as **Name**, **Author**, **Version**, **Homepage**, **SDK version**, and **Description**. The **Version** field is of particular importance; with it, you can indicate that your app needs a specific version of a package (such as 2.1.0) or a major version number of 1 (>= 1.0.0 < 2.0.0); it locks your app to these versions of the dependencies. To use the installed unittest package, write the following code line at the top of unittest_v1.dart:

```
import 'package:unittest/unittest.dart';
```

The path to a Dart source file after `package:` is searched for in the `packages` folder. As a second example and in preparation for the next chapter, we will install the `dartlero` package from Pub (although the `unittest_v1.dart` program will not use its specific functionality). Add a dependency called `dartlero` via the pubspec screen; any version is good. Take the default value `hosted` from the **Source** drop-down list and fill in `https://github.com/dzenanr/dartlero` for the path. Save this and then run **Pub Get**. Pub will install the project from GitHub, install it in the `packages` folder, and update the `pubspec.lock` file. To make it known to your app, use the following `import` statement:

```
import 'package:dartlero/dartlero.dart';
```

The command `pub publish` checks whether your package conforms to certain conditions and then uploads it to pub's central repository at `pub.dartlang.org`.

> Dart Editor stores links to the installed packages for each app; these get invalid when you move or rename your code folders. If Editor gives you the error `Cannot find referenced source: package: somepkg/pkg.dart`, do this: close the app in the editor and restart the editor. In most cases, the problem is solved; if not, clean out the Editor cache by deleting everything in `C:\users\yourname\DartEditor`. When you reopen the app in the Editor the problem is solved.

Here is a summary of how to install packages:

- Change `pubspec.yaml` and add dependencies through the **Details** screen
- Run the `pub get` command
- Add an import statement to your code for every installed package

Unit testing in Dart

Dart has a built-in unit-test framework. We learned how to import it in our app in the previous section. Every real app, and certainly the ones that you're going to deploy somewhere, should contain a sufficient amount of unit tests. Test programs will normally be separated from the main app code, residing in their own directory called `test`. Unit testing offers quite a lot of features; we will apply them in the forthcoming projects. Here we want to show you the basics, and we will do so by creating a `BankAccount` object, making some transactions on it, and verifying the results so that we can trust our `BankAccount` methods are doing fine (we continue to work in `unittest_v1.dart`). Let's create a `BankAccount` constructor and do some transactions:

```
var ba1 = new BankAccount("John Gates","075-0623456-72", 1000.0);
ba1.deposit(500.0);
```

```
ba1.withdraw(300.0);
ba1.deposit(136.0);
```

After this, `ba1.balance` is equal to `1336.0` (because *1000 + 500 – 300 + 136 = 1336*). We can test whether our program calculated this correctly with the following statement:

```
test('Account Balance after deposit and withdrawal', () {
  expect(ba1.balance, equals(1336.0));
});
```

Or we can use a shorter statement as follows:

```
test('Account Balance after deposit and withdrawal', () =>
  expect(ba1.balance, equals(1336.0)));
```

The function `test` from `unittest` takes two parameters:

- A test name (`String`); here, this is `Account Balance after deposit and withdrawal`

- A function (here anonymous) that calls the `expect` function; this function also takes two parameters:

    ○ The value as given by the program
    ○ The expected value, here given by `equals` (*expected value*)

Now running the program gives this output:

```
unittest-suite-wait-for-done
PASS: Account Balance after deposit and withdrawal
All 1 tests passed.
unittest-suite-success
```

Of course, here `PASS` indicates that our program tested successfully. If this were not the case (suppose the balance had to be 1335.0 but the program produced 1336.0) we would get an exception with the message `Some tests failed`:

```
unittest-suite-wait-for-done
FAIL: Account Balance after deposit and withdrawal
  Expected: <1335.0>
       but: was <1336.0>
0 PASSED, 1 FAILED, 0 ERRORS
```

There would also be screen output showing you which test went wrong, the expected (correct) value, and the program value (it is important to note that the tests run after all other statements in the method have been executed). Usually, you will have more than one test, and then you can group them as follows using the same syntax as `test`:

```
group('Bank Account tests', () {
  test('Account Balance after deposit and withdrawal', () =>
    expect(ba1.balance, equals(1336.0)));
  test('Owner is correct', () => expect(ba1.owner, equals
    ("John Gates")));
  test('Account Number is correct', () => expect
    (ba1.number, equals("075-0623456-72")));
});
```

We can even prepare the tests in a setUp function (in this case, that would be creating the account and doing the transactions, setUp is run before each test) and clean up after each test executes in a tearDown function (indicating that the test objects are no longer needed):

```
group('Bank Account tests', () {
  setUp(() {
    ba1 = new BankAccount("John Gates","075-0623456-72", 1000.0);
    ba1.deposit(500.0);
    ba1.withdraw(300.0);
    ba1.deposit(136.0);
  });
  tearDown(() {
    ba1 = null;
  });
  test('Account Balance after deposit and withdrawal', () =>
    expect(ba1.balance, equals(1336.0)));
  test('Owner is correct', () => expect(ba1.owner, equals
    ("John Gates")));
  test('Account Number is correct', () => expect
    (ba1.number, equals("075-0623456-72")));
});
```

The preceding code produces the following output:

```
unittest-suite-wait-for-done
PASS: Bank Account tests Account Balance after
  deposit and withdrawal
PASS: Bank Account tests Owner is correct
PASS: Bank Account tests Account Number is correct
All 3 tests passed.
unittest-suite-success
```

In general, the second parameter of expect is a so-called **matcher** that tests whether the value satisfies some constraint. Here are some matcher possibilities: isNull, isNotNull, isTrue, isFalse, isEmpty, isPositive, hasLength(m), greaterThan(v), closeTo(value, delta), inInclusiveRange(low, high) and their variants. For a more detailed discussion of their use, see the documentation at http://www.dartlang.org/articles/dart-unit-tests/#basic-synchronous-tests. We'll apply unit testing in the coming projects, notably in the example that illustrates Dartlero in the next chapter.

Project – word frequency

We will now develop systematically a small but useful web app that takes as input ordinary text and produces as output an alphabetical listing of all the words appearing in the text, together with the number of times they appear (their frequency). For an idea of the typical output, see the following screenshot (`word_frequency.dart`):

Word frequency app

The user interface is easy: the text is taken from the `textarea` tag with `id` text in the top half. Clicking on the frequency button sets the processing in motion, and the result is shown in the bottom half with `id` words. Here is the markup from `word_frequency.html`:

```
<!DOCTYPE html>
<html>
  <head>
    <meta charset="utf-8">
    <title>Word frequency</title>
    <link rel="stylesheet" href="word_frequency.css">
  </head>
  <body>
    <h1>Word frequency</h1>

    <section>
      <textarea id="text" rows=10 cols=80></textarea>
      <br/>
      <button id="frequency">Frequency</button>
             
      <button id="clear">Clear</button>
      <br/>
```

```
        <textarea id="words" rows=40 cols=80></textarea>
    </section>

    <script type="application/dart"
      src="word_frequency.dart"></script>
      <script src="packages/browser/dart.js"></script>
    </body>
</html>
```

In the last line, we see that the special script dart.js (which checks for the existence of the Dart VM and starts the JavaScript version if that is not found) is also installed by pub. In *Chapter 1, Dart – A Modern Web Programming Language*, we learned how to connect variables with the HTML elements through the querySelector function:

```
variable = querySelector('#id')
```

So that's what we will do first in main():

```
// binding to the user interface:
var textArea = querySelector('#text');
var wordsArea = querySelector('#words');
var wordsBtn = querySelector('#frequency');
var clearBtn = querySelector('#clear');
```

Our buttons listen to click events with the mouse; this is translated into Dart as:

```
wordsBtn.onClick.listen((MouseEvent e) { ... }
```

Here is the processing we need to do in this click-event handler:

1. The input text is a String; we need to clean it up (remove spaces and special characters).

2. Then we must translate the text to a list of words. This will be programmed in the following function:

   List fromTextToWords(**String** text)

3. Then, we traverse through the List and count for each word the number of times it occurs; this effectively constructs a map. We'll do this in the following function:

   Map analyzeWordFreq(**List** wordList)

4. From the map, we will then produce a sorted list for the output area:

   List sortWords(**Map** wordFreqMap)

With this design in mind, our event handler becomes:

```
wordsBtn.onClick.listen((MouseEvent e) {
  wordsArea.value = 'Word: frequency \n';
  var text = textArea.value.trim();
  if (text != '') {
    var wordsList = fromTextToWords(text);
    var wordsMap = analyzeWordFreq(wordsList);
    var sortedWordsList = sortWords(wordsMap);
    sortedWordsList.skip(1).forEach((word) =>
    wordsArea.value = '${wordsArea.value} \n${word}');
  }
});
```

In the last line, we append the output for each word to `wordsArea`.

Now we fill in the details. Removing unwanted characters can be done by chaining `replaceAll()` for each character like this:

```
var textWithout = text.replaceAll(',', '').replaceAll
  (';', '').replaceAll('.', '').replaceAll('\n', ' ');
```

This is very ugly code! We can do better by defining a regular expression that assembles all these characters. We can do this with the expression \W that represents all noncharacters (letters, digits, or underscores), and then we only have to apply `replaceAll` once:

```
List fromTextToWords(String text) {
  var regexp = new RegExp(r"(\W\s?)");           (1)
  var textWithout = text.replaceAll(regexp, '');
  return textWithout.split(' ');                  (2)
}
```

We use the class `RegExp` in line (1), which is more often used to detect pattern matches in a `String`. Then we apply the `split()` method of `String` in line (2) to produce a list of words `wordsList`. This list is transformed into a Map with the following function:

```
Map analyzeWordFreq(List wordList) {
  var wordFreqMap = new Map();
  for (var w in wordList) {
    var word = w.trim();
    wordFreqMap.putIfAbsent(word, () => 0);       (3)
    wordFreqMap[word] += 1;
  }
  return wordFreqMap;
}
```

Note the use of putIfAbsent instead of if...else in line (3).

Then we use the generated Map to produce the desired output in the method sortWords:

```
List sortWords(Map wordFreqMap) {
  var temp = new List<String>();
  wordFreqMap.forEach((k, v) => temp.add('${k}:
    ${v.toString()}'));
  temp.sort();
  return temp;
}
```

The resulting list is shown in the bottom text area. You can find the complete listing in the file word_frequency.dart.

Summary

Congratulations! You can call yourself a Dart programmer now. By working through this and the previous chapter, you have acquired a lot of technical skills and gained insights into how Dart works. The main ideas to take away from this chapter are:

- Modeling the data of your project in classes, perhaps extending another class or implementing the interface of some classes
- The library concept to structure your code at a higher level using packages from other developers and eventually publishing your own app with pub
- The basic ways of unit testing a Dart app

In the next chapter, we will graphically design a model for our app and base the code on a modeling framework, all in Dart.

4
Modeling Web Applications with Model Concepts and Dartlero

Up until now, the apps we discussed were quite simple; there was no real need to design a model. However, when developing more complex (web) applications, a good model to start from will lay a more stable foundation for the code. In this chapter we will build a project from scratch, designing its model graphically, and start implementing it with a framework. The good thing is that we will use tools developed in Dart to do this. Because most of the projects we will develop are hosted on GitHub, we start by looking at how Git and GitHub work. We will cover the following topics:

- A short introduction to Git and GitHub
- What a model is and why we need it in programming
- Model concepts – a graphical design tool for our models
- Dartlero – a simple domain model framework
- The categories and links model

A short introduction to Git and GitHub

Git is an open source software tool that allows groups of people to work together harmoniously on the same code project at the same time. So, it's a distributed version control system. The projects are published in the cloud, for example, in the GitHub repository `https://github.com/` (there are other websites that accept Git projects, for example, Bitbucket at `https://bitbucket.org/`). Git maintains local copies of these projects on your computer(s). For this to work, the Git tool must be installed locally as well. To get started, create an account on the GitHub website or sign in if you already have one. Go to the site `https://help.github.com/articles/set-up-git` and click on the **Download and install the latest version of Git** link. If necessary, choose your OS and then let the wizard install Git on your machine with the default options. The code from this book resides in the following GitHub repository: `https://github.com/Ivo-Balbaert/learning_dart`. To create a local copy of the code examples:

1. Make a folder where you store your Git downloads (for example, `/home/git` or `d:\git`)

2. Start the Git Bash command-line tool and go to that folder:

   cd git

3. Clone the remote repository into your local repository by using the following command:

   git clone git://github.com/Ivo-Balbaert/learning_dart.git

A subfolder `learning_dart` is created and then all files are copied in it locally. Afterwards, if you want to get the latest changes from the remote repository, go to the local directory and use the following command:

git pull

Creating a repository on GitHub and a local version

This is easy; just follow the steps given here:

1. Sign in into GitHub, click on the **New Repository** button, and fill in a repository name, say `dart_projects`. Then click on the **Create Repository** button (we follow the Dart style guidelines here and name it as a directory: `lowercase_with_underscores`). Now, your remote repository is created with the URL `https://github.com/your_name/dart_projects.git`.

2. Create a folder for your local version of this repository, say `git/dart_projects`. Start Git bash and go to that folder with `cd`.

3. Initialize an empty Git repository with the following command:

   `git init`

4. Every project needs a readme file; so create an empty text file `README.md` in a simple text editor, and put some useful information in it with Dart Editor (or your favorite text-editor).

5. We add this file to our local repository with the command:

   `git add README.md.`

   In general, the `git add` command will put all that is inside the directory into a waiting room (called a staging area or index). The `git status` command will show these new changes that are yet to be committed to your project. At this time, you make these changes permanent by committing our project with the following command:

   `git commit -m 'created first version'`

   Here, `-m` provides a message. You can also provide a text file called `gitignore` to contain files (or patterns of files) that are not to be included in the version control system.

6. To push your local changes to your remote GitHub repository, use the following commands:

   ```
   git remote add origin https://github.com/your_name
     /dart_projects.git
   ```

   and

   `git push -u origin master`

   (You will be asked to authenticate with your GitHub username and password).

7. The next time you work on your project and want to store the changes in the repository (local and on GitHub), you can simply use the following command:

   ```
   git add .
   git commit -m 'verb something'
   git push
   ```

8. If you deleted a file, just use `git rm filename` before `commit`. You can also indicate a version of your project by giving it a tag, for example, s00:

```
git tag -a s00 -m 'spiral 00'
```

9. To push these tags to the remote repository, use the following command:

```
git push --tags
```

Collaborating on a GitHub project

If you want to invite someone else to join your project in order to make changes, select the repository of your project, use the **Settings** menu, and then select the **Collaborators** option. Add that person by using his or her GitHub name. If you are not alone on your project, you should always start your working session with the `git pull` command to get the latest changes and to avoid conflicts. Watch the videos at this link to get a good introduction to Git: http://git-scm.com/videos. Also, the basic concepts are explained in this course: https://www.codeschool. com/courses/try-git.

What a model is and why we need it in programming

Most applications that go beyond simple exercises are too complex to start developing them from the start; a model that describes the entities in the application domain and their relations is needed. To fully support such a domain-driven development, we need three things:

- A **graphical tool** for model design and import/export of the model definitions; this is the Model Concepts tool

- A **domain model framework** — Dartlero for simple cases and Dartling for more complicated business domains

- A **web component framework** for rapid development of dynamic web applications: the `Polymer.dart` package

The first two were developed by *Dzenan Ridjanovic*, one of the authors, and the third was developed by the Google Dart team. All are written in Dart and are available as free, open source software. The remainder of this chapter will show how to use model concepts and Dartlero, and we will apply them in constructing a simple model of categories and links. Web components, which are essentially chunks of reusable HTML5, are explained in *Chapter 8, Developing Business Applications with Polymer Web Components*. We will also build a web component application for the category-links model. Dartling is discussed in depth in *Chapter 9, Modeling More Complex Applications with Dartling*. Both of them will be used in the projects from *Chapter 10, MVC Web and UI Frameworks in Dart – An Overview*, onwards. First we will explore the model concepts.

Model concepts – a graphical design tool for our models

This project is also hosted on GitHub. To get a local copy open your Git bash terminal, go to the folder where you want to store the code and issue the following command:

```
git clone git://github.com/dzenanr/model_concepts.git
```

After a few seconds, the `model_concepts` folder is created. It contains the whole project. Open the folder in Dart Editor to get a feel of how it is constructed. It is a web app containing the script tag `<script type="application/dart" src="model_concepts.dart"></script>` and it starts the Dart VM with `model_concepts.dart`. When you run the app, the graphical designer appears in Chrome (Dartium). If you want to run it in another browser without Dart VM, first generate the JavaScript version through **Tools | Generate JavaScript**, and then paste the URL in the address window of your favorite browser (something like `http://127.0.0.1:3030/F:/git/model_concepts/web/model_concepts.html`). The web folder contains the HTML file and the startup script `model_concepts.dart`, which contains the following code snippet:

```
import 'dart:html';
import 'package:model_concepts/model_concepts.dart';          (1)

void main() {
  // Get a reference to the canvas.
  CanvasElement canvas = document.query('#canvas');           (2)
  Board board = new Board(canvas);                            (3)
}
```

Line (1) loads in the model_concepts library from the packages folder; the original source code of the library resides in the lib directory. The library header file, also called model_concepts.dart, shows the dart libraries that we need (html, async, and convert) as well as all the part files:

```
library model_concepts;

import 'dart:html';
import 'dart:async';
import 'dart:convert';


part 'board.dart';
part 'box.dart';
part 'item.dart';
part 'json_panel.dart';
part 'line.dart';
part 'menu_bar.dart';
part 'png_panel.dart';
part 'tool_bar.dart';
```

This app uses canvas painting in HTML5 (we'll explore that bottom-up in the coming chapters). In line (2), the <canvas> tag with the ID canvas is bound to a canvas object of the CanvasElement class. Then in line (3), an object of the Board class (the file board.dart) is instantiated with a reference to this canvas, starting up the program.

We shall not provide further explanation of how the code works here. The app was built up in versions (called **spirals**, so far there are 14). On the *On Dart* blog (http://dzenanr.github.io/), under the **Magic Boxes** posts, you can find a detailed description of how the code evolved from **Spiral s00** to the current app (magic boxes grew into model concepts), along with a summary of the development on http://goo.gl/DqF7d. This is a truly great way to learn Dart!

When the app starts up, we see the following screen:

Model concepts start screen

Working with model concepts

The purpose of this tool is to graphically design a **domain model** of your app. Concepts or entities are drawn as rectangular boxes; these contain **items** that represent the **attributes**. The boxes are connected with **lines** that represent the **relationships** between the entities; their multiplicity (that is, how many entities of kind B are associated with an entity of kind A, for example, many employees working in one department) can be indicated with *0..N* or *1..1*. The tool itself contains a (tiny) user guide, which is revealed on scrolling down the screen.

Explaining the model

We will learn how to work with this tool by designing the model for our next app: the category-links application. This app is all about subjects (called categories here) such as HTML5, Dart, Apple, Google, Programming, the economic crisis, and hyperlinks (called links here) to web postings about these subjects. Here are some examples of links for HTML5: `www.html5rocks.com`, `http://diveintohtml5.info/` and `http://animateyourhtml5.appspot.com/`. Clearly, a category can have multiple links but it may also have none; so, the relationship from category to link is *0..N*.

Our app (that will be developed in *Chapter 8, Developing Business Applications with Polymer Web Components*) will show all categories and the corresponding links for each category. Furthermore, we will be able to edit, remove, and add categories as well as links. But first we will draw a model with two concepts (**Category/Link**) and one relationship (**links**). It will look like the following figure:

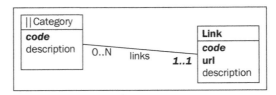

The graphical model of category-links

The category concept has two attributes: a code (name) such as Dart and a description such as Web programming language, tools, and how to. The code attribute is drawn in italics because it is an identifier and in bold because its value is required. The link concept has the code identifier, the required URL attribute, and an optional description attribute. For example, the URL for Dart could be www.dartlang.org and the description could be Official Google site for Dart. In our model, a link has exactly one category, so a *1..1* relation is applied (this is, a simplification of a more realistic situation where a link could belong to many categories). A relationship between two concepts has two directions (**neighbours**). The category-link direction, where **Link** is a neighbor of **Category**, has a min cardinality of *0* (a category need not have any link) and a max cardinality of *N* (many). In addition, it has the link's name. The link-category direction has no name. Hence, it will not be represented explicitly in Dart; its min and max cardinalities are in bold and italics. Together with the code, it is the identifier of the link (note that *1..1* is in italics and bold). Within the same category, all links must have a unique code value. Category is the only entry (| | as a door) into the model. This means that the model will have a collection of categories and each category will have a collection of links.

Drawing the model

The steps to draw a model are given as follows:

1. Click on the box tool icon in the tool bar (brown background, refer to the model concepts' start screen) and create a box for the category concept by clicking on an empty space in the board.

2. Click on the box to select it (four squares appear in the corners) and click again to deselect it. The selected box is displayed in the tool bar and you can enter the name Category for it in the concept field of the tool bar. The name will not appear in the selected box until you use the *Enter* key.

3. Check the entry checkbox; Category is marked with | |. To move a box, select it and keep the mouse down while moving it. If there are connecting lines, they will follow.

The size of selected boxes may be changed by menu items in the **View** menu. If you want to create several boxes, double-click on the box tool to stay active. To return to the select mode, double-click on the select tool.

A box item (an attribute of a concept) may be created by entering its name in the attribute field of the toolbar and by using the *Enter* key.

1. Select the identifier from the drop-down list; the default type String is ok. Enter code and the item appears in the **Category** box. Repeat the steps for the item description, but select the attribute from the list.

2. Now design the link concept with its attributes, and mark the URL attribute from the list as per your requirements.

3. Click on the line tool to create a line between the last two clicked boxes by clicking on an empty space in the board.

The first box is a parent and the second box is a child. By default, the parent box has *0..N* cardinalities. The min is *0* and the max is *N*. By default, the child box has *1..1* cardinalities. For more details, see the tiny user guide in the program screen beneath the brown toolbar.

1. To make a PNG image from our model, scroll down to the **To image** button above the PNG panel and click on the button. The created image becomes visible in the panel; right-click to save it to a file (**Save Image as**) or copy (**Copy Image**) and paste it into another file (for example, as documentation).

2. Name the current model in the **Model** menu as Category_Links and save it in the local storage of your browser (we will see how this works in *Chapter 11, Local Data and Client-Server Communication*). In a later session, simply enter the model name (it is case-sensitive!) and open it.

Exporting the model

Drawing the model clarifies our thoughts about it, but it won't be of much use if we can't get to code from it. We can export the semantics of a model (only the non-hidden boxes and lines) in the JSON format by clicking on the **From model to json** button above the JSON panel. After doing this, the JSON text appears in the JSON panel; copy it and save it into a local text file category_links.json. It also works the other way around: the JSON text may be used to recreate the graphical model in magic boxes. Paste the JSON text from a previous model into the JSON panel and click on the **From json to model** button to visualize the model. For a pretty JSON version of the model, click on the **Pretty json** button, but only after clicking on the **From model to json** button. Open the .json file in a text editor and see how the information about our model is contained in it:

```json
{
    "width":990,
    "lines":[
        {
            "box2box1Max":"1",
            "box1Name":"Category",
            "box1box2Min":"0",
            "box2Name":"Link",
            "box1box2Id":false,
            "box2box1Id":false,
            "box2box1Name":"",
            "box1box2Max":"N",
            "box1box2Name":"",
            "box2box1Min":"1",
            "category":"relationship",
            "internal":true
        }
    ],
    "height":580,
    "boxes":[
        {
            "width":120,
            "entry":true,
            "name":"Category",
            "x":125,
            "height":80,
            "y":63,
            "items":[
                {
                    "sequence":10,
```

```
                          "name":"code",
                          "category":"identifier",
                          "type":"String",
                          "init":""
                     },
                     {

                          "sequence":20,
                          "name":"description",
                          "category":"attribute",
                          "type":"String",
                          "init":""
                     }
                ]
           },
     // omitted analogous entry for link
       ]
    }
```

What is JSON?

JSON (JavaScript Object Notation) is a simple text format (easy to be read and
written by humans and machines) for representing structured objects and collections,
and exchanging data between applications or computers. For example, when a client
sends data to or receives data from a server through a web service, this data is often
in JSON format. It arose from the open source world, more or less as a competitor to
the *heavier* XML format; but it is used everywhere now. Any production language
has special functions (in library `dart:convert`) to make it easy to use, Dart being no
exception. Let us examine a simple JSON example and see how it connects to list and
map: look at the `BankAccount` object from `banking_v3.dart` (*Chapter 2*, *Getting to
Work with Dart*):

```
var ba1 = new BankAccount("John Gates","075-0623456-72", 1000.0);
```

It contains three data items: the owner, the number, and the balance of the account.
The JSON representation of this data (object) is:

```
{
    "owner": "John Gates",
    "number": "075-0623456-72",
    "balance": 1000.0
}
```

In a Dart app, this could be typed as a multiline string (see line (1) in json.dart at code\chapter_3). Looking at it from the Dart perspective, this is a map where the names of the object properties are the keys and the values are the map's values; there is a close relationship between objects and JSON (hence the name). This object notation can be nested (for example, the owner could be an object itself with a name, address, and telephone number). To express that there are many of these objects, you can use the [ ] notation, as in the following code snippet:

```
[
    {
        "owner": "John Gates",
        "number": "075-0623456-72",
        "balance": 1000.0
    },
    {
        "owner": "Bill O'Connor",
        "number": "081-0731645-91",
        "balance": 2500.0
    }
]
```

This effectively corresponds to a list of maps in Dart.

You can encode a Dart object into a JSON string with the JSON.encode() function from the dart:convert library, for example, the bankAccounts variable in line (2). The resulting JSON can be sent over the network, or it could be the return value of a call to a web service. The Dart object to encode needs to be of the type null, bool, int, double, String, List, or Map; any other object needs to have a toJson() method that is called when encoding. The other way around, decoding a JSON string into a Dart object is done with the JSON.decode method (see line (3) in json.dart):

```
import 'dart:convert';

var jsonStr1 = '''                                              (1)
{
    "owner": "John Gates",
    "number": "075-0623456-72",
    "balance": 1000.0
}
''';
var jsonStr2 = '''
[
    {
        "owner": "John Gates",
        "number": "075-0623456-72",
```

```
        "balance": 1000.0
    },
    {
        "owner": "Bill O'Connor",
        "number": "081-0731645-91",
        "balance": 2500.0
    }
]
''';
var bankAccounts = [{ "owner": "John Gates","number": "075-0623456-
72",
                    "balance": 1000.0 },
                { "owner": "Bill O'Connor", "number": "081-
0731645-91",
                    "balance": 2500.0 }];
main() {
  // encoding a Dart object (here a List of Maps) to a JSON string:
  var jsonText = JSON.encode(bankAccounts);                    (2)
  print('$jsonText'); // all white space is removed
  // decoding a JSON string into a Dart object:
  var obj = JSON.decode(jsonText);                             (3)
  assert(obj is List);
  assert(obj[0] is Map);
  assert(obj[0]['number']=="075-0623456-72");

  var ba1 = new BankAccount("John Gates","075-0623456-72", 1000.0);
  var json = JSON.encode(ba1);
}

class BankAccount {
  // other properties and methods ...
  String toJson() {
    return '{"owner":"$owner", "number":"$number", "balance:
      "$balance"}';
  }
}
```

In the previous section, data were exported from model concepts in the JSON format and this data can be imported in the domain model framework Dartling (see *Chapter 9, Modeling More Complex Applications with Dartling*) in order to generate the code for it. We will use JSON again as the format to store data in, or to send data to the server, in some of the forthcoming projects. In the dartlero_tasks project of *Chapter 12, Data-driven Web Applications with MySQL and MongoDB*, we will read and write the JSON files. For a more in-depth look, refer to http://en.wikipedia.org/wiki/JSON.

Dartlero – a simple domain model framework

We will now discuss Dartlero to get an idea of what a domain model framework is all about and how you can build upon it. Dartlero is a limited model framework used in teaching and learning basic data structures in Dart. Get your copy of Dartlero from Pub or from GitHub with the following command:

```
git clone git://github.com/dzenanr/dartlero.git
```

Open the `dartlero` folder in your Dart Editor. Dartlero's code sits in the `lib` folder and the library file `dartlero.dart`, referencing three part files in the `model` subdirectory (lines (3) to (5)):

```
library dartlero;
import 'package:unittest/unittest.dart';

part 'model/concept_model.dart';                              (3)
part 'model/concept_entities.dart';                           (4)
part 'model/concept_errors.dart';                             (5)
```

Dartlero is just a library; it cannot be started by itself. We see that the central concepts are entities and models, and it builds heavily on the built-in `List` and `Map` classes. The code is quite *abstract* but it is instructive to dig into it (use the editor to see the code in its entirety). In the `concept_entities.dart` file, the abstract class `ConceptEntityApi` is defined. It describes the properties and methods of an entity in this framework. We see that an entity has only one property named `code` (with get and set), and there are abstract methods to create (`newEntity`), to copy, and to transform an entity into a map (`toJson`) and vice versa (`fromJson`).

```
abstract class ConceptEntityApi<T extends ConceptEntityApi<T>>
    implements Comparable {

  String get code;
  set code(String code);
  ConceptEntityApi<T> newEntity();                            (1)
  T copy();
  Map<String, Object> toJson();                               (2)
  void fromJson(Map<String, Object> entityMap);               (3)
}
```

The `newEntity` method (line (1)) is used to provide a specific object within the generic code of the `ConceptEntity` class. The `toJson` and `fromJson` methods (lines (2) and (3)) provide the export and import of entities, which will be used in the saving and loading of data.

This class is implemented by `ConceptEntity`, which also contains methods to display an entity and compare two entities. Although all methods contain code, this class is meant as an interface to be implemented by concrete entity classes (that's why it is called `ConceptEntity`):

```
abstract class ConceptEntity<T extends ConceptEntity<T>>
    implements ConceptEntityApi {
    // code left out
}
```

The abstract class `ConceptEntitiesApi` defines a number of properties and methods, such as `length`, `forEach`, `add`, `toList`, and `toJson`, for a collection of entities; in fact, it contains a list and a map of entities:

```
abstract class ConceptEntitiesApi<T extends ConceptEntityApi<T>> {
    int get length;
    bool get isEmpty;
    Iterator<T> get iterator;
    ConceptEntitiesApi<T> newEntities();
    ConceptEntityApi<T> newEntity();
    void forEach(Function f);
// other code left out
}
```

Again, this class is implemented by the class `ConceptEntities`:

```
abstract class ConceptEntities<T extends ConceptEntity<T>>
    implements ConceptEntitiesApi {
    // code left out
}
```

All of the above classes are defined for a generic type `T`, for example:

```
abstract class ConceptEntity<T extends ConceptEntity<T>>
```

When the framework is applied in a concrete domain, `T` is replaced by a concrete type. This type has to be a child class of `ConceptEntity<T>`. This will become clearer when we discuss the example in the next section.

In the `concept_model.dart` file, an abstract class `ConceptModelApi` is defined, which is implemented by `ConceptModel`. This is essentially a map connecting names to `ConceptEntities`:

```
abstract class ConceptModelApi {
    Map<String, ConceptEntitiesApi> newEntries();
    ConceptEntitiesApi getEntry(String entryConcept);
}
```

```
abstract class ConceptModel implements ConceptModelApi {
  Map<String, ConceptEntities> _entryMap;
  ConceptModel() {
    _entryMap = newEntries();
  }

  ConceptEntities getEntry(String entryConcept) => _
entryMap[entryConcept];
}
```

The third file `concept_errors.dart` defines some specific `Error` classes:

```
class DartleroError implements Error {
  final String msg;
  DartleroError(this.msg);
  toString() => '*** $msg ***';
}

class JsonError extends DartleroError {
  JsonError(String msg) : super(msg);
}
```

Dartlero mostly hides the use of the list and map data structures (by looking at the code, you can see how list and map are used internally). It does not support identifiers and relationships and it doesn't have a code generator.

An example of using Dartlero

To get a better feeling of what using a framework entails, let us examine the project that exists as the example folder in the `dartlero` project and as a separate project called `dartlero_example` at GitHub (there are slight differences due to the pub specifications). Get your copy in a separate folder with:

```
git clone git://github.com/dzenanr/dartlero_example.git
```

Then, open the folder `dartlero_example` in Dart Editor.

This app defines the simplest possible model: a project model with only one concept, a `Project`. We will now use the Dartlero framework. The dependency on this package is indicated in the `pubspec.yaml` file so that it can be managed by pub:

```
name: dartlero_example
version: 1.0.0
author: Dzenan Ridjanovic <dzenanr@gmail.com>
description: An example how to use Dartlero, a model framework for
educational purposes.
```

```
homepage: http://ondart.me/
dependencies:
  dartlero:
  git: git://github.com/dzenanr/dartlero.git
```

The library file `dartlero_example.dart` in the `lib` folder imports Dartlero and references two files in a subfolder model:

```
library dartlero_example;
import 'package:dartlero/dartlero.dart';

part 'model/project_entities.dart';
  part 'model/project_model.dart';
```

In the `project_entities.dart` file, we see a `Project` class that extends the framework class `ConceptEntity<Project>` and the collection class `Projects` that extends the `ConceptEntities<Project>` class:

```
class Project extends ConceptEntity<Project> { ... }
class Projects extends ConceptEntities<Project> { ... }
```

What has happened here? The `<Project>` type argument is passed to the `ConceptEntity` class (or `ConceptEntities`) and its `T` parameter is replaced by `Project`. If we replace this, the class `signature` in the abstract class `ConceptEntity<T extends, ConceptEntity<T>` becomes more specific: `abstract class ConceptEntity<Project extends ConceptEntity<Project>>`.

After that, wherever we see `T`, Dart (or the Dart Editor) sees project; the same is true for the `ConceptEntities` class. This means that a collection of entities will contain only projects. Thus, if we want to add a task to projects (let's say of the `Task` type), Dart Editor will complain. Without generics, Dart Editor would happily accept a new task in the projects collection. Using generics makes a framework more general. It can be used with all kinds of concrete types, constraining data so that the model is valid. The following is the complete code of `project_entities.dart`:

```
part of dartlero_example;

class Project extends ConceptEntity<Project> {

  String _name;
  String description;

  String get name => _name;
  set name(String name) {
    _name = name;
    if (code == null) {
      code = name;
```

```
      }
    }

    Project newEntity() => new Project();

    Project copy() {
      var project = super.copy();
      project.name = name;
      project.description = description;
      return project;
    }

    String toString() {
      return '  {\n '
             '    ${super.toString()}, \n '
             '    name: ${name}, \n '
             '    description: ${description}\n'
             '  }';
    }

    Map<String, Object> toJson() {
      Map<String, Object> entityMap = super.toJson();
      entityMap['name'] = name;
      entityMap['description'] = description;
      return entityMap;
    }

    fromJson(Map<String, Object> entityMap) {
      super.fromJson(entityMap);
      name = entityMap['name'];
      description = entityMap['description'];
    }

    bool get onProgramming =>
        description.contains('Programming') ? true : false;

    int compareTo(Project other) {
      return name.compareTo(other.name);
    }
  }

  class Projects extends ConceptEntities<Project> {
    Projects newEntities() => new Projects();
    Project newEntity() => new Project();
  }
```

The `Project` and `Projects` classes also contain the methods `newEntity` and `newEntities` to create concrete objects, implementing the abstract methods of their parent classes. A project has a name and a description; some of its methods (such as `copy`, `toString`, `toJson`, and `fromJson`) extend the methods inherited from `ConceptEntity` by using the `super` keyword. The inherited `compareTo` method gets a new implementation in project: it is completely overridden. Furthermore, `Project` adds a new `onProgramming` method, which is a get only property to see from the description whether the project has something do to with programming.

The `subfolder` model also contains `project_model.dart` with a `ProjectModel` class that extends the `ConceptModel` class from the Dartlero framework. Three projects are created in the `init()` method, and the `display()` method on the model delegates work to the inherited (from `ConceptEntities`) `display()` method on the `projects` object. The following is the code from `project_model.dart`:

```
part of dartlero_example;

class ProjectModel extends ConceptModel {

  static final String project = 'Project';

  Map<String, ConceptEntities> newEntries() {
    var projects = new Projects();
    var map = new Map<String, ConceptEntities>();
    map[project] = projects;
    return map;
  }

  Projects get projects => getEntry(project);

  init() {
    var design = new Project();
    design.name = 'Dartling Design';
    design.description =
        'Creating a model of Dartling concepts based on MagicBoxes.';
    projects.add(design);

    var prototype = new Project();
    prototype.name = 'Dartling Prototype';
    prototype.description =
        'Programming the meta model and the generic model.';
    projects.add(prototype);

    var production = new Project();
```

```
      production.name = 'Dartling';
      production.description =
          'Programming Dartling.';
      projects.add(production);
    }

    display() {
      print('Project Model');
      print('=============');
      projects.display('Projects');
      print(
        '============ ============ ============ '
        '============ ============ ============ '
      );
    }
  }
}
```

In the packages folder, we will see not only dartlero but also unittest, because Dartlero needs that library. This project model is exercised in the accompanying test program project_model_test.dart in test/model, and it contains the following code:

```
import 'package:unittest/unittest.dart';
import 'package:dartlero/dartlero.dart';
import 'package:dartlero_example/dartlero_example.dart';

testProjects(Projects projects) {
  group("Testing Projects", () {
    setUp(() { ...   });
    tearDown(() { ...   });
    test('Add Project', () { ... });
    // various other tests
    });
}

initDisplayModel() {
  ProjectModel projectModel = new ProjectModel();
  projectModel.init();
  projectModel.display();
}

testModel() {
  ProjectModel projectModel = new ProjectModel();
  Projects projects = projectModel.projects;
  testProjects(projects);
}
```

```
main() {
  // initDisplayModel();
  testModel();
}
```

The `main()` method calls `testModel()`, which in turn calls `testProjects()` that uses the `unittest` framework. It contains one `group ("Testing Projects", () {...}` method with `setUp`, `tearDown`, and a number of test methods. In the `setUp()` function, some projects and a collection containing them are created and displayed. Running this test program gives the following output:

```
Project Model
=============

Projects
[
  {
    code: Dartling Design,
    name: Dartling Design,
    description: Creating a model of Dartling concepts based on
MagicBoxes.
  }
]
// some output omitted for brevity //
unittest-suite-wait-for-done
PASS: Testing Projects Add Project
// some output omitted for brevity //
PASS: Testing Projects From JSON to Project Model

All 13 tests passed.
unittest-suite-success
```

Some of the applied tests are given as follows:

- When instantiating an object:
  ```
  var design = new Project();
  expect(design, isNotNull);
  ```

- When adding a project to projects counting the number of Projects:
  ```
  expect(projects.length, equals(++projectCount));
    var added = projects.add(project);
    expect(added, isTrue);
  ```

- When projects is cleared:
  ```
  expect(projects.isEmpty, isTrue);
  ```

- When searching for a project:

```
var project = projects.find(searchName); expect(project.name,
equals(searchName));
```

- Testing that every project has a name:

```
expect(projects.every((p) => p.name != null), isTrue);
```

So what are the advantages of using a domain model framework? Clearly, by inheriting from the model classes we get (a lot of) code that we don't have to write ourselves. So, we get a head start in the functionality of our app. For the simple Dartlero framework, there are methods such as `copy`, `toJson`, `fromJson`, `contains`, `find`, and `display`.

The categories and links application

Let us now apply Dartlero to a model with two concepts and one relationship, our category-links model. Once again, clone the project from GitHub with:

```
git clone git://github.com/dzenanr/dartlero_category_links.git
```

The model is implemented in the `lib` folder of the `dartlero_category_links` application (refer to the following screenshot):

The code structure of categories-links

There are three dart files in the `model` folder, one for the model and two for the two entities. The `dartlero_category_links` library is defined in the `dartlero_category_links.dart` file:

```
library dartlero_category_links;

import 'package:dartlero/dartlero.dart';

part 'model/category_entities.dart';
part 'model/category_links_model.dart';
part 'model/link_entities.dart';
```

There are two classes in the `category_entities.dart` file, one for the entity definition and the other for a collection of entities. The `Category` class of the model extends the `ConceptEntity` class of `Dartlero` (line (1)), while the `Categories` class inherits its properties and methods from the `ConceptEntities` class (line (2)):

```
part of dartlero_category_links;
class Category extends ConceptEntity<Category> {   (1)

  String description;
  Links links = new Links();

  Category newEntity() => new Category();

  String toString() {
    return '  {\n '
           '    ${super.toString()}, \n '
           '    description: ${description}\n'
           '  }\n';
  }

  Map<String, Object> toJson() {
    Map<String, Object> entityMap = super.toJson();
    entityMap['description'] = description;
    entityMap['links'] = links.toJson();
    return entityMap;
  }

  fromJson(Map<String, Object> entityMap) {
```

```
        super.fromJson(entityMap);
        description = entityMap['description'];
        links.fromJson(entityMap['links']);
    }

    bool get onProgramming =>
        description.contains('programming') ? true : false;

}


class Categories extends ConceptEntities<Category> {      (2)
    Categories newEntities() => new Categories();
    Category newEntity() => new Category();
}
```

The `Category` class inherits the code property from the `ConceptEntity` class; it has its own description and links properties. Note that a parent-child relationship direction is represented as the links property in the `Category` class. In addition, the `Category` class inherits the public application interface of the `ConceptEntityApi` class. The `Categories` class (line `(2)`) is simple because most of its behavior is defined in the `ConceptEntities` class of Dartlero. The `Link` and `Links` classes are created in a similar way (refer `link_entities.dart`).

The `CategoryLinksModel` class extends the `ConceptModel` class of Dartlero (refer to `category_links_model.dart`). The `newEntries` method in the `CategoryLinksModel` class provides the only entry into the model. The `init` method creates a few categories and links. The `display` method shows data of the model in the console. To see the model in action, run the following programs in the `test` folder: `category_links_model_test.dart`, `category_entities_test.dart`, or `link_entities_test.dart`. They exercise the same methods and tests as we saw in the first Dartlero example. For example, the model test program calls the `init` and `display` methods:

```
    import 'package:unittest/unittest.dart';
    import 'package:dartlero/dartlero.dart';
    import 'package:dartlero_category_links/dartlero_category_links.dart';

    testModel() {
      CategoryLinksModel categoryLinksModel;
      Categories categories;
      group("Testing Model: ", () {
        setUp(() {
          categoryLinksModel = new CategoryLinksModel();
          categoryLinksModel.init();
          categories = categoryLinksModel.categories;
```

```
      });
      tearDown(() {
        categories.clear();
        expect(categories.isEmpty, isTrue);
      });
      test('Display model', () {
        categoryLinksModel.display();
      });
    });
}

main() {
  testModel();
}
```

This code produces output similar to the previous code snippet.

Summary

In this chapter, we acknowledged the importance of defining a domain model before starting the development of the app. We used a graphical tool (model concepts) to design a model for categories and links, which can be exported in JSON format. Also, we saw how JSON can be used in Dart. A simple domain model framework Dartlero was explored, and we implemented that in two models: a project model and a category-links model. By doing this, we exercised the knowledge of classes, interfaces, generics, lists, maps, and unit testing that we acquired in *Chapter 2, Getting to Work with Dart*. The next few chapters are more practical in nature. We learned how to work with the **Document Object Model** (**DOM**) in HTML pages, how to build forms, how to draw, and how to use audio and video in web pages.

5
Handling the DOM in a New Way

A Dart web application runs inside the browser (HTML) page that hosts the app; a single-page web app is more and more common. This page may already contain some HTML elements or nodes, such as `<div>` and `<input>`, and your Dart code will manipulate and change them, but it can also create new elements. The user interface may even be entirely built up through code. Besides that, Dart is responsible for implementing interactivity with the user (the handling of events, such as button-clicks) and the dynamic behavior of the program, for example, fetching data from a server and showing it on the screen. In previous chapters, we explored some simple examples of these techniques. Compared to JavaScript, Dart has simplified the way in which code interacts with the collection of elements on a web page (called the DOM tree). This chapter teaches you this new method using a number of simple examples, culminating with a Ping Pong game. The following are the topics:

- Finding elements and changing their attributes
- Creating and removing elements
- Handling events
- Manipulating the style of page elements
- Animating a game
- Ping Pong using style(s)
- How to draw on a canvas – Ping Pong revisited

Finding elements and changing their attributes

All web apps import the Dart library `dart:html`; this is a huge collection of functions and classes needed to program the DOM (look it up at `api.dartlang.org`). Let's discuss the base classes, which are as follows:

- The `Navigator` class contains info about the browser running the app, such as the product (the name of the browser), its vendor, the MIME types supported by the installed plugins, and also the geolocation object.

- Every browser window corresponds to an object of the `Window` class, which contains, amongst many others, a `navigator` object, the `close`, `print`, `scroll` and `moveTo` methods, and a whole bunch of event handlers, such as `onLoad`, `onClick`, `onKeyUp`, `onMouseOver`, `onTouchStart`, and `onSubmit`. Use an alert to get a pop-up message in the web page, such as in `todo_v2.dart`:

  ```
  window.onLoad.listen( (e) =>
  window.alert("I am at your disposal") );
  ```

- If your browser has tabs, each tab opens in a separate window. From the `Window` class, you can access local storage or IndexedDB to store app data on the client (see *Chapter 10, MVC Web and UI Frameworks in Dart – An Overview*).

- The `Window` object also contains an object document of the `Document` class, which corresponds to the HTML document. It is used to query for, create, and manipulate elements within the document. The document also has a list of stylesheets (objects of the `StyleSheet` class) — we will use this in our first version of the Ping Pong game.

- Everything that appears on a web page can be represented by an object of the `Node` class; so, not only are tags and their attributes nodes, but also text, comments, and so on. The `Document` object in a `Window` class contains a `List<Node>` element of the nodes in the document tree (DOM) called `childNodes`.

- The `Element` class, being a subclass of `Node`, represents web page elements (tags, such as `<p>`, `<div>`, and so on); it has subclasses, such as `ButtonElement`, `InputElement`, `TableElement`, and so on, each corresponding to a specific HTML tag, such as `<button>`, `<input>`, `<table>`, and so on. (For example, see `prorabbits_v3.dart` and `todo_v1.dart` in *Chapter 1, Dart – A Modern Web Programming Language*). Every element can have embedded tags, so it contains a `List<Element>` element called children.

Let us make this more concrete by looking at `todo_v2.dart`, (a modified version of `todo_v1.dart` from *Chapter 1, Dart – A Modern Web Programming Language*; see the next screenshot) solely for didactic purposes—the HTML file contains an `<input>` tag with the `id` value `task`, and a `<ul>` tag with the `id` value `list`:

```
<div><input id="task" type="text" placeholder="What do you want to
do?"/>
    <p id="para">Initial paragraph text</p>
</div>
<div id="btns">
    <button class="backgr">Toggle background color of header</button>
    <button class="backgr">Change text of paragraph</button>
    <button class="backgr">Change text of placeholder in input
field and the background color of the buttons</button>
</div>
<div><ul id="list"/>
</div>
```

In our Dart code, we declare the following objects representing them:

```
InputElement task;
UListElement list;
```

The following list object contains objects of the `LIElement` class, which are made in `addItem()`:

```
var newTask = new LIElement();
```

You can see the different elements and their layout in the following screenshot:

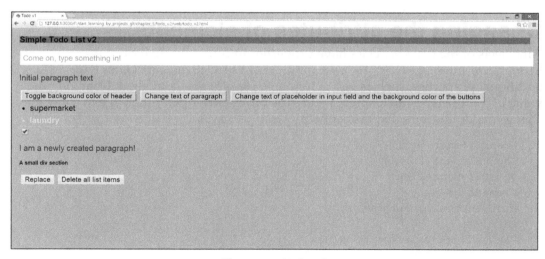

The screen of todo_v2

Finding elements

Now we must bind these objects to the corresponding HTML elements. For that, we use the top-level functions querySelector and querySelectorAll; for example, the InputElement task is bound to the <input> tag with the id value task using: **task = querySelector('#task');**.

Both functions take a string (a CSS selector) that identifies the element, where the id value task will be preceded by #. CSS selectors are patterns that are used in .css files to select elements that you want to style. There are a number of them, but, generally, we only need a few basic selectors (for an overview visit http://www.w3schools.com/cssref/css_selectors.asp).

- If the element has an id attribute with the value abc, use querySelector('#abc')

- If the element has a class attribute with value abc, use querySelector('.abc')

- To get a list of all elements with the tag <button>, use querySelectorAll('button')

- To get a list of all text elements, use querySelectorAll('input[type="text"]') and all sorts of combinations of selectors; for example, querySelectorAll('#btns .backgr') will get a list of all elements with the backgr class that are inside a tag with the id value btns

These functions are defined on the document object of the web page, so in code you will also see document.querySelector() and document.querySelectorAll().

Changing the attributes of elements

All objects of the Element class have properties in common, such as classes, hidden, id, innerHtml, style, text, and title; specialized subclasses have additional properties, such as value for a ProgressElement method. Changing the value of a property in an element makes the browser re-render the page to show the changed user interface. Experiment with todo_v2.dart:

```
import 'dart:html';
InputElement task;
UListElement list;
Element header;
List<ButtonElement> btns;
main() {
  task = querySelector('#task');
  list = querySelector('#list');
```

```
    task.onChange.listen( (e) => addItem() );
    // find the h2 header element:
    header = querySelector('.header');                      (1)
    // find the buttons:
    btns = querySelectorAll('button');                      (2)
    // attach event handler to 1st and 2nd buttons:
    btns[0].onClick.listen( (e) => changeColorHeader() );   (3)
    btns[1].onDoubleClick.listen( (e) => changeTextPara() ); (4)
    // another way to get the same buttons with class backgr:
    var btns2 = querySelectorAll('#btns .backgr');          (5)
    btns2[2].onMouseOver.listen( (e) => changePlaceHolder() );(6)
    btns2[2].onClick.listen((e) => changeBtnsBackColor() );  (7)
    addElements();
}
changeColorHeader() => header.classes.toggle('header2');  (8)
changeTextPara() => querySelector('#para').text = "You changed my
text!";      (9)
changePlaceHolder() => task.placeholder = 'Come on, type something
in!';           (10)
changeBtnsBackColor() => btns.forEach( (b) => b.classes.add('btns_
backgr'));   (11)
void addItem() {
    var newTask = new LIElement();          (12)
    newTask.text = task.value;              (13)
    newTask.onClick.listen( (e) => newTask.remove());
    task.value = '';
    list.children.add(newTask);             (14)
}
addElements() {
    var ch1 = new CheckboxInputElement();   (15)
    ch1.checked = true;
    document.body.children.add(ch1);        (16)
    var par = new Element.tag('p');         (17)
    par.text = 'I am a newly created paragraph!';
    document.body.children.add(par);
    var el = new Element.html('<div><h4><b>A small div
section</b></h4></div>');                  (18)
    document.body.children.add(el);
    var btn = new ButtonElement();
    btn.text = 'Replace';
    btn.onClick.listen(replacePar);
    document.body.children.add(btn);
    var btn2 = new ButtonElement();
    btn2.text = 'Delete all list items';
    btn2.onClick.listen( (e) => list.children.clear() );  (19)
```

```
    document.body.children.add(btn2);
}
replacePar(Event e) {
    var el2 = new Element.html('<div><h4><b>I replaced this div!</b>
</h4></div>');
    el.replaceWith(el2);                    (20)
}
```

Comments for the numbered lines are as follows:

1. We find the `<h2>` element via its class.

2. We get a list of all the buttons via their tags.

3. We attach an event handler to the `Click` event of the first button, which toggles the class of the `<h2>` element, changing its background color at each click (line `(8)`).

4. We attach an event handler to the `DoubleClick` event of the second button, which changes the text in the `<p>` element (line `(9)`).

5. We get the same list of buttons via a combination of CSS selectors.

6. We attach an event handler to the `MouseOver` event of the third button, which changes the placeholder in the input field (line `(10)`).

7. We attach a second event handler to the third button; clicking on it changes the background color of all buttons by adding a new CSS class to their classes collection (line `(11)`).

Every HTML element also has an attribute Map where the keys are the attribute names; you can use this Map to change an attribute, for example:

```
    btn.attributes['disabled'] = 'true';
```

Please refer to the following document to see which attributes apply to which element:

```
https://developer.mozilla.org/en-US/docs/HTML/Attributes
```

Creating and removing elements

The structure of a web page is represented as a tree of nodes in the Document Object Model (DOM). A web page can start its life with an initial DOM tree, marked up in its HTML file, and then the tree can be changed using code; or, it can start off with an empty tree, which is then entirely created using code in the app, that is every element is created through a constructor and its properties are set in code. Elements are subclasses of `Node`; they take up a rectangular space on the web page (with a width and height). They have, at most, one parent Element in which they are enclosed and can contain a list of Elements — their children (you can check this with the function `hasChildNodes()` that returns a `bool` function). Furthermore, they can receive events. Elements must first be created before they can be added to the list of a parent element. Elements can also be removed from a node. When elements are added or removed, the DOM tree is changed and the browser has to re-render the web page.

An Element object is either bound to an existing node with the `querySelector` method of the `document` object or it can be created with its specific constructor, such as that in line (12) (where `newTask` belongs to the class `LIElement` — List Item element) or line (15). If useful, we could also specify the `id` in the code, such as in `newTask.id = 'newTask';`

 If you need a DOM element in different places in your code, you can improve the performance of your app by querying it only once, binding it to a variable, and then working with that variable.

After being created, the element properties can be given a value such as that in line (13). Then, the object (let's name it `elem`) is added to an existing node, for example, to the body node with `document.body.children.add(elem)`, as in line (16), or to an existing node, as `list` in line (14). Elements can also be created with two named constructors from the Element class:

1. Like `Element.tag('tagName')` in line (17), where `tagName` is any valid HTML tag, such as `<p>`, `<div>`, `<input>`, `<select>`, and so on.

2. Like `Element.html('htmlSnippet')` in line (18), where `htmlSnippet` is any valid combination of HTML tags.

Use the first constructor if you want to create everything dynamically at runtime; use the second constructor when you know what the HTML for that element will be like and you won't need to reference its child elements in your code (but by using the `querySelector` method, you can always find them if needed).

You can leave the type of the created object open using `var`, or use the type `Element`, or use the specific class name (such as `InputElement`)—use the latter if you want your IDE to give you more specific code completion and warnings/errors against the possible misuse of types.

When hovering over a list item, the item changes color and the cursor becomes a hand icon; this could be done in code (try it), but it is easier to do in the CSS file:

```
#list li:hover {
  color: aqua;
  font-size:20 px;
  font-weight: bold;
  cursor: pointer;
}
```

To delete an Element `elem` from the DOM tree, use `elem.remove()`. We can delete list items by clicking on them, which is coded with only one line:

```
newTask.onClick.listen( (e) => newTask.remove() );
```

To remove all the list items, use the List function `clear()`, such as in line (19). Replace `elem` with another element `elem2` using `elem.replaceWith(elem2)`, such as in line (20).

Handling events

When the user interacts with the web form, such as when clicking on a button or filling in a text field, an event fires; any element on the page can have events. The DOM contains hooks for these events and the developer can write code (an event handler) that the browser must execute when the event fires. How do we add an event handler to an element (which is also called registering an event handler)?. The general format is:

```
element.onEvent.listen( event_handler )
```

(The spaces are not needed, but can be used to make the code more readable). Examples of events are `Click`, `Change`, `Focus`, `Drag`, `MouseDown`, `Load`, `KeyUp`, and so on. View this as the browser listening to events on elements and, when they occur, executing the indicated event handler. The argument that is passed to the `listen()` method is a callback function and has to be of the type `EventListener`; it has the signature: `void EventListener(Event e)`

The event handler gets passed an Event parameter, succinctly called e or ev, that contains more specific info on the event, such as which mouse button should be pressed in case of a mouse event, on which object the event took place using e.target, and so on. If an event is not handled on the target object itself, you can still write the event handler in its parent, or its parent's parent, and so on up the DOM tree, where it will also get executed; in such a situation, the target property can be useful in determining the original event object. In todo_v2.dart, we examine the various event-coding styles. Using the general format, the Click event on btns2[2] can be handled using the following code:

```
btns2[2].onClick.listen( changeBtnsBackColor );
```

where changeBtnsBackColor is either the event handler or callback function. This function is written as:

```
changeBtnsBackColor(Event e) => btns.forEach( (b) =>
b.classes.add('btns_backgr'));
```

Another, shorter way to write this (such as in line (7)) is:

```
btns2[2].onClick.listen( (e) => changeBtnsBackColor() );
changeBtnsBackColor() => btns.forEach( (b) =>
b.classes.add('btns_backgr'));
```

When a Click event occurs on btns2[2], the handler changeBtnsBackColor is called.

In case the event handler needs more code lines, use the brace syntax as follows:

```
changeBtnsBackColor(Event e) {
        btns.forEach( (b) => b.classes.add('btns_backgr'));
  // possibly other code
}
```

Familiarize yourself with these different ways of writing event handlers.

Of course, when the handler needs only one line of code, there is no need for a separate method, as in the following code:

```
newTask.onClick.listen( (e) => newTask.remove() );
```

For clarity, we use the function expression syntax => whenever possible, but you can inline the event handler and use the brace syntax along with an anonymous function, thus avoiding a separate method. So instead of executing the following code:

```
task.onChange.listen( (e) => addItem() );
```

we could have executed:

```
task.onChange.listen( (e) {
    var newTask = new LIElement();
    newTask.text = task.value;
    newTask.onClick.listen( (e) => newTask.remove());
    task.value = '';
    list.children.add(newTask);
  } );
```

JavaScript developers will find the preceding code very familiar, but it is also used frequently in Dart code, so make yourself acquainted with the code pattern ((e) {...});. The following is an example of how you can respond to key events (in this case, on the window object) using the keyCode and ctrlKey properties of the event e:

```
window.onKeyPress.listen( (e) {
    if (e.keyCode == KeyCode.ENTER) {
      window.alert("You pressed ENTER");
    }
    if (e.ctrlKey && e.keyCode == CTRL_ENTER) {
      window.alert("You pressed CTRL + ENTER");
    }
});
```

In this code, the constant const int CTRL_ENTER = 10; is used.

(The list of keyCodes can be found at http://www.cambiaresearch.com/ articles/15/javascript-char-codes-key-codes).

Manipulating the style of page elements

CSS style properties can be changed in the code as well: every element elem has a classes property, which is a set of CSS classes. You can add a CSS class as follows:

```
elem.classes.add('cssclass');
```

as we did in changeBtnsBackColor (line (11)); by adding this class, the new style is immediately applied to the element. Or, we can remove it to take away the style:

```
elem.classes.remove('cssclass');
```

The toggle method (line (8)) elem.classes.toggle('cssclass'); is a combination of both: first the cssclass is applied (added), the next time it is removed, and, the time after that, it is applied again, and so on.

Working with CSS classes is the best way to change the style, because the CSS definition is separated from the HTML markup. If you do want to change the style of an element directly, use its style property `elem.style`, where the cascade style of coding (see *Chapter 2, Getting to Work with Dart*) is very appropriate, for example:

```
newTask.style
      ..fontWeight = 'bold'
      ..fontSize = '3em'
      ..color = 'red';
```

Animating a game

People like motion in games and a movie is nothing but a quick succession of image frames. So, we need to be able to redraw our screen periodically to get that effect; with Dart screen frame rates of 60 fps or higher, this becomes possible. A certain time interval is represented in Dart as an object of the type `Duration`. To do something periodically in Dart, we use the `Timer` class from the `dart:async` library and its `periodic` method. To execute a function `moveBall()` at every `INTERVAL` ms (you could call it a periodic event), use the following method:

```
new Timer.periodic( const Duration(milliseconds: INTERVAL),
             (t) => moveBall()  );
```

The first parameter is the time period, the second is the callback function that has to be periodically executed, and `t` is the `Timer` object. If the callback function has to be executed only once, just write a new `Timer(.,.)` method, omitting the `periodic` function. When drawing on canvas, the first thing that the periodically called function will have to do is erase the previous drawing. To stop a `Timer` object (usually in a game-over situation), use the `cancel()` method.

Another way of doing this is by using the `animationFrame` method from the `window` class, as we will demonstrate in the memory game in *Chapter 7, Building Games with HTML5 and Dart*.With this technique, we start `gameLoop` in the `main()` function and let it call itself recursively, as in the following code:

```
main() {
 // code left out
 // redraw
 window.animationFrame.then(gameLoop);
}

gameLoop(num delta) {
 moveBall();
 window.animationFrame.then(gameLoop);
}
```

Ping Pong using style(s)

To show these DOM possibilities, here is a Ping Pong game using styles, based on a similar JavaScript project described in the book at http://www.packtpub.com/html5-games-development-using-css-javascript-beginners-guide/book. Normally, you would write an HTML Dart game using canvas as we do in the next section, but it is interesting to see what is possible just by manipulating the styles. Download the project from GitHub with: git clone git://github.com/dzenanr/ping_pong_dom.git.

This project was developed in spirals; if you want to see how the code was developed, explore the seven stages in the subfolder spirals (spiral s07, especially, contains a function examineCSS() that show you how to read the rules in the stylesheet of Dart code; also, the game screen contains some useful links to learn more about reading and changing CSS rules).

The following is the Dart code of the master version; we have commented on it using line numbers:

```
import 'dart:html';
import 'dart:async';
const int INTERVAL = 10;  // time interval in ms to redraw the screen
const int INCREMENT = 20; // move increment in pixels
CssStyleSheet styleSheet;                   (1)
var pingPong = {                 (2)
  'ball': {
    'speed': 3,
    'x'    : 195,
    'y'    : 100,
    'dx'   : 1,
    'dy'   : 1
  },
  'key': {
    'w'    : 87,
    's'    : 83,
    'up'   : 38,
    'down' : 40
  },
  'paddleA' : {
    'width'  : 20,
    'height' : 80,
    'left'   : 20,
    'top'    : 60,
    'score'  : 0
  },
```

```
    'paddleB' : {
      'width'  : 20,
      'height' : 80,
      'left'   : 360,
      'top'    : 80,
      'score'  : 0
    },
    'table' : {
      'width'       : 400,
      'height'      : 200
    }
  };

main() {
  styleSheet = document.styleSheets[0];           (3)
  document.onKeyDown.listen(onKeyDown);           (4)
  // Redraw every INTERVAL ms.
  new Timer.periodic(const Duration(milliseconds: INTERVAL),
          (t) => moveBall());                     (5)
}
String ballRule(int x, int y) {
  String rule = '''
    #ball {
      background: #fbbfbb;
      position: absolute;
      width: 20px;
      height: 20px;
      left: ${x.toString()}px;
      top: ${y.toString()}px;
      border-radius: 10px;
    }
  ''';
  return rule;
}
String paddleARule(int top) {
  String rule = '''
    #paddleA {
      background: #bbbbff;
      position: absolute;
      width: 20px;
      height: 80px;
      left: 20px;
      top: ${top.toString()}px;
    }
```

```
      ''';
    return rule;
  }
  String paddleBRule(int top) {
    String rule = '''
      #paddleB {
        background: #bbbbff;
        position: absolute;
        width: 20px;
        height: 80px;
        left: 360px;
        top: ${top.toString()}px;
      }
    ''';
    return rule;
  }
  updateBallRule(int left, int top) {
    styleSheet.removeRule(1);
    styleSheet.insertRule(ballRule(left, top), 1);
  }
  updatePaddleARule(int top) {
    styleSheet.removeRule(2);
    styleSheet.insertRule(paddleARule(pingPong['paddleA']['top']), 2);
  }
  updatePaddleBRule(int top) {
    styleSheet.removeRule(3);
    styleSheet.insertRule(paddleBRule(pingPong['paddleB']['top']), 3);
  }
  onKeyDown(e) {
    var paddleA = pingPong['paddleA'];
    var paddleB = pingPong['paddleB'];
    var key = pingPong['key'];
    if (e.keyCode == key['w']) {                    (6)
      paddleA['top'] = paddleA['top'] - INCREMENT;
      updatePaddleARule(paddleA['top']);
    } else if (e.keyCode == key['s']) {
      paddleA['top'] = paddleA['top'] + INCREMENT;
      updatePaddleARule(paddleA['top']);
    } else if (e.keyCode == key['up']) {
      paddleB['top'] = paddleB['top'] - INCREMENT;
      updatePaddleBRule(paddleB['top']);
    } else if (e.keyCode == key['down']) {
      paddleB['top'] = paddleB['top'] + INCREMENT;
      updatePaddleBRule(paddleB['top']);
```

```
    }
  }
moveBall() {
  var ball = pingPong['ball'];
  var table = pingPong['table'];
  var paddleA = pingPong['paddleA'];
  var paddleB = pingPong['paddleB'];
  // check the table boundary
  // check the bottom edge
  if (ball['y'] + ball['speed'] * ball['dy'] > table['height']) {
    ball['dy'] = -1;              (7)
  }
  // check the top edge
  if (ball['y'] + ball['speed'] * ball['dy'] < 0) {
    ball['dy'] = 1;
  }
  // check the right edge
  if (ball['x'] + ball['speed'] * ball['dx'] > table['width']) {
    // player B lost           (8)
    paddleA['score']++;
    document.querySelector('#scoreA').innerHtml
    paddleA['score'].toString();
    // reset the ball;
    ball['x'] = 250;
    ball['y'] = 100;
    ball['dx'] = -1;
  }
  // check the left edge
  if (ball['x'] + ball['speed'] * ball['dx'] < 0) {
    // player A lost           (9)
    paddleB['score']++;
    document.querySelector('#scoreB').innerHtml =
paddleB['score'].toString();
    // reset the ball;
    ball['x'] = 150;
    ball['y'] = 100;
    ball['dx'] = 1;
  }
  ball['x'] += ball['speed'] * ball['dx'];
  ball['y'] += ball['speed'] * ball['dy'];
  // check the moving paddles
  // check the left paddle
  if (ball['x'] + ball['speed'] * ball['dx'] <        (10)
      paddleA['left'] + paddleA['width']) {
```

```
      if (ball['y'] + ball['speed'] * ball['dy'] <=
          paddleA['top'] + paddleA['height'] &&
          ball['y'] + ball['speed'] * ball['dy'] >= paddleA['top']) {
        ball['dx'] = 1;
      }
    }
    // check the right paddle
    if (ball['x'] + ball['speed'] * ball['dx'] >= paddleB['left']) {
      if (ball['y'] + ball['speed'] * ball['dy'] <=
          paddleB['top'] + paddleB['height'] &&
          ball['y'] + ball['speed'] * ball['dy'] >= paddleB['top']) {
        ball['dx'] = -1;                      (11)
      }
    }
    // update the ball rule
    updateBallRule(ball['x'], ball['y']);
}
```

The screen looks like as shown in the following screenshot:

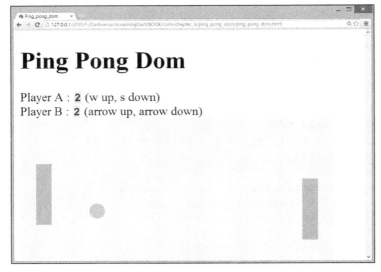

The screen of Ping Pong DOM

Basically, the mechanism is that we change the `left` and `top` property values in the style rules for the ball, `paddleA` and `paddleB` in the function `ballRule`, `paddlARule`, and so on. When this new style rule is attached to our document, the HTML element moves on the screen. In line (1), we declare a stylesheet that we append to our document in line (3). The variable `pingPong` in line (2) is a Map with the keys `ball`, `key`, `paddleA`, `paddleB`, and `table` (these correspond with HTML element IDs), and their values are, themselves, maps containing variables and their values (for example, `top` has the value 60). These maps are further referenced using variables, as follows:

```
var paddleA = pingPong['paddleA'];
```

In line (4), an `onKeyDown` event handler is defined. This tests the key that was pressed along with `if (e.keyCode == key['w'])` (line (6)), and so on, and, when the key is recognized, the value of the `top` variable in the corresponding paddle Map is incremented or decremented (the value of `Top` is 0 at the top of the screen and increases towards the bottom of the screen. `w` means that the value is going up; this means the value of `top` is decreasing, so we have to subtract `INCREMENT` from the current `top` value, and likewise for the other directions). An `updatePaddle(A-B)Rule` function is called; in it, a new style rule is inserted into the stylesheet, updating the `top` value for the style rule of the corresponding paddle HTML element (the style rules are multiline strings).

Let's then see what happens in the periodic function `moveBall()`. Basically, this method changes the `x` and `y` coordinates of the ball:

```
ball['x'] += ball['speed'] * ball['dx'];
ball['y'] += ball['speed'] * ball['dy'];
```

However, we have to check a number of boundary conditions (such as the ball crossing the edges of the table); if the ball is going down toward the bottom edge of the table (line (7)), `dy` becomes `-1`, so the new `ball['y']` value will be smaller and the inverse will occur for when the ball goes along the top edge. If the ball goes over the right edge (line (8)), **Player A** wins a point, so their score is updated on the screen and the ball is reset. In line (9), the inverse is true and **Player B** wins a point. In lines (10) and (11), we test for the collision of the ball and `paddleA` or `paddleB` respectively; using `paddleA`, we want to send the ball to the right, so we set `dx = 1`; with `paddleB`, we want to send it to the left, so `dx = -1`. Then, in the same way as for the paddles, we update the style rule for the ball.

How to draw on a canvas – Ping Pong revisited

Canvas is a way to draw graphics on a web page in a straightforward manner. It is an important part of HTML5 and provides apps with a resolution-dependent bitmap canvas, which can be used for rendering graphs, game graphics, art, or other visual images on-the-fly. We will rewrite our Ping Pong game using the canvas drawing technique (this project is based on the Dart port of the canvas tutorial at http://billmill.org/static/canvastutorial/ by Chris Buckett (https://github.com/chrisbu/Bounce)). Download the project from GitHub using git clone git://github.com/dzenanr/ping_pong.

When you open the project in Dart Editor, you see the latest master version and you can run and play it immediately. In the spirals subfolder, you see how the project has grown in 11 stages and we will learn about canvas drawing by exploring this evolution. The spiral approach to learning is used to advance step-by-step from simple spirals at the beginning to more complex ones close to the last version of the project. This is also an excellent development approach that encourages refactoring and, thus, produces clear, understandable code.

Spiral 1 – drawing a circle and a rectangle

Open the project spirals/ping_pong_01. The goal of this spiral is to display a small, black circle and a small, white rectangle with a black border; in other words, to learn how to draw. Take a look at the HTML file—all drawing is done within the <canvas> tag:

```
<canvas id="canvas" width="300" height="300">
  Canvas is not supported in your browser.
</canvas>
```

Adjusting the width and height values to the app's needs, you can also include text that which will be displayed in older browsers that do not support canvas (it is widely supported, but only in Internet Explorer from 9.0 onwards). Now we look at the code of ping_pong.dart in the following spiral:

```
library ping_pong;            (1)

import 'dart:html';
import 'dart:math';

part 'board.dart';            (2)

void main() {
```

```
    //get a reference to the canvas
    CanvasElement canvas = querySelector('#canvas');         (3)
    Board board = new Board(canvas);         (4)
    board.circle(75, 75, 10);         (5)
    board.rectangle(95, 95, 20, 20);         (6)
}
```

Following good practice, we make our app a library in line (1). The file containing the library declaration contains the starting point main(); all other code resides in other parts (see line (2)). In line (3), we make a reference to <canvas> using an object of the type CanvasElement (in dart:html). Then, we have to make a context object (which can be either 2d or webgl (3d)) to draw on:

```
CanvasRenderingContext2D context = canvas.getContext('2d');
```

In this app, we will draw on a Board object made in line (4); this object has the methods circle and rectangle that contain the details for drawing these shapes and they are called in lines (5) and (6). Line (4) passes the canvas object to the Board constructor (line (7)) in the part file board.dart, where the context object is created:

```
part of ping_pong;
class Board {
  CanvasRenderingContext2D context;
  Board(CanvasElement canvas) {         (7)
    context = canvas.getContext('2d');
  }
  //draw a circle
  void circle(x, y, r) {
    context.beginPath();         (8)
    context.arc(x, y, r, 0, PI*2, true);         (9)
    context.closePath();         (10)
    context.fill();         (11)
  }
  //draw a rectangle
  void rectangle(x, y, w, h) {
    context.beginPath();
    context.rect(x,y,w,h);         (12)
    context.closePath();
    context.stroke();         (13)
  }
}
```

When drawing an arbitrary shape, we draw, in fact, a path. This usually involves a number of steps enclosed within a call to `beginPath()` (line (8)) and a call to `closePath()` (line (10)); this also closes the shape; when drawing basic shapes, such as lines, rectangles, and circles, as in this example, they can be left out. A black line or an open figure is drawn using `context.stroke()`, such as in line (13); for a filled-in shape, you need to use `context.fill()`, such as in line (13). When we run this script, it shows:

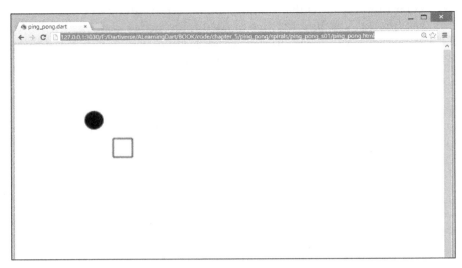

The screen of Ping Pong spiral 1

To further explore how lines and arcs are drawn, we create an additional web app `canvas_1`:

```
import 'dart:html';
import 'dart:math';
CanvasRenderingContext2D context;
var width, height;
void main() {
  //get a reference to the canvas
  CanvasElement canvas = querySelector('#canvas');
  width = canvas.width;                 (1)
  height = canvas.height;
  context = canvas.getContext('2d');
  lines();
  arcs();
}
//drawing lines
void lines() {
  context.moveTo(100, 150);
  context.lineTo(450, 50);
```

```
    context.lineWidth = 2;
    context.lineCap = 'round'; // other values: 'square' or 'butt'
    context.stroke();
}
//drawing arcs
void arcs() {
    var x = width / 2;              (2)
    var y = height / 2;
    var radius = 75;
    var startAngle = 1.1 * PI;
    var endAngle = 1.9 * PI;
    var antiClockWise = false;
    context.arc(x, y, radius, startAngle, endAngle, antiClockWise);
    context.lineWidth = 8;
    context.stroke();
}
```

We obtain the `width` and `height` parameters of the `canvas` object (line (1)) in order to draw proportionally to the space that we have, for example, in choosing the center of a circle (for our arc), such as in line (2).

Canvas uses an (x, y) coordinate system, measured in pixels to locate points: the origin (0,0) is the upper-left corner of the drawing area, the x axis goes from left to right, and the y axis from top to bottom. `moveTo(x, y)` positions the drawing cursor at the `point (x, y)` method and the `lineTo(x', y')` method draws a straight line from (x, y) to (x', y') when the `stroke` or `fill` methods are called; `lineWidth` is an obvious property. To draw a circular arc, you use the method with the same name `arc`; this method takes no less than six parameters: `context.arc(x, y, radius, startAngle, endAngle, antiClockWise);` x and y are the coordinates of the circle's center; the third parameter is the circle's radius; parameters `startAngle` and `endAngle` are the start and end angles (in radians); the parameter `antiClockWise` is `true` or `false` (the default value is `anticlockwise`, that is from end to start) and defines the direction of the arc between its two end points: see the next figure for clarification and the example in the `arcs()` method (comment out the call to `lines()`). Now we see how a circle can be drawn by going from a 0 PI angle to a 2 PI angle, such as in the `board.dart` line (9), which is called using line (5).

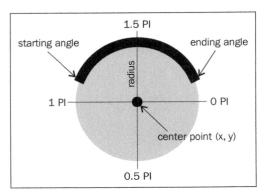

Drawing an arc

Using the `lineTo` method, it takes three calls to draw a triangle and four for a rectangle. The latter case was considered common enough to provide a `rect(x,y,w,h)` method (line (12) in `board.dart`), where x and y are the coordinates of the upper-left corner, w is the width, and h is the height of the rectangle; this is applied in the `rectangle()` method called on `board` (line (6)). To erase all drawing in a rectangular area, use the `context.clearRect(x,y,w,h)` method (first used in *Spiral 3 – moving a ball*).

Spiral 2 – colored circles and rectangles

In the project `spirals/ping_pong_02`, the goal is to display two circles and two rectangles in different colors; that is: how can we get some color in our drawing? For that, we need two new properties: `context: strokeStyle` sets the drawing color for the border and `fillStyle` sets the fill color; if you do not use these, black is the default color. The color itself is given as a string, containing:

- a predefined color name, such as `context.strokeStyle = 'red';`
- a hexadecimal number, such as `context.strokeStyle = '#ff0000';`
- an `rgba` string containing the `red`, `green`, `blue` values (between 0 and 255) and an alpha value (the opacity of the color having a value between 0 and 1), such as `context.fillStyle ="rgba(55, 55, 0, .75)"`

For example, a `rectangle` method can be given a border color and an inside color by calling:

```
board.rectangle(15, 150, 120, 120,
        "rgba(55, 55, 0, .75)", "rgba(155, 155, 0, .5)");
while the rectangle method is now changed to:
void rectangle(x, y, w, h, strokeStyle, fillStyle) {
    context.beginPath();
```

```
        context.strokeStyle = strokeStyle;
        context.fillStyle = fillStyle;
        context.rect(x,y,w,h);
        context.stroke();
        context.fill();
        context.closePath();
    }
```

Do experiment with the possibilities.

We now know everything we need to draw our Ping Pong game; we'll start doing this and developing the game logic in the next spiral. But, often, you need other techniques in drawing applications: you'll find more of them in `canvas_2.dart` To see clearly what each code section does, comment all code and uncomment only the section you want to run. In this code file, you can find the methods for drawing quadratic curves and Bezier curves, combining them in paths, custom shapes, linear and radial gradients, and drawing images and text. For more details on the different parameters, refer to `http://www.html5canvastutorials.com/ tutorials`. You can find a lot more code examples in the GitHub repository git at `http://github.com/dzenanr/ondart_examples` especially the folders `ondart_dom`, `ondart_html5`, and `ondart_canvas`; these accompany the course presentations found at `http://ondart.me/web_programming.md`.

Spiral 3 – moving a ball

In the project `spirals/ping_pong_03`, the goal is to change the position of a small, black circle (a ball) in a straight line using subsequent calls of the `move` method.

Run the app: we see a ball moving down diagonally from the upper-left corner to the right and then disappearing out of sight. In the main file `ping_pong.dart`, nothing much has changed; a new part file `ball.dart` has appeared (line (1)). To describe the ball and its behavior in the `Ball` class; and; in line (2), the `ball` object is created, giving it a reference to the `board` object.

```
    library ping_pong;
    import 'dart:html';
    import 'dart:async';
    import 'dart:math';
    part 'board.dart';
    part 'ball.dart';                   (1)
    void main() {
      CanvasElement canvas = querySelector('#canvas');
      Board board = new Board(canvas);
      Ball ball = new Ball(board, 0, 0, 10);        (2)
```

```
      new Timer.periodic(const Duration(milliseconds: 10),
         (t) => ball.move());                      (3)
   }
```

In `ball.dart`, we see that in the constructor (line (4)), our ball is drawn by calling `context.arc` on the `board` object.

```
      part of ping_pong;
      class Ball {
        Board board;
        int x, y, r;
        int dx = 2;
        int dy = 4;
        Ball(this.board, this.x, this.y, this.r) {           (4)
          draw();
        }
        void draw() {
          board.context.beginPath();
          board.context.arc(x, y, r, 0, PI*2, true);
          board.context.closePath();
          board.context.fill();
        }
        void move() {
          board.clear();                       (5)
          board.context.beginPath();
          board.context.arc(x, y, r, 0, PI*2, true);
          board.context.closePath();
          board.context.fill();
          x += dx;                    (6)
          y += dy;                    (7)
        }
      }
```

In (line (3)) in the `main()` method in the preceding code, a `Timer` invokes periodically the `move()` method on the ball. In the `move()` method, the board is first cleared (line (5)). Within the `clear()` method, this is done through a new `clearRect()` method on the `context` object:

```
      void clear() {
          context.clearRect(0, 0, width, height);
      }
```

In lines (6) and (7), the values of the x and y coordinates of the center of the ball are increased using dx and dy respectively. As these remain the same, the ball runs from left to right and top to bottom; it disappears when it leaves the canvas area determined by the width and height parameters. We will improve on this in *Spiral 5 – a bouncing ball*; for now, let's give the board object the same dimensions as the canvas element:

```
Board(CanvasElement canvas) {
    context = canvas.getContext("2d");
    width = canvas.width;
    height = canvas.height;
}
```

Spiral 4 – reorganizing the code

In this spiral, we pause and reorganise (refactor) our code a bit (we wrote duplicate code in draw() and move() –horror!). In our main() method, we now only create the board object, and call a new method init() on it:

```
void main() {
  CanvasElement canvas = querySelector('#canvas');
  Board board = new Board(canvas);
  board.init();
}
```

This method in board.dart creates the ball object, passing it as a reference to the board object using the this parameter:

```
void init() {
  Ball ball = new Ball(this, 0, 0, 10);
  new Timer.periodic(const Duration(milliseconds: 10), (t) =>
}
```

The common code in draw() and move() from the *Spiral 3 – moving a ball* section is eliminated by letting move() call draw() from ball.dart:

```
void draw() {
  board.context.beginPath();
  board.context.arc(x, y, r, 0, PI*2, true);
  board.context.closePath();
  board.context.fill();
}
void move() {
  board.clear();
  draw();
  x += dx;
  y += dy;
}
```

We have applied a fundamental principle called DRY (Don't Repeat Yourself, at least not in code).

Spiral 5 – a bouncing ball

In most games, the ball has to stay on the board, so let's try to bounce the ball on the board's edges. The code that lets the ball move is the `move()` method, so that is the only code that has to expand. For both coordinates, we now have to check the boundary that the ball will cross on the board's edge lines:

- For x, this means that `(x + dx)` must not equal to `> board.width (right border)` or equal to `< 0 (left border)`; if any of these situations do occur (that's why we use or: `||`), for example, `if (x + dx > board.width || x + dx < 0)`,, the ball must change its direction (the value of x must decrease instead of increase and vice versa); this we can obtain by reversing the sign of dx: `dx = -dx`;

- For y, this means that `(y + dy)` must not equal to `> board.height (bottom border)` and must not equal to `< 0 (top border)`; if it does, for example, `if (y + dy > board.height || y + dy < 0)`, the ball must change its direction (y must decrease instead of increase and vice versa); this we can obtain by reversing the sign of dy: `dy = -dy`;

Verify that this procedure works (although the movement is rather boring at this stage).

Spiral 6 – displaying the racket

In this spiral, we add a racket that is displayed as a small, black rectangle. From the beginning of the code, we represent it through its own class in `racket.dart`. In it, we provide a constructor and the `draw` method that uses `context.rect`; the racket also has a reference to the `board` object.

```
part of ping_pong;
class Racket {
  Board board;
  num x, y, w, h;
  Racket(this.board, this.x, this.y, this.w, this.h) {
    draw();
  }
  void draw() {
    board.context.beginPath();
    board.context.rect(x, y, w, h);
    board.context.closePath();
    board.context.fill();
  }
}
```

To enhance the adaptability of the game, we start by defining a number of constant values upfront in the Board class:

```
const num START_X = 0;
const num START_Y = 0;
const num BALL_R = 10;
const num RACKET_W = 75;
const num RACKET_H = 10;
```

These are used in the init() method to construct the ball and racket objects:

```
void init() {
    ball = new Ball(this, START_X, START_Y, BALL_R);
    racket = new Racket(this, width/2, height-RACKET_H, RACKET_W,
    RACKET_H);
        timer = new Timer.periodic(const Duration(milliseconds: 10),
            (t) => redraw());
}
```

Since we now have to draw two objects, we rename the periodic function to redraw() and give the responsibility to the board object, which calls the draw methods on the ball and racket objects (lines (1) and (2)).

```
void redraw() {
    clear();
    ball.draw();                    (1)
    racket.draw();                  (2)
    if (ball.x + dx > width || ball.x + dx < 0) {
        dx = -dx;
    }
    if (ball.y + dy > height || ball.y + dy < 0) {
        dy = -dy;
    } else if (ball.y + dy > height) {          (3)
        if (ball.x > racket.x && ball.x < racket.x + racket.w) {
            dy = -dy;
        } else {
            timer.cancel();
        }
    }
    ball.x += dx;
    ball.y += dy;
}
```

It also does all the checks for the boundary conditions and we add in line (3) that the ball is bounced (`dy = -dy`) only when it touches the racket (`ball.x > racket.x && ball.x < racket.x + racket.w`); if it falls outside the racket, the game is over and we cancel the timer, stopping the animation (line (4)). Due to the start location of the ball, the game-over condition does not occur in this spiral.

Spiral 7 – moving the racket using keys

Here, the goal is to move the racket using the left and right keys of the keyboard. To this end, the racket will have to listen to key events; the following is the code of `racket.dart`:

```
part of ping_pong;
class Racket {
  Board board;
  num x, y, w, h;
  bool rightDown = false;              (1)
  bool leftDown = false;
  Racket(this.board, this.x, this.y, this.w, this.h) {
    draw();
    document.onKeyDown.listen(_onKeyDown);       (2)
    document.onKeyUp.listen(_onKeyUp);
  }
  void draw() { ... } // see Spiral 6
  _onKeyDown(event) {                  (3)
    if (event.keyCode == 39) rightDown = true;
    else if (event.keyCode == 37) leftDown = true;
  }
  _onKeyUp(event) {                    (4)
    if (event.keyCode == 39) rightDown = false;
    else if (event.keyCode == 37) leftDown = false;
  }
}
```

In line (2), we register for the KeyDown event and attach the handler _onKeyDown, which is also done in the following line for the KeyUp event. _onKeyDown and _ onKeyUp are private methods that could have been used anonymously in the event definition. In these handlers, we test for the keyCode of the pressed key: the left arrow has keyCode 37 and the right arrow 39. We catch their state in two Boolean variables leftDown and rightDown: if the left arrow is pressed, we set leftDown to true and, when the right arrow is pressed, we set rightDown to true (line (3)). In the KeyUp event handler in line (4) that fires when the key is released, the boolean is reset to false. As long as the arrow key is pressed, its corresponding boolean is true. This is tested in the redraw() method of the Board class, where the following lines are added before racket.draw():

```
if (racket.rightDown)      racket.x += 5;
else if (racket.leftDown) racket.x -= 5;
```

When the right arrow is pressed, the racket moves to the right and vice versa.

This is the first playable version of our game; but, we see that our racket can disappear and, perhaps, we want to be able to move the racket using the mouse as well.

Spiral 8 – moving the racket using the mouse

To accomplish moving the racket using the mouse, we listen for a MouseMove event and attach the event handler to the racket constructor: document.onMouseMove. listen(_onMouseMove).

We also define two variables that define the canvas width:

```
canvasMinX = 0;
canvasMaxX = canvasMinX + board.width;
```

We use the preceding code statements to perform a test in the mouse event handler: if the x coordinate of the mouse pointer (given by event.pageX) is situated in our canvas, set the x coordinate of our racket object to the same value:

```
_onMouseMove(event) {
   if (event.pageX > canvasMinX && event.pageX < canvasMaxX)
   x = event.pageX;
}
```

Spiral 9 – a real game

The goals for this spiral are as follows:

1. The board should have a border.

2. We want two rackets.

3. The rackets cannot be moved outside the border.

The border is easy; call the `border()` method from `init()` to draw a rectangle around the canvas:

```
void border() {
    context.beginPath();
    context.rect(X, Y, width, height);
    context.closePath();
    context.stroke();
}
```

We add a second racket to the top of the screen, which moves synchronously with the bottom racket. Our `board` object will now contain two racket objects `racketNorth` and `racketSouth`, both of which are created in the `init()` method:

```
racketNorth = new Racket(this, width/2, 0, RACKET_W, RACKET_H);
racketSouth = new Racket(this, width/2, height-RACKET_H, RACKET_W,
RACKET_H);
```

The code from *Spiral 7 – moving the racket using keys* is applied to both the objects.

The third goal is accomplished by adding a test to the `MouseMove` event handler:

```
_onMouseMove(event) {
    if (event.pageX > board.X && event.pageX < board.width) {
        x = event.pageX - board.X - w/2;
        if (x < board.X) x = board.X;
        if (x > board.width - w) x = board.width - w;
    }
}
```

By introducing an X constant for `board`, we have simplified the condition we saw in *Spiral 8 – moving the racket using the mouse*. The racket movements are now more synchronous with the mouse movement, and the last two if tests make it impossible for the rackets to go outside the borders of the board. Now we have a minimally decent game.

Spiral 10 – title and replay

In this spiral, we add a title and a button to restart the game; both are done in HTML. The button is placed in a `<div>` tag outside the canvas:

```
<button type="button" id="play">Play</button>
```

We now change the constructor of `board` to only start `init()` when the button with the ID `play` is clicked: `query Selector('#play').onClick.listen( (e) => init() );`

That's it!

Spiral 11 – the master version

No new Dart code is added here, but we improve the display using CSS. Additionally, some relevant web links are added along with a section for each new spiral to indicate what is new. Take a look at `ping_pong.html` (in both the source and the browser) to learn how to use the document features of HTML5:

- The title within the screen is displayed in a `<header>` tag.

- The different parts of the document are placed in their own `<section>` tag with an appropriate ID, such as `side` or `main`; sections can be nested. The two columns' layout design style is applied using the `float` property in `layout2.css`. The `side` section is the playground and contains a `<button>` tag to start the game, placed within a `<footer>` tag. The hyperlinks beneath it are placed within a `<nav>` tag; the design from `link.css` uses a background image to better display the links.

- The `<footer>` tags are used to separate the different spirals at the bottom of the screen.

The preceding points are shown in the following screenshot:

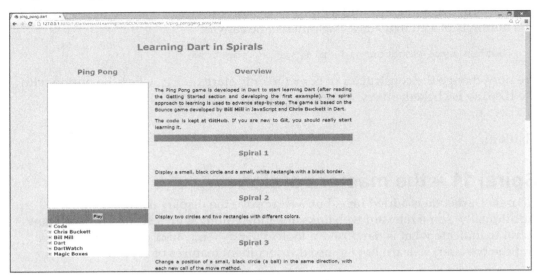

Ping Pong, the master version

As an exercise, you could decouple the rackets so that we have two independent players and then keep score of the game (see the DOM version of the game for inspiration). Also, place the timer interval in a variable if you want to change the game's difficulty level.

Summary

You now know all the techniques for finding, manipulating, and styling web page elements using Dart code to change the user interface and you can respond to events that take place on the page. You have learned how to change the CSS properties in DOM in order to move game objects, how to draw on a canvas for developing game screens, and how to build a complete game project. We found that it is advisable to develop in a spiral way, building upon the previous spirals as the project acquires more functionality. The different entities are represented by classes; in that way, our project is naturally modularized. In the next chapter, we will focus on the web page as a way to show, gather, and validate data, because that's what we will need to do in business apps.

6
Combining HTML5 Forms with Dart

In business applications, data is structured through model classes and stored permanently, but the first step, controlling the input of data, is essential. In this chapter the new input and validation functionalities of HTML5 are explored. You will learn how to:

- Process input data by validating them through HTML5 and Dart
- Store and retrieve data in the browser's local storage
- Show data in HTML5 forms

We will expand on our Bank Account example to show these features, gradually building it up in spirals.

Spiral 1 – the power of HTML5 forms

We will make a form that will enable us to create objects for the BankAccount class that we encountered in code examples in *Chapter 1, Dart – A Modern Web Programming Language*, and *Chapter 2, Getting to Work with Dart*. Moreover, we will be able to deposit or withdraw money from these accounts, calculating and adding interest to them.

 For code files of this section, refer to chapter 6\ bank_terminal_s1 in the code bundle.

In this first spiral, we construct our model classes and lay out a form to create and update a bank account, using the new specialized input fields of HTML5. The code for the classes is kept in the subfolder `model` and these are part of our application, as shown in the initial code of `bank_terminal_s1.dart`:

```
library bank_terminal;
import 'dart:html';
part '../model/bank_account.dart';
part '../model/person.dart';
void main() {
```

A bank account is owned by a person, as we see in the starting code of (`bank_account.dart`):

```
part of bank_terminal;
class BankAccount {
  String number;
  Person owner;
  double balance;
  int pin_code;
  final DateTime date_created;
  DateTime date_modified;
  // constructors:
  BankAccount(this.owner, this.number, this.balance, this.pin_code):
date_created = new DateTime.now();
  // rest of code omitted
}
```

The final item `date_created` is initialized to the current date in the initializer list of the constructor. The person's data is kept in objects of a separate `Person` class in `person.dart`:

```
part of bank_terminal;
class Person {
  // Person properties and methods
  String name, address, email, gender;
  DateTime date_birth;
  // constructor:
  Person(this.name, this.address, this.email, this.gender,
  this.date_birth);
  // methods:
  String toString() => 'Person: $name, $gender';
}
```

After applying some CSS3 to the form attribute, our input screen looks like the following screenshot:

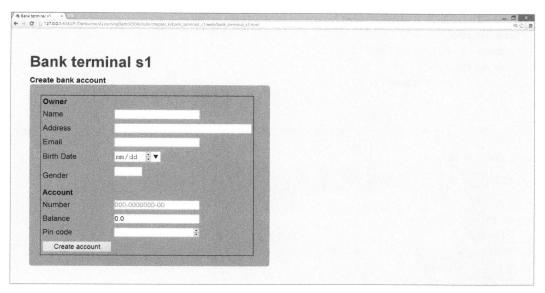

The Bank Account input screen

We surround all input fields in this form tag: `<form name="account" autocomplete>`. The `autocomplete` attribute makes sure that the browser shows a list based on values that the user has entered before. When all the data is filled in, clicking on the button **Create account** will create the objects and then store them. The name of the owner certainly is a required field, but how do we enforce this in HTML5? Take a look at the source code in `bank_terminal_s1.html`:

```
<input id="name" type="text" required autofocus/>
```

The `required` attribute does exactly that: clicking on the button with an empty name field shows a pop up with the text **Please fill out this field**; this is achieved by using the corresponding CSS3 pseudoclass `:required`:

```
:required {
  border-color: #1be032;
  box-shadow:
    0 0 5px rgba(57, 237, 78, .5);

    }
```

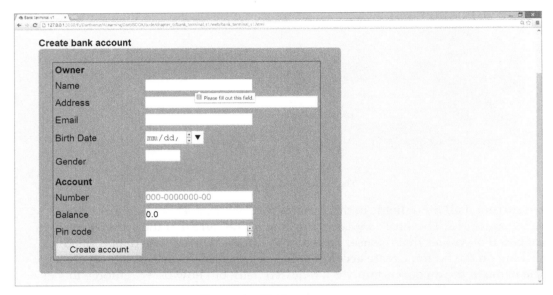

The required field pop-up screen

To automatically focus on the **Name** input field when the screen loads, use the **autofocus** attribute. The **Email** input field is required, but it is also of type **email**:

```
<input id="email" type="email" required/>
```

This will check whether the value conforms to a standard e-mail address pattern of the form "*@-.-"; likewise, there is also a field of type `url`. The **Birth Date** field is of HTML5 type `date`. You can type in the date by filling it in the mm/dd/yyyy pattern, and you can also use the spinner buttons to choose the year. The big down button shows all days in the selected month, and allows changing the month and day. The **Gender** field shows a pre-populated list of values; this can be attached to the field through the `list` attribute and the `<datalist>` tag. The **Account Number** and **Balance** fields use the `placeholder` attribute to give the user a hint on what the input should be; this value, however, is not taken as the default input value, hence use the `value` attribute instead. To control the input format, use the `pattern` attribute; for example, `pattern="[0-9]{3}-[0-9]{7}-[0-9]{2}"`, where the string can be any valid regular expression. For a HTML5 url field type, use the pattern, `"https?://.+"`. The **Pin code** field is of type `number`, which checks the integer numerical input, possibly indicating a minimum and maximum value. Try out the validations by using different input values. Other valid HTML5 input types include `color`, `date`, `datetime`, `datetime-local`, `month`, `search`, `tel` (for a telephone number, use it with a pattern), `time`, `week`, `range`, and `url`.

Spiral 2 – how to validate data with Dart

If you have tested the *Spiral 1 – the power of HTML5 forms* version thoroughly, you would have come across some things that could be improved:

1. The HTML5 control only does its checks when the **Create Account** button is clicked on; it would be better if the user is alerted earlier, preferably after filling in each field.
2. The **Birth Date** value is checked to be a correct `DateTime` value, but a value in the future is accepted.
3. The **Gender** field will gladly accept other values than M or F.
4. The **Balance** field accepts a negative number.

So HTML5 doesn't give us full validation possibilities; to remedy and supplement that, we must add code validation, see `bank_terminal_s2.dart`:

> For code files of this section, refer to chapter 6\
> bank_terminal_s2 in the code bundle.

```
InputElement name, address, email, birth_date, gender;
InputElement number, balance, pin_code;
void main() {
  // bind variables to DOM elements:
```

```dart
      name = querySelector('#name');
      address = querySelector('#address');
      email = querySelector('#email');
      birth_date = querySelector('#birth_date');
      gender = querySelector('#gender');
      number = querySelector('#number');
      balance = querySelector('#balance');
      pin_code = querySelector('#pin_code');
      lbl_error = querySelector('#error');
      lbl_error.text = "";
      lbl_error.style..color = "red";
      // attach event handlers:
      // checks for not empty in onBlur event:
      name.onBlur.listen(notEmpty);              (1)
        email.onBlur.listen(notEmpty);
          number.onBlur.listen(notEmpty);
      pin_code.onBlur.listen(notEmpty);
      // other checks:
      birth_date.onChange.listen(notInFuture);    (2)
      birth_date.onBlur.listen(notInFuture);      (3)
      gender.onChange.listen(wrongGender);       (4)
      balance.onChange.listen(nonNegative);       (5)
      balance.onBlur.listen(nonNegative);        (6)
    }
  notEmpty(Event e) {
    InputElement inel = e.currentTarget as InputElement;
    var input = inel.value;
    if (input == null || input.isEmpty) {
      lbl_error.text = "You must fill in the field ${inel.id}!";
      inel.focus();
    }
  }
  notInFuture(Event e) {
    DateTime birthDate;
    try {
      birthDate = DateTime.parse(birth_date.value);
    } on ArgumentError catch(e) {                (7)
      lbl_error.text = "This is not a valid date!";
      birth_date.focus();
      return;
    }
    DateTime now = new DateTime.now();
    if (!birthDate.isBefore(now)) {
      lbl_error.text = "The birth date cannot be in the future!";
      birth_date.focus();
    }
  }
```

```
wrongGender(Event e) {
  var sex = gender.value;
  if (sex != 'M' && sex != 'F') {
    lbl_error.text = "The gender must be either M (male) or F
    (female)!";
    gender.focus();
  }
}
nonNegative(Event e) {
  num input;
  try {
    input = int.parse(balance.value);
  } on ArgumentError catch(e) {
    lbl_error.text = "This is not a valid balance!";
    balance.focus();
    return;
  }
  if (input < 0) {
    lbl_error.text = "The balance cannot be negative!";
    balance.focus();
  }
}
```

When the user leaves a field, the `blur` event fires; so, to check whether a value was given in the field, use the `onBlur` event handler. For example, for the `name` field in line (1) we show an alert window and use the `focus` method to put the cursor back in the field. Notice that the `notEmpty` method can be used for any input field. Controlling a given value is best done in the `onChange` event handler, as we do for `birth_date` in line (2); we use a `try` construct to `catch` the `ArgumentError` exception that occurs in line (7) when no date is given or selected (leave the method with return in the error case, so that no further processing is done). To ensure that the user cannot leave the field, call the same method in `onBlur` (in line (3)). For checking gender and balance, we also use the `onChange` handlers (lines (4) and (5)). Check the e-mail address with a regular expression pattern in an `onChange` event handler as an exercise. Now we are ready to store the data; we add the following line after line (6):

```
btn_create.onClick.listen(storeData);
```

In the method `storeData`, we first create the objects:

```
storeData(Event e) {
// creating the objects:
Person p = new Person(name.value, address.value, email.value,
gender.value, DateTime.parse(birth_date.value));
BankAccount bac = new BankAccount(p, number.value, double.
parse(balance.value), int.parse(pin_code.value)); }
```

Notice that we have to perform data conversions here; the value from the `balance` and `pin_code` Element objects is always a string!

Validation in the model

For a more robust application, we should also include validations in the model classes themselves, that way, they are independent of the front-end graphical interface and could be re-used in another application (provided we place them in their own library to import in this application, instead of using the part construct). We illustrate this with the `number` field in `BankAccount` (the class code in this spiral also contains the validations for the other fields). First, we make the field private by prefixing it with an _:

```
String  _number;
```

Then, we make a `get` and `set` method for this property; it is in the setter that we can validate the incoming value:

```
String get number => _number;
set number(value) {
  if (value == null || value.isEmpty)
    throw new ArgumentError("No number value is given");   (1)
  var exp = new RegExp(r"[0-9]{3}-[0-9]{7}-[0-9]{2}");    (2)
  if (exp.hasMatch(value)) _number = value;         (3)
}
```

In the model classes, we don't have the possibility to show an error window, but we can throw an error or exception in line (1). To catch this error, we have to change the code in `storeData`, where the `BankAccount` object is created:

```
try {
  BankAccount bac = new BankAccount(p, number.value, double.
parse(balance.value),
      int.parse(pin_code.value));
}
  catch(e) {
    window.alert(e.toString());
}
```

To test the particular format, we make use of the `RegExp` class in the built in `dart:core` library. We construct an object exp of this class by passing the regular expression as a raw string in line (2); then, we use `hasMatch` to test whether the value conforms to the format of exp (line (3)).

Using this mechanism, it turns out that we cannot use the short version of the constructors any more, because a setter can only be called from within the constructor body; so the BankAccount constructor changes to:

```
BankAccount(this.owner, number, balance, pin_code):
    date_created = new DateTime.now() {
    this.number = number;
    this.balance = balance;
    this.pin_code = pin_code;
}
```

Spiral 3 – how to store data in local storage

When a fully validated bank account object is created, we can store it in local storage, also called the Web Storage API, that is widely supported in modern browsers. In this mechanism, the application's data are persisted locally (on the client-side) as a Map-like structure: a dictionary of key/value pairs. This is yet another example of the universal use of JSON for storage and transport of data (see *Chapter 4, Modeling Web Applications with Model Concepts and Dartlero*). Unlike cookies, local storage does not expire, but every application can only access its own data, up to a certain limit depending on the browser. With it, our application can also have an offline mode of functioning, when the server is not available to store the data in a database. Web Storage also has another way of storing data called sessionStorage, but this limits the persistence of the data to only the current browser session. So data is lost when the browser is closed or another application is started in the same browser window. In the localStorage mechanism, which we will use here, JSON strings are stored and retrieved, so we need a two-way mechanism to convert our objects to and from JSON and the corresponding toJson and fromJson methods in our classes, for example, in person.dart:

> For code files of this section, refer to chapter 6\ bank_terminal_s3 in the code bundle.

```
Map<String, Object> toJson() {
    var per = new Map<String, Object>();
    per["name"] = name;
    per["address"] = address;
    per["email"] = email;
    per["gender"] = gender;
    per["birthdate"] = date_birth.toString();
    return per;
}
```

The preceding method is called from the `toJson` method in the following `BankAccount` class (see `bank_terminal_s3\bank_account.dart`):

```
String toJson() {
  var acc = new Map<String, Object>();
  acc["number"] = number;
  acc["owner"] = owner.toJson();
  acc["balance"] = balance;
  acc["pin_code"] = pin_code;
  acc["creation_date"] = date_created.toString();
  acc["modified_date"] = date_modified.toString();
  var accs = JSON.encode(acc); // use only once for the root
          // object (here a bank account)
  return accs;
}
```

We will store our bank account object `bac` in `localStorage` using its number as the key:

```
window.localStorage["Bankaccount:${bac.number}"] = bac.toJson();
```

Now we can create bank accounts and store them on the browser's machine. In Chrome, verify this in **Tools | Developer | Tools | Resources | Local Storage | http:127.0.0.1:port** (where port is the port number, usually **3030**):

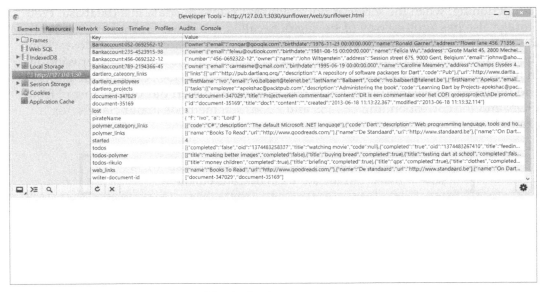

Viewing local storage screen

Local Storage can be disabled (by user action, or via an installed plug-in or extension) so we must alert the user when this needs to be changed; we can do this by catching the Exception that occurs in this case:

```
try {
    window.localStorage["Bankaccount:${bac.number}"] =
    bac.toJson();
} on Exception catch (ex) {
    window.alert("Data not stored: Local storage has been
    deactivated!");
}
```

Local Storage is in fact of type `Map<String, String>`; so it has a `length` property; you can query whether it contains something with `isEmpty`, and you can loop through all stored values with:

```
for (var key in window.localStorage.keys) {
    String value = window.localStorage[key];
}
```

Spiral 4 – reading and showing data

Having stored our data in local storage, it is just as easy to read this data from local storage. Here is a simple screen that takes a bank account number as input, and reads its data when the number field is filled in:

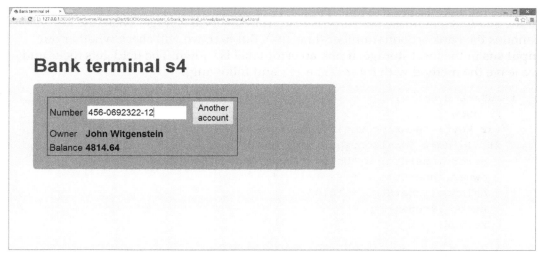

Bank terminal screen

For code files of this section, refer to `chapter 6\`
`bank_terminal_s4` in the code bundle.

We clean up our code making `main()` shorter by calling methods:

```
void main() {
  bind_elements();
  attach_event_handlers();
}
bind_elements() {
  owner = querySelector('#owner');
  balance = querySelector('#balance');
  number = querySelector('#number');
  btn_other = querySelector('#btn_other');
  error = querySelector('#error');
}
attach_event_handlers() {
  number.onInput.listen(readData);
  btn_other.onClick.listen(clearData);
}
```

Apply this refactoring from now on when coding a form. When the number is filled in, its Input event listener is triggered:

```
number.onInput.listen(readData);
```

In the `readData` handler, the value is read from the local storage where the key contains the bank account number (line (2)). But first, we will check whether our input sits in the local storage; if not, an error label is shown. The field gets focus and we leave the method with return (line (1) and following):

```
readData(Event e) {
  // show data:
  var key = 'Bankaccount:${number.value}';
  if (!window.localStorage.containsKey(key)) {         (1)
    error.innerHtml = "Unknown bank account!";
    owner.innerHtml = "----------";
    balance.innerHtml = "0.0";
    number.focus();
    return;
  }
  error.innerHtml = "";
  // read data from local storage:
  String acc_json = window.localStorage[key];          (2)
```

```
bac = new BankAccount.fromJson(JSON.decode(acc_json));    (3)
// show owner and balance:
owner.innerHtml = "<b>${bac.owner.name}</b>";      (4)
balance.innerHtml = "<b>${bac.balance.toStringAsFixed(2)}</b>";
}
```

The bank account object `bac` is now created in line (3), and the `owner` and `balance` labels can then be filled in line (4). Let's examine this in some detail. The resulting string `acc_json` has the structure of a map, and the `JSON.decode` method of the convert package transforms this string into a map. We will enhance our model classes with functionality to convert this map into an object. The best way to do this is with a named constructor (called appropriately `fromJson`) that takes this map and makes a new object from it. So in the `person` class, we add the following named constructor:

```
Person.fromJson(Map json) {
    this.name = json["name"];
    this.address = json["address"];
    this.email = json["email"];
    this.gender = json["gender"];
    this.date_birth = DateTime.parse(json["birthdate"]);
}
```

This is used by the `fromJson` constructor in the `BankAccount` class:

```
BankAccount.fromJson(Map json):  date_created =
  DateTime.parse(json["creation_date"]) {
    this.number = json["number"];
    this.owner = new Person.fromJson(json["owner"]);
    this.balance = json["balance"];
    this.pin_code = json["pin_code"];
    this.date_modified = DateTime.parse(json["modified_date"]);
}
```

Spiral 5 – changing and updating data

Now that we have our bank account back on screen, we add an input field with ID #number (and of type number) that captures the amount of money that we want to deposit or withdraw from our account. We add a button "**Deposit-Withdrawal**" to initiate that action, and also a button "**Add interest**" to calculate and add interest to our account. Our screen now looks like the following screenshot:

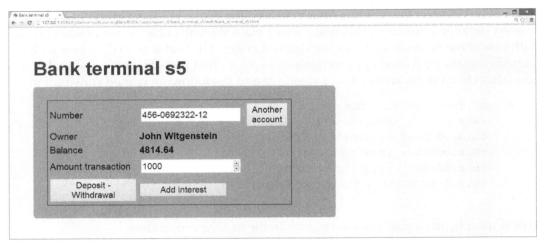

Changing data screen

 For code files of this section, refer to chapter 6\ bank_terminal_s5 in the code bundle.

Here is the code of bank_terminal_s5.dart (declarations are left out for brevity):

```dart
void main() {
  bind_elements();            (1)
  attach_event_handlers();      (2)
  disable_transactions(true);   (3)
}
bind_elements() {
  owner = query('#owner');
  balance = query('#balance');
  number = query('#number');
  btn_other = query('#btn_other');
  amount = query('#amount');
  btn_deposit = query('#btn_deposit');
  btn_interest = query('#btn_interest');
  error = query('#error');
}
```

```
attach_event_handlers() {
  number.onInput.listen(readData);
  amount.onChange.listen(nonNegative);
  amount.onBlur.listen(nonNegative);
  btn_other.onClick.listen(clearData);
  btn_deposit.onClick.listen(deposit);
  btn_interest.onClick.listen(interest);
}
readData(Event e) {
  // same code as in Spiral 4
  // enable transactions part:
  disable_transactions(false);                                 (4)
}
clearData(Event e) {
  number.value = "";
  owner.innerHtml = "----------";
  balance.innerHtml = "0.0";
  number.focus();
  disable_transactions(true);
}
disable_transactions(bool off) {
  amount.disabled = off;
  btn_deposit.disabled = off;
  btn_interest.disabled = off;
}
changeBalance(Event e) {
  // read amount:
  double money_amount = double.parse(amount.value);            (5)
  // call deposit on BankAccount object:
  if (money_amount >= 0) bac.deposit(money_amount);            (6)
  else bac.withdraw(money_amount);
  window.localStorage["Bankaccount:${bac.number}"] = bac.toJson();
  // show new amount:
  balance.innerHtml = "<b>${bac.balance.toStringAsFixed(2)}</b>";
  // disable refresh screen:
  e.preventDefault();                                          (7)
  e.stopPropagation();
}
interest(Event e) {
  bac.interest();
  window.localStorage["Bankaccount:${bac.number}"] =  bac.toJson();
                                                               (8)
  balance.innerHtml = "<b>${bac.balance.toStringAsFixed(2)}</b>";
  e.preventDefault();
  e.stopPropagation();
}
```

The main() method in lines ((1) and (2)) calls methods to create objects for the DOM elements, and creates the event handlers. When the screen displays for the first time, the **Amount transaction** field and the buttons are best shown as disabled; this is accomplished by line (3), which calls a handy method disable_transactions to disable or enable DOM elements by passing a boolean value. When data is shown, the readData method performs as in *Spiral 4, reading and showing data*, and the second part of the screen is enabled line (5). The **Deposit-Withdrawal** button can perform both functions whether the amount is greater or less than 0. The double.parse method in line (5) will not throw an exception, because we checked the number input. The corresponding methods on the object are called to change its balance in line (6), for example, the deposit method in BankAccount class:

```
deposit(double amount) {
    balance += amount;
    date_modified = new DateTime.now();
}
```

The changed object is again stored in local storage in line (8). The two lines starting at line (7) are necessary to stop the event from propagating; if they are not used, the change is not visible because the screen is refreshed immediately. The interest calculation follows the same pattern.

Spiral 6 – working with a list of bank accounts

In this spiral, we will read all our Bank Account data from the local storage and display the numbers in a dropdown list. Upon selection, all details of the bank account are shown in a table. This is how our page looks, at the start, upon opening the selection list:

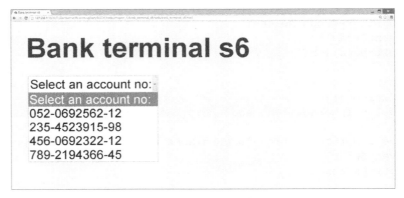

Selecting a bank account number screen

For code files of this section, refer to `chapter 6\`
`bank_terminal_s6` in the code bundle.

In this spiral, we will let the code construct the web page:

```
void main() {
  readLocalStorage();                    (1)
  constructPage();                       (2)
  sel.onChange.listen(showAccount);      (3)
}
```

In line (1), the account numbers are read from local storage, extracted, and put into a list:

```
readLocalStorage() {
  account_nos = [];
  for (var key in window.localStorage.keys) {
    account_nos.add(key.substring(12)); // extract account number
  }
}
```

The method in line (2) calls two other methods, `constructSelect` (line (4)) and `constructTable` (line (5)), to build up the select list and the empty table respectively:

```
constructPage() {
// make dropdown list and fill with data:
  var el = new Element.html(constructSelect());      (4)
  document.body.children.add(el);
// prepare html table for account data:
  var el1 = new Element.html(constructTable());      (5)
  document.body.children.add(el1);
  sel = query('#accounts');
  table = query('#accdata');
  table.classes.remove('border');
}
String constructSelect() {
  var sb = new StringBuffer();                       (6)
  sb.write('<select id="accounts">');
  sb.write('<option selected>Select an account no:</option>');
  account_nos.forEach( (acc) =>
  sb.write('<option>$acc</option>'));                (7)
  sb.write('</select>');
  return sb.toString();
}
```

```
String constructTable() {
  var sb = new StringBuffer();
  sb.write('<table id="accdata" class="border">');
  sb.write('</table>');
  return sb.toString();
}
```

Both methods `constructSelect` and `constructTable` use a `StringBuffer` method for efficiency (line (6)) and we use string interpolation (line (7)) to merge the data with the HTML. Upon selection, using the `onChange` event (line (3)), the following method is called:

```
showAccount(Event e) {
  // remove previous data:
  table.children.clear();                              (8)
  table.classes.remove('border');                      (9)
  // get selected number:
  sel = e.currentTarget;
  if (sel.selectedIndex >= 1) { // an account was chosen  (10)
    var accountno = account_nos[sel.selectedIndex - 1];
    var key = 'Bankaccount:$accountno';
    String acc_json = window.localStorage[key];
    bac = new BankAccount.fromJson(parse(acc_json));
    // show data:
    table.classes.add('border');
    constructTrows();
  }
}
```

To make sure no previous data is shown, the table is cleared in lines (8) and (9), and we also make sure that we select one of the accounts with line (10). The rest of the code is straightforward, using `constructTrows` to fill in the table. We inserted all the `<tr>` tags in one `Element.html`; because of this we are forced to include a `<p>` tag to surround all table rows, because the HTML method needs a surrounding tag. The following screenshot shows the detail screen:

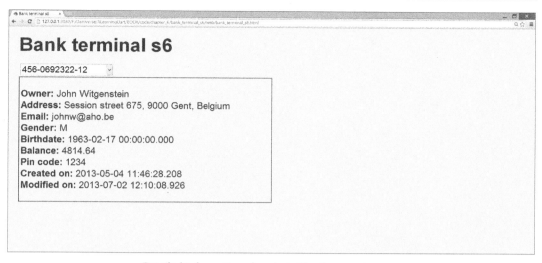

Detailed information of a selected bank account screen

Summary

You have now gained experience with the techniques for building HTML5 screens with input fields that know how to validate data, further controlling data through Dart, and storing them in the browser's local storage for offline use. Along the way, we perfected our skills to work with JSON, and how to (de)construct Dart objects to/from JSON. All these can be used in the frontend of your business application. If you need a more complex user interface, web components are the way to go, and we explore them in detail in *Chapter 8, Developing Business Applications with Polymer Web Components*. In the next chapter, we will sharpen our modeling and game-building skills, adding multimedia functionality to our applications.

7
Building Games with HTML5 and Dart

In this chapter, you will use the knowledge of the previous chapters to create a well-known memory game. But instead of presenting and explaining the code completed in the previous chapters, a model is designed first, and you work up your way from a modest beginning to a completely functional game, spiral by spiral. You will also learn how to enhance the attractiveness of web games with audio and video techniques. The following topics will be covered in this chapter:

- The model for the memory game
- Spiral 1 – drawing the board
- Spiral 2 – drawing cells
- Spiral 3 – coloring the cells
- Spiral 4 – implementing the rules
- Spiral 5 – game logic (bringing in the time element)
- Spiral 6 – some finishing touches
- Spiral 7 – using images
- Adding audio to a web page
- Using an audio library – Collision clones
- Adding video to a web page

The model for the memory game

When started, the game presents a board with square cells. Every cell hides an image that can be seen by clicking on the cell, but this disappears quickly. You must remember where the images are because they come in pairs. If you quickly click on two cells that hide the same picture, the cells are "flipped over" and the pictures stay visible. The objective of the game is to turn over all pairs of matching images in a very short time.

 The code for this project can be downloaded from GitHub using the following command:

```
git clone git://github.com/dzenanr/
educ_memory_game.git
```

After some thinking, we came up with the following model, which describes the data handled by the application. In our game we have a number of pictures, which could belong to a **Catalog.** For example, a travel catalog with a collection of photos from our trips or something similar. Furthermore, we have a collection of cells, and each cell is hiding a picture. Also, we have a structure that we will call memory, and this contains the cells in a grid of rows and columns. Using our Model Concepts graphical design tool from *Chapter 4, Modeling Web Applications with Model Concepts and Dartlero,* we could draw it as shown in the following figure. You can import the model from the file `game_memory_json.txt` that contains its JSON representation:

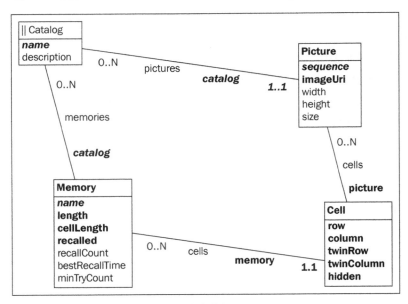

A conceptual model of the memory game

The **Catalog** ID is its `name`, which is mandatory, but the description is optional. The **Picture** ID consists of the `sequence` number within the Catalog. The `imageUri` field stores the location of the image file. `width` and `height` are optional properties since they may be derived from the image file. The size may be small, medium, or large to help us select an image. The ID of a **Memory** is its `name` within the Catalog, the collection of cells is determined by the memory length, for example, 4 cells per side. Each cell is of the same length `cellLength`, which is a property of the memory. A memory is recalled when all image pairs are discovered. Some statistics must be kept, such as recall count, the best recall time in seconds, and the number of cell clicks to recover the whole image (`minTryCount`). The **Cell** has the `row` and `column` coordinates and also the coordinates of its twin with the same image. Once the model is discussed and improved, model views may be created: a **Board** would be a view of the Memory concept and a Box would be a view of the Cell concept. Application would be based on the Catalog concept. If there is no need to browse photos of a catalog and display them within a page, there would not be a corresponding view. Now, we start developing this game from scratch.

Spiral 1 – drawing the board

The app starts with `main()` in `educ_memory_game.dart`:

```
library memory;

import 'dart:html';
import 'dart:async';

part 'board.dart';

void main() {
  // Get a reference to the canvas.
  CanvasElement canvas = querySelector('#canvas');          (1)
  new Board(canvas);                                        (2)
}
```

 For code files of this section refer to `chapter 7\educ_memory_game\spirals\s01` in the code bundle.

As we did in *Chapter 5, Handling the DOM in a New Way*, we'll draw a board on a canvas element. So, we need a reference that is given in line (1). The Board view is represented in code as its own Board class in the board.dart file. Since everything happens on this board, we construct its object with canvas as argument (line (2)). Our game board is periodically drawn as a rectangle in line (4) by using the animationFrame method from the Window class in line (3):

```
part of memory;

class Board {
  // The board is drawn every INTERVAL in ms.
  static const int INTERVAL = 8;

  CanvasElement canvas;
  CanvasRenderingContext2D context;
  num width, height;

  Board(this.canvas) {
    context = canvas.getContext('2d');
    width = canvas.width;
    height = canvas.height;
    // Draw every INTERVAL in ms.
    window.animationFrame.then(gameLoop);                      (3)
  }

  void gameLoop(num delta) {
    draw();
    window.animationFrame.then(gameLoop);
  }

  void draw() {
    clear();
    border();
  }

  void clear() {
    context.clearRect(0, 0, width, height);
  }

  void border() {
    context..rect(0, 0, width, height)..stroke();              (4)
  }
}
```

And this is our first result:

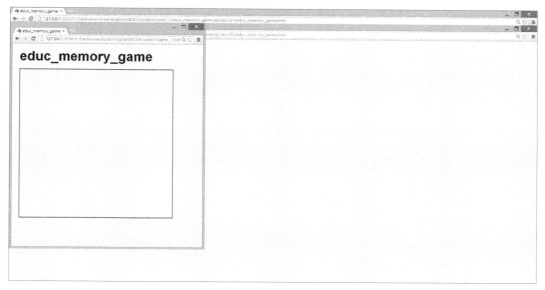

The game board

Spiral 2 – drawing cells

In this spiral, we will give our app code some structure: Board is a view, so board. dart is moved to the view folder. We also introduce here the Memory class from our model in its own code file memory.dart in the model folder. So, we have to change the part statements to the following:

```
part 'model/memory.dart';
part 'view/board.dart';
```

For code file of this section refer to chapter 7\educ_memory_game\spirals\s02.

The Board view needs to know about Memory. So, we will include it in the Board class and make its object in the Board constructor:

```
new Board(canvas, new Memory(4));
```

The Memory class is still very rudimentary with only its length property:

```
class Memory {
  num length;
  Memory(this.length);
}
```

Our `Board` class now also needs a method to draw the lines, which we decided to make private because it is specific to `Board`, as well as the methods `clear()` and `border()`:

```
void draw() {
    _clear();
    _border();
    _lines();
}
```

The `lines` method is quite straightforward; first draw it on a piece of paper and then translate it to code using `moveTo` and `lineTo`. Remember that x goes from top left to right and y goes from top left to bottom:

```
void _lines() {
    var gap = height / memory.length;
    var x, y;
    for (var i = 1; i < memory.length; i++) {
      x = gap * i;
      y = x;
      context
        ..moveTo(x, 0)
        ..lineTo(x, height)
        ..moveTo(0, y)
        ..lineTo(width, y);
    }
}
```

The result is a nice grid:

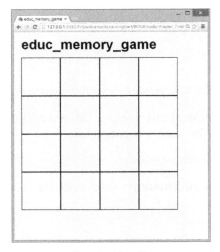

Board with cells

Spiral 3 – coloring the cells

To simplify, we will start using colors instead of pictures to show in the grid. Up until now, we didn't implement the cell from the model. Let's do that in `model\cell.dart`. We start simple by saying that the `Cell` class has the `row`, `column`, and `color` properties, and it belongs to a `Memory` object passed in its constructor:

```
class Cell {
    int row, column;
    String color;
    Memory memory;
    Cell(this.memory, this.row, this.column);
}
```

 For code files of this section, refer to `chapter 7\educ_memory_game\spirals\s03` in the code bundle.

Because we need a collection of cells, it is a good idea to make a `Cells` class, which contains `List`. We give it an `add` method and also an iterator, so that we will be able to use a `for...in` statement to loop over the collection:

```
class Cells {
    List _list;

    Cells() {
        _list = new List();
    }

    void add(Cell cell) {
        _list.add(cell);
    }

    Iterator get iterator => _list.iterator;
}
```

We will need colors that are randomly assigned to the cells. We will also need some utility variables and methods that do not specifically belong to the model and don't need a class. Hence, we code them in a folder called `util`. To specify the colors for the cells, we use two utility variables: a `List` variable of colors (`colorList`), which has the named colors, and a `colorMap` variable that maps the names to their RGB values. Refer to `util\color.dart`, later on we can choose some fancier colors:

```
var colorList = ['black', 'blue', //other colors  ];
var colorMap = {'black': '#000000', 'blue': '#0000ff', //... };
```

To generate (pseudo) random values (ints, doubles, or Booleans), Dart has the class `Random` from `dart:math`. We will use the `nextInt` method, which takes an integer (the maximum value) and returns a positive random integer in the range from 0 (inclusive) to `max` (exclusive). We build upon this in `util\random.dart` to make methods that give us a random color:

```
int randomInt(int max) => new Random().nextInt(max);
randomListElement(List list) => list[randomInt(list.length - 1)];
String randomColor() => randomListElement(colorList);
String randomColorCode() => colorMap[randomColor()];
```

Our `Memory` class now contains an instance of the class `Cells`:

```
Cells cells;
```

We build this in the `Memory` constructor in a nested `for` loop, where each cell is successively instantiated with a row and column, given a random color, and added to `cells`:

```
Memory(this.length) {
  cells = new Cells();
  var cell;
  for (var x = 0; x < length; x++) {
    for (var y = 0; y < length; y++) {
      cell = new Cell(this, x, y);
      cell.color = randomColor();
      cells.add(cell);
    }
  }
}
```

We know from *Chapter 5, Handling the DOM in a New Way*, that we can draw a rectangle and fill it with a color at the same time. So, we realize we don't need to draw lines as we did in the previous spiral! The `_boxes` method is called from the draw animation: with a for...in statement we loop over the collection of cells, and then call the `_colorBox` method that will draw and color the cell for each cell:

```
void _boxes() {
  for (Cell cell in memory.cells) {
    _colorBox(cell);
  }
}

void _colorBox(Cell cell) {
  var gap = height / memory.length;
  var x = cell.row * gap;
```

```
        var y = cell.column * gap;
        context
          ..beginPath()
          ..fillStyle = colorMap[cell.color]
          ..rect(x, y, gap, gap)
          ..fill()
          ..stroke()
          ..closePath();
    }
```

And now we have a colored board:

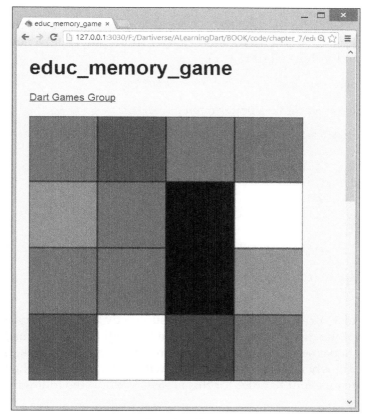

The colored board

Spiral 4 – implementing the rules

But wait, our game can only work if the same color only appears in two cells: a cell and its twin cell. Moreover, a cell can be hidden or not, that is, the color can be seen or not? To take care of this, the Cell class gets two new attributes:

```
Cell twin;
bool hidden = true;
```

 [For code files of this section, refer to chapter 7\
educ_memory_game\spirals\s04 in the code bundle.]

The method _colorBox in the Board class can now show the color of the cell when hidden is false (line (2)); when hidden = true (the default state) a neutral gray color will be used for that cell (line (1)):

```
static const String COLOR_CODE = '#f0f0f0';
```

We also gave the gap variable a better name, boxSize:

```
void _colorBox(Cell cell) {
    var x = cell.column * boxSize;
    var y = cell.row * boxSize;
    context.beginPath();
    if (cell.hidden) {
      context.fillStyle = COLOR_CODE;                    (1)
    } else {
      context.fillStyle = colorMap[cell.color];          (2)
    }
// same code as in Spiral 3
}
```

The lines (1) and (2) can also be stated more succinctly with the ternary operator ?. Remember that the drawing changes because the method _colorBox is called via draw at 60 frames per second and the board can react to a mouse click. In this spiral, we will show a cell when it is clicked together with its twin cell and then they stay visible. Attaching an event handler for this is easy. We add the following line to the Board constructor:

```
querySelector('#canvas').onMouseDown.listen(onMouseDown);
```

The onMouseDown event handler has to know on which cell the click occurred. The mouse event e contains the coordinates of the click in its e.offset.x and e.offset.y (lines (3) and (4) beneath). We obtain the cell's row and column by using a truncating division ~/ operator dividing the x (which gives the column) and y (which gives the row) values by boxSize:

```
void onMouseDown(MouseEvent e) {
    int row = e.offset.y ~/ boxSize;                    (3)
    int column = e.offset.x ~/ boxSize;                 (4)
    Cell cell = memory.getCell(row, column);            (5)
    cell.hidden = false;                                (6)
    cell.twin.hidden = false;                           (7)
}
```

Memory has a collection of cells. To get the cell with a specified row and column value, we add a getCell method to memory and call it in line (5). When we have the cell, we set its hidden property and that of its twin cell to false (lines (6) to (7)). The getCell method must return the cell at the given row and column. It loops through all the cells in line (8) and checks each cell whether it is positioned at that row and column (line (9)). If yes, it returns that cell:

```
Cell getCell(int row, int column) {
    for (Cell cell in cells) {                  (8)
        if (cell.intersects(row, column)) {     (9)
            return cell;
        }
    }
}
```

For this purpose, we add an intersects method to the Cell class. This checks whether its row and column match the given row and column for the current cell (see line (10)):

```
bool intersects(int row, int column) {
    if (this.row == row && this.column == column) {     (10)
        return true;
    }
    return false;
}
```

Now, we have already added a lot of functionality, but the drawing of the board needs some more thinking:

- How to give a cell (and its twin cell) a random color that is not yet used?
- How to attach randomly a cell to a twin cell that is not yet used?

To this end, we will have to make the constructor of Memory a lot more intelligent:

```dart
Memory(this.length) {
    if (length.isOdd) {                                          (1)
      throw new Exception(
          'Memory length must be an even integer: $length.');
    }
    cells = new Cells();
    var cell, twinCell;
    for (var x = 0; x < length; x++) {
      for (var y = 0; y < length; y++) {
        cell = getCell(y, x);                                    (2)
        if (cell == null) {                                      (3)
          cell = new Cell(this, y, x);
          cell.color = _getFreeRandomColor();                   (4)
          cells.add(cell);
          twinCell = _getFreeRandomCell();                      (5)
          cell.twin = twinCell;                                 (6)
          twinCell.twin = cell;
          twinCell.color = cell.color;
          cells.add(twinCell);
        }
      }
    }
}
```

The number of pairs given by *((length * length) / 2)* must be even. This is only true if the length parameter of Memory itself is even, so we check that in line (1). Again, we code a nested loop and we get the cell at that row and column. But when the cell at that position has not yet been made (line (3)), we continue to construct it and assign its color and twin. In line (4), we call _getFreeRandomColor to get a color which is not yet used:

```dart
String _getFreeRandomColor() {
    var color;
    do {
      color = randomColor();
    } while (usedColors.any((c) => c == color));              (7)
    usedColors.add(color);                                     (8)
    return color;
}
```

The do...while loop continues as long as the color is already in a list of usedColors (this is elegantly checked with the functional any from *Chapter 3, Structuring Code with Classes and Libraries*). On exiting from the loop, we found an unused color, which is added to usedColors in line (8) and also returned. Then, we have to set everything for the twin cell. We search for a free one with the _getFreeRandomCell method in line (5). Here, the do...while loop continues until a (row, column) position is found where cell == null, meaning we haven't yet created a cell there (line (9)). We promptly do this in line (10):

```
Cell _getFreeRandomCell() {
    var row, column;
    Cell cell;
    do {
      row = randomInt(length);
      column = randomInt(length);
      cell = getCell(row, column);
    } while (cell != null);                                (9)
    return new Cell(this, row, column);                    (10)
}
```

From line (6) onward, the properties of the twin cell are set and it is added to the list. That's all we need to produce the following result:

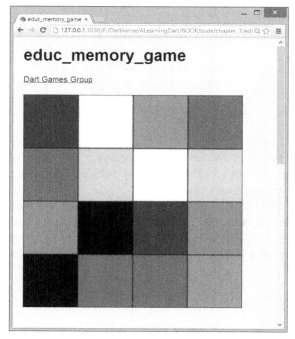

Paired colored cells

Spiral 5 – game logic (bringing in the time element)

Our app isn't playable yet:

- When a cell is clicked, its color must only show for a short period of time (say one second)

- When a cell and its twin cell are clicked within a certain time interval, they must remain visible

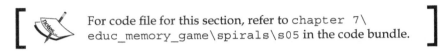

For code file for this section, refer to `chapter 7\`
`educ_memory_game\spirals\s05` in the code bundle.

All of this is coded in the `mouseDown` event handler, and we also need a variable `lastCellClicked` of type `Cell` in the `Board` class. Of course, this is exactly the cell which we get in the `mouseDown` event handler. So, we set this in line (5) in the following code snippet:

```
void onMouseDown(MouseEvent e) {
  // same code as in Spiral 4 -
  if (cell.twin == lastCellClicked && lastCellClicked.shown) {   (1)
    lastCellClicked.hidden = false;                              (2)
      if (memory.recalled)    memory.hide();                     (3)
  } else {
    new Timer(const Duration(milliseconds: 1000), () =>
                    cell.hidden = true);                         (4)
  }
  lastCellClicked = cell;                                        (5)
}
```

In line (1), we check whether the last clicked cell was the twin cell, and if this is still shown. Then we make sure in (2) that it stays visible. `shown` is a new getter in the `Cell` class to make the code more readable: `bool get shown => !hidden;`. If at that moment all cells are shown (the memory is recalled), we again hide them all in line (3). If the last clicked cell was not the twin cell, we hide the current cell after one second in line (4). `recalled` is a simple getter (read-only property) in the `Memory` class, and it makes use of a Boolean variable in `Memory` that is initialized to `false` (`_recalled = false;`):

```
bool get recalled {
    if (!_recalled) {
        if (cells.every((c) => c.shown)) {                       (6)
          _recalled = true;
```

```
    }
  }
  return _recalled;
}
```

In line (6), we test that if every cell is shown then this variable is set to true (the game is over). every is a new method in Cells and a nice functional way to write this is given as follows:

```
bool every(Function f) => list.every(f);
```

The hide method is straightforward: hide every cell and reset the _recalled variable to false:

```
hide() {
    for (final cell in cells) cell.hidden = true;
    _recalled = false;
}
```

That's it, our game works!

Spiral 6 – some finishing touches

A working program always gives its developer a sense of joy, and rightfully so. However, this doesn't mean you can leave the code as it is. On the contrary, carefully review your code for some time to see if there is room for improvement or optimization. For example, are the names you used clear enough? The color of a hidden cell is now named simply COLOR_CODE in board.dart, renaming it to HIDDEN_CELL_COLOR_CODE makes its meaning explicit. The List used in the Cells class can indicate that it is a List<Cell>, by applying the fact that Dart lists are generic. The parameter of the every method in the Cell class is more precise—it is a function that accepts a cell and returns bool. Our onMouseDown event handler contains our game logic, so it is very important to tune it if possible. After some thought we see that the code from the previous spiral can be improved; in the line below the second condition after && is in fact unnecessary:

```
if (cell.twin == lastCellClicked && lastCellClicked.shown) {...}
```

 For code files of this section, refer to chapter 7\ educ_memory_game\spirals\s06 in the code bundle.

When the player has guessed everything correctly, showing the completed screen for a few seconds will be more satisfactory (line (2)). So, this portion of our event handler code changes to:

```
if (cell.twin == lastCellClicked) {                              (1)
    lastCellClicked.hidden = false;
    if (memory.recalled) { // game over
        new Timer(const Duration(milliseconds: 5000), () =>
                memory.hide());                                  (2)
    }
} else if (cell.twin.hidden) {
    new Timer(const Duration(milliseconds: 800), () =>
            cell.hidden = true);
}
```

And why not show a banner "YOU HAVE WON!"? We will do this by drawing the text on the canvas (line (3)), so we must do it in the draw() method (otherwise, it would disappear after INTERVAL milliseconds):

```
void draw() {
  _clear();
  _boxes();
  if (memory.recalled) { // game over
   context.font = "bold 25px sans-serif";
   context.fillStyle = "red";
   context.fillText("YOU HAVE WON !", boxSize, boxSize * 2);   (3)
  }
}
```

Then the same game with the same configuration can be played again.

We could make it more obvious that a cell is hidden by decorating it with a small circle in the _colorBox method (line (4)):

```
if (cell.hidden) {
    context.fillStyle = HIDDEN_CELL_COLOR_CODE;
    var centerX = cell.column * boxSize + boxSize / 2;
    var centerY = cell.row * boxSize + boxSize / 2;
    var radius = 4;
    context.arc(centerX, centerY, radius, 0, 2 * PI, false);    (4)
}
```

We do want to give our player a chance to start over by supplying a **Play again** button. The easiest way is to simply refresh the screen (line (5)) by adding this code to the startup script:

```
void main() {
  canvas = querySelector('#canvas');
  ButtonElement play = querySelector('#play');
  play.onClick.listen(playAgain);
  new Board(canvas, new Memory(4));
}

playAgain(Event e) {
  window.location.reload();                                      (5)
}
```

Spiral 7 – using images

One improvement that certainly comes to mind is use of pictures instead of colors, as shown in the *Using images* screenshot. How difficult would that be? It turns out that this is surprisingly easy because we already have the game logic firmly in place!

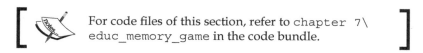

> For code files of this section, refer to chapter 7\
> educ_memory_game in the code bundle.

In the images folder, we supply a number of game pictures. Instead of the color property we give the cell a String property (image), which will contain the name of the picture file. We replace util\color.dart with util\images.dart, which contains a variable imageList with the image filenames. In util\random.dart, we replace the color methods with the following code:

```
String randomImage() => randomListElement(imageList);
```

The changes to `memory.dart` are also straightforward: replace the `usedColor` list with `List usedImages = [];` and the method `_getFreeRandomColor` with `_getFreeRandomImage`, which uses the new list and method:

```
List usedImages = [];

String _getFreeRandomImage() {
    var image;
    do {
      image = randomImage();
    } while (usedImages.any((i) => i == image));
    usedImages.add(image);
    return image;
}
```

In `board.dart`, we replace `_colorBox(cell)` with `_imageBox(cell)`. The only new thing is how to draw the image on canvas. For this, we need `ImageElement` objects. Here, we have to be careful to create these objects only once and not over and over again in every draw cycle because this produces a flickering screen. We will store the `ImageElements` object in a `Map`:

```
var imageMap = new Map<String, ImageElement>();
```

Then populate this in the `Board` constructor with a for...in loop over `memory.cells`:

```
for (var cell in memory.cells) {
    ImageElement image = new Element.tag('img');        (1)
    image.src = 'images/${cell.image}';                 (2)
    imageMap[cell.image] = image;                       (3)
}
```

We create a new `ImageElement` object in line (1), giving it the complete file path to the image file as a `src` property in line (2) and store it in `imageMap` in line (3). The image file will then be loaded into memory only once. We don't do any unnecessary network access and effectively cache the images. In the draw cycle, we load the image from our `imageMap` and draw it in the current cell with the `drawImage` method in line (4):

```
if (cell.hidden) {
    // see previous code
} else {
    ImageElement image = imageMap[cell.image];
    context.drawImage(image, x, y); // resize to cell size (4)
}
```

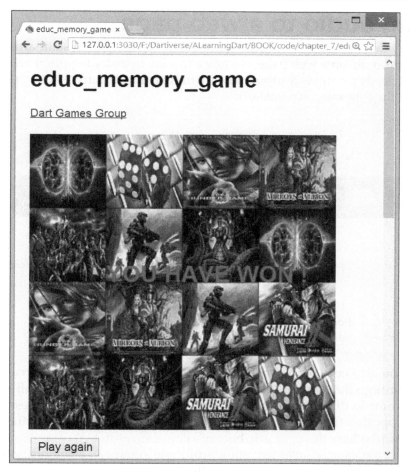

Using images

Perhaps you can think of other improvements? Why not let the player specify the game difficulty by asking the number of boxes. It is 16 now. Check that the input is a square of an even number. Do you have enough colors from which to choose? Perhaps dynamically building a list with enough random colors is a better idea. Calculating and storing the statistics discussed in the model would also make the game more attractive. For ideas, see the *Using an audio library – Collision clones* section. Another enhancement from the model is supporting different catalogs of pictures. Exercise your Dart skills!

Adding audio to a web page

HTML5 provides us with the `<audio>` element, which specifies a standard way to embed an audio file on a web page. No more trouble in installing plugins in your browsers! It needs a *controls* attribute to add audio controls, such as play, pause, and volume (see the following screenshot):

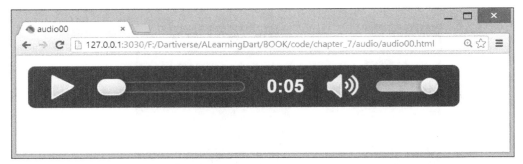

The controls attribute

 For code file for this section, refer to chapter 7\audio\ and chapter 7\audio_dart\ in the code bundle.

Of course, you also need to indicate where the browser can find the source of the sound file through the `<source>` element and its `src` attribute. But, we all know that media files come in different formats, such as MP3, WAV, and OGG. These are the currently supported file formats, and only Chrome supports all three of them. The format is described via the `type` attribute of `<source>`, as in `type="audio/mpeg"` for MP3. Luckily, the `<audio>` element allows multiple `<source>` elements, so that we can link to different audio file formats and the browser will use the first recognized format. Try it out with `audio00.html`:

```
<audio controls>
<source src="dog.mp3" type="audio/mpeg" />
 <source src="dog.ogg" type="video/ogg" />
   The audio tag is not supported in your browser.
   Download the audio <a href="dog.mp3">here</a>.
 </audio>
```

 Best practice is to provide both MP3 and OGG sources in order to take full advantage of HTML5 audio. The browser takes the first recognized format.

Note that Dartium doesn't support the `<audio>` format MP3 with local sounds until now. To set up HTML5 audio in the most robust manner, you can also add the `codecs` info to the `type` attribute, as we did in `audio01.html`:

```
<source src="dog.ogg" type="audio/ogg; codecs='vorbis'" />
```

The source can also be a URL reference as in `audio02.html`:

```
src= "http://www.html5rocks.com/en/tutorials/audio/quick/test.mp3"
```

Refer to `http://html5doctor.com/html5-audio-the-state-of-play/` to find out more information. To use sound in from Dart is very easy too (see `audio_dart`), just give the `<audio>` element an ID so that you can reference it from code like this

```
AudioElement thip = querySelector('#thip');
  thip.play();
```

Now the sound file starts to play. We apply this to enhance our game – we play a sound when two similar images are found and another when the memory is recalled (in `board.dart`):

```
void onMouseDown(MouseEvent e) {
    // code left out
    if (cell.twin == lastCellClicked) {
      lastCellClicked.hidden = false;
      // play sound found same 2 images:
      AudioElement thip = querySelector('#thip');
      thip.play();
      if (memory.recalled) { // game over
        AudioElement fireballs= querySelector('#fireballs');
        fireballs.play();
    // code left out
}
```

For more serious sound applications, HTML5 introduced the **Web Audio** API. Dart incorporated this in its `dart:web_audio` library. This package makes it possible to process, mix, filter, and synthesize sound in your web applications. A Dart game that uses this is Pop Pop Win, a MineSweeper variant by *Kevin Moore*. You can play it at `https://www.dartlang.org/samples/` and find the source at `https://github.com/dart-lang/pop-pop-win`. You can find more detailed info on Web Audio at `http://www.html5rocks.com/en/tutorials/webaudio/intro/`.

If you need less sophistication, you can use the `simple_audio` library written by *John McCutchan*, you can find at `https://github.com/johnmccutchan/simple_audio`.

The `AudioManager` class is the main entry point in this library. You can create `AudioClips` and `AudioSources` with the manager and play clips from sources with the manager. This library is used in the game Collision clones, which comes next.

Using an audio library – Collision clones

This game shows a field of moving cars of different sizes and colors. The player controls the red car (initially at the top-left corner) through the mouse cursor. The objective is to move the red car within the time limit with as few collisions as possible. The lower the speed limit, the slower the cars. The game runs until the time limit is over (in minutes). You will lose if the number of collisions during that time is greater than the time elapsed in seconds. You win if you survive the time limit. If the red car is hit, it shrinks to a small black car. In order to revive it, move the cursor to one of the borders of the board. After a certain number of collisions, clone cars appear. Here is a typical game screen:

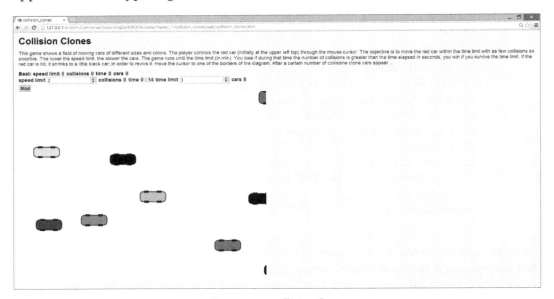

Game screen collision clones

For code file of this section, refer to `chapter 7\collision_clones` and `chapter 7\car_collisions` in the code bundle. You can also get them from GitHub using the following commands:

```
git clone git://github.com/dzenanr/collision_clones.git
git clone git://github.com/dzenanr/car_collisions.git
```

This is our first example of a web app where all code is assembled in a `collision_clones` library that resides in its own `lib` folder. Because it is also stored in the `packages` folder, it can be imported (line `(1)`) in the startup script `web\collision_clones.dart`, where a new object of the class `Board` is created:

```
import 'package:collision_clones/collision_clones.dart';        (1)

main() {
  new Board();
}
```

Now, look at `pubspec.yaml`:

```
dependencies:
  browser: any
  simple_audio:
    git: https://github.com/johnmccutchan/simpleaudio.git
```

We see that the `simple_audio` library, which was briefly discussed at the end of the *Adding audio to a web page* section, is also imported in the `lib\collision_clones.dart` library file along with all the other constituent packages and source files:

```
library collision_clones;

import 'dart:html';
import 'dart:async';
import "dart:json";
import 'dart:math';
import 'package:simple_audio/simple_audio.dart';

part 'view/game_board.dart';
part 'model/cars.dart';
part 'model/score.dart';
part 'sound/audio.dart';
part 'util/color.dart';
part 'util/random.dart';
```

Again, the `view` class is called `Board` (in `view\game_board.dart`) and its instantiation starts and animates the game. The viewable objects in this game are the cars, and specifically the red car. They have corresponding classes in `lib\model\cars.dart` and the `Board` class contains `List<Car>` and a variable `redCar`. Because they share many properties, we let them both inherit from an abstract class `Vehicle`:

```
abstract class Vehicle
class Car extends Vehicle
class RedCar extends Vehicle
```

The abstract class contains all that is needed to draw a car in its constructor and the draw method: getting the canvas context, calculating a random position (x, y) and color code, and the methods on the canvas context we saw in *Chapter 5, Handling the DOM in a New Way*, are put to use. The draw method is given as follows:

```
draw() {
    context
      ..beginPath()
      ..fillStyle = colorCode
      ..strokeStyle = 'black'
      ..lineWidth = 2;
    roundedCorners(context, x, y, x + width, y + height, 10);
    context
      ..fill()
      ..stroke()
      ..closePath();
    // wheels
    context
      ..beginPath()
      ..fillStyle = '#000000'
      ..rect(x + 12, y - 3, 14, 6)
      ..rect(x + width - 26, y - 3, 14, 6)
      ..rect(x + 12, y + height - 3, 14, 6)
      ..rect(x + width - 26, y + height - 3, 14, 6)
      ..fill()
      ..closePath();
}
```

Every Car object has a different speed specified in its constructor: a random number that is lower than the speed limit.

```
Car(canvas, speedLimit) : super(canvas) {
    var speedNumber = int.parse(speedLimit);
    dx = randomNum(speedNumber);
    dy = randomNum(speedNumber);
}
```

The Car class contains a move method, which is called from displayCars() in Board, that changes the position (line (1)), taking into account that cars must bounce from the borders (line (4)). In line (2) we test if the car referred to by this has had a collision with the red car, and in line (3), we test if this car has had a collision with the red car:

```
move(RedCar redCar, List<Car> cars) {
    x += dx;                    (1)
    y += dy;
    if (redCar.big) {
```

```
      redCar.collision(this);                       (2)
    }
    for (Car car in cars) {                          (3)
      if (car != this) {
        car.collision(this);
      }
    }
    if (x > canvas.width || x < 0) dx = -dx;         (4)
    if (y > canvas.height || y < 0) dy = -dy;
  }
```

The red car creates an AudioManager object (line (1) in the following code snippet) in its constructor to make a sound when it collides with another car. The red car also contains some Booleans to determine whether it is in its big or small state and when it is movable. The onMouseDown and onMouseMove events are defined on document property of canvas, and are also there in the red car constructor:

```
RedCar(canvas) : super(canvas) {
    audioManager = new Audio().audioManager;            (1)
    colorCode = bigColorCode;
    width = bigWidth;
    height = bigHeight;
    canvas.document.onMouseDown.listen((MouseEvent e) {  (2)
      movable = !movable;
      if (small) {
        bigger();
      }
    });
    canvas.document.onMouseMove.listen((MouseEvent e) {  (3)
      if (movable) {
        x = e.offset.x - 35;
        y = e.offset.y - 35;
        if (x > canvas.width) {
          bigger();
          x = canvas.width - 20;
        }
      }
// some code left out for brevity
```

The first event handler (line (2)) makes the red car movable after a click on the **Play** button at the beginning of the game or after a click on the **Stop** button. The second handler (line (3)) makes sure the red car is contained within the board's dimensions and that it is revived at the limits of the board after a collision. When the red car collides with another car, the collision method in RedCar invokes smaller():

```
smaller() {
    if (big) {
      small = true;
```

```
        audioManager.playClipFromSourceIn(0.0, 'game', 'collision');
        colorCode = smallColorCode;
        width = smallWidth;
        height = smallHeight;
        collisionCount++;
      }
    }
```

This plays a typical collision sound from web\sound\collision.ogg. We have added an Audio class (in lib\sound\audio.dart) that wraps functionality from the simple_audio library:

```
class Audio {
  AudioManager _audioManager;

  Audio() {
    _audioManager = new AudioManager('${demoBaseUrl()}/sound');
    AudioSource audioSource = _audioManager.makeSource('game');
    audioSource.positional = false;
    AudioClip collisionSound =
        _audioManager.makeClip('collision', 'collision.ogg');
    collisionSound.load();
  }
  // code left out
  AudioManager get audioManager => _audioManager;
}
```

The Board class constructs a Score object, a Red Car object, and the other cars. Then displays them in displayCars() every INTERVAL milliseconds in line (1). In line (2), the score is updated, displayed, and stored in local storage every ACTIVE millisecond (see save() and load() in the class Score):

```
Board() {
    var bestScore = new Score();
    // code left out
  redCar = new RedCar(canvas);
  cars = new List();
  for (var i = 0; i < carCount; i++) {
    var car = new Car(canvas, score.currentSpeedLimit);
    cars.add(car);
  }
  // code left out
  // active play time:
  new Timer.periodic(const Duration(milliseconds: 1000), (t) {
    if (!stopped && redCar.big) {                                (2)
  // code left out
}
```

Here is a portion of the `displayCars()` code:

```
displayCars() {
   // code left out
   clear();              // nested function !
   for (var i = 0; i <cars.length; i++) {
     cars[i].move(redCar, cars);
     cars[i].draw();
   }
   redCar.draw();
   // code left out
```

The `Score` class also contains supporting code to keep track of the counters. That's it, you can find some suggestions for change or improvement in `doc\todo.txt`.

An important improvement can still be made. The `Car` class contains both state information (position, color, and so on) as well as the way to draw itself. The model should not concern itself with the user interface. This separation is achieved in the `car_collisions` variant where everything related to drawing is moved to the `view` class `Board`. Also, in this variant the built-in `AudioElement` class is used. Compare both versions and see how the separation makes the project much easier to understand and maintain.

Adding video to a web page

Adding video to a web page is as easy to do as adding audio: just add a `<video>` tag to the HTML with an embedded `<source>` tag specifying `src` and `type`, and Dartium renders this nicely (see `video01.html`):

```
<video poster="wildlife.jpg" controls>
   <source src="wildlife.ogv" type='video/ogg; codecs="theora,
vorbis"' />
   <source src="wildlife.webm" type='video/webm; codecs="vp8,
vorbis"' />
      The video tag is not supported in your browser. Download the
video <a href="wildlife.webm">here</a>.
</video>
```

 For code file of this section, refer to `chapter 7\video\` in the code bundle.

The `poster` attribute from `<video>` serves to provide the initial image, see the following screenshot:

The poster image with the <video> tag

The three important formats you should care about are WEBM, MP4, and OGV. For MP4, use the following type:

```
type='video/mp4; codecs="avc1.42E01E, mp4a.40.2"'
```

Both `<audio>` and `<video>` support other attributes, such as `autoplay` and `loop`.

 For more info, check the following link:
http://www.html5rocks.com/en/tutorials/video/basics/

Calling a video from Dart is nothing more than creating a `VideoElement` class that references the `<video>` tag, as in `video2.dart`. The `loop` property shows the video continuously:

```
VideoElement video = querySelector('#video');
video.loop = true;
```

Summary

By thoroughly investigating two games applying all of Dart we have already covered, your Dart star begins to shine. For other Dart games, visit `http://www.builtwithdart.com/projects/games/`.

`http://www.dartgamedevs.org/` is the site where you can find more information about building games. In the next chapter, we embark on the quest for the holy grail of modern web development: web components.

8

Developing Business Applications with Polymer Web Components

Web components are the hottest new thing where everybody is looking into and working on in the web universe. We show you how they fit together with HTML5, why they are needed in the web applications of the future, and how Dart brings this to you through Polymer. The following topics will be covered:

- How web components change web development
- Web components with `Polymer.dart`
- Two-way data binding in `Polymer.dart`
- The polymer links project
- The category links project
- The project tasks application

How web components change web development

Developers in object-oriented languages, such as Java (for example, in Swing) and C# / VB.NET (for example, in Windows Forms, ASP.NET, WPF, and Silverlight) are keen to apply inheritance and re-use the components of their app user interfaces (in short UI). Controls are adapted to specific needs by extending basic UI classes, and controls are assembled into reusable parts of screens (commonly user or custom controls). Web developers want to be able to do the same: for example, extend a `<button>` tag, or encapsulate a piece of markup for re-use, or have a simple way to bind data to an HTML element. But until now this wasn't possible in web development. This is exactly the promise of web components: extending HTML, they bring to web development what OO-developers expect in their toolkit. Web components enable you to specialize HTML elements with style and code, and W3C is actively engaged in the standardization of this technology. They can be thought of as extending (often they extend `<div>`, `<span>` or `<section>` tags) or even as new HTML elements: they create encapsulated reusable views to embed in several places of your application or even across several applications. So web components give you what you need in order to write data-driven scalable web applications, namely:

- **Encapsulation**: This is a concept in which structure, style, and behavior are defined separate from the pages in which the component is used

- **Reusability**: This is used by importing components into web pages; a direct consequence from encapsulation

- **Data-binding**: This is to view (one-way) and change (two-way) model data

The code that we need to write is considerably simplified: Dart doesn't manipulate the DOM directly anymore. In effect, we won't need to write code referencing DOM elements to get or change their value, nor do we need to register event handlers in code as we did in *Chapter 5, Handling the DOM in a New Way*, and *Chapter 6, Combining HTML5 Forms with Dart*.

The first package which the Dart team developed for this was named **Web UI**, and some projects were built using it (see *Chapter 10, MVC Web and UI Frameworks in Dart – An Overview*). However, in mid July 2013, the Dart team announced `Polymer. dart`, a Dart port of the Polymer framework (`http://www.polymer-project.org`), in close collaboration with the Google Polymer developers. The Polymer project is a new library on top of Web (or Custom) Components, Model-Driven Views, Shadow DOM, and many more emerging standards for the web platform to simplify and improve the development process. Although the work is still in progress, Polymer promises to provide a broad set of reusable custom components for developers.

Web components with Polymer.dart

The `Polymer.dart` framework provides a set of Polymer (UI and other) components, but it will only work in the most recent versions of browsers: IE9, IE10, Safari 6, Firefox, and the latest Chrome (also for Android). It is important that in Polymer you can only have a single Dart script tag on an HTML document. Get started with creating a new Polymer application **polymer1** by selecting the project template **Web application** (using the `polymer` library) in Dart Editor:

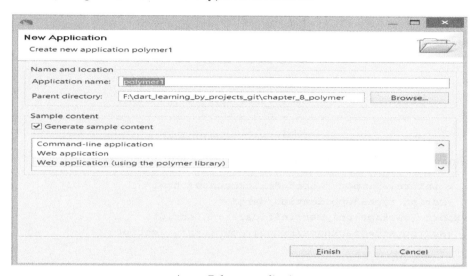

A new Polymer application

Inspecting `pubspec.yaml` will reveal the polymer dependency:

```
dependencies:
    polymer: any
```

Pub is invoked automatically, and installs polymer and a whole group of packages needed by polymer (such as `mdv`, `observe`, `polymer_expressions`, `shadow_dom`, and so on). We'll now examine in detail how a web component is defined in Polymer.

Declaring and instantiating a web component

This is what we see when `polymer1.html` file is run: again a counter button, defined as a web component (also called a Polymer element):

The clickable counter in polymer1

The main `polymer1.html` file contains the following important sections:

```
<link rel="import" href="clickcounter.html">      (1)
<script type="application/dart">
export 'package:polymer/init.dart'; </script>     (2)
<script src="packages/browser/dart.js"></script>
</head>
<body>
  <h1>Polymer1</h1>
  <p>Hello world from Dart!</p>
  <div id="sample_container_id">
    <click-counter count="5"></click-counter>      (3)
  </div>
</body>
```

In addition to the `dart.js` file we now need `polymer/init.dart` in line (2) to initialize polymer elements automatically. Alternatively, if you do want to replace it with your own Dart script, be sure to include a call to the `initPolymer()` method:

```
main() {
      initPolymer();
      doSomething();
}
```

In line (3), we see the web component `<click-counter>`, which as before is imported through the `<link rel ="import">` tag in line (1).

A Polymer element definition should always be in its own HTML source file. That way it is self contained, so it can easily be included by other files to re-use it in other projects and changes have only to be done in one place.

The name of a component must contain a dash (-); in general, the first half of the name should make it unique (for example, by including a project or a business name) so as to avoid conflicts with the other components. Now, let's turn our attention to the definition of the web component. The structure and style of the <click-counter> web component is defined in clickcounter.html file inside a <template> in a <polymer-element> tag whose name attribute in line (4) is the name of the web component:

```
<polymer-element name="click-counter">                     (4)
  <template>
    <style>
      div {
        font-size: 24pt;
        text-align: center;
        margin-top: 140px;
      }
      button {
        font-size: 24pt;
        margin-bottom: 20px;
      }
    </style>
    <div>
     <button on-click="{{increment}}">Click me</button><br>  (5)
      <span>(click count: {{count}})</span>                   (6)
    </div>
  </template>
  <script type="application/dart"
  src="clickcounter.dart"></script>                          (7)
</polymer-element>
```

In general, the <template> section contains markup outlining the UI appearance of the web component. We observe that an HTML file containing a Polymer element definition does not need <html>, <head>, or <body> tags. Line (5) shows that <click-counter> is a button that reacts on the click event by calling an increment method. Line (6) tells us that a count variable is shown with the polymer expression {{count}}. This is the typical syntax {{ expression }} used for data binding to an expression, but as shown in line (5), an event handler is called in the same way.

The behavior of the component is defined in the Dart script `clickcounter.dart` referenced in the `<script>` tag in line (7). This does a lot of things:

```
import 'package:polymer/polymer.dart';                        (8)
@CustomTag('click-counter')                                   (9)
class ClickCounter extends PolymerElement {                  (10)
  @published int count = 0;                                  (11)
    ClickCounter.created() : super.created() { }             (12)
  void increment() {                                         (13)
    count++;
  }
}
```

In line (8), the `polymer` package is imported, `@CustomTag` in line (9) registers `click-counter` as an element in the Polymer framework. Our model is represented by the `ClickCounter` class in line (10), which has to inherit from the `PolymerElement` class and override its `created()` constructor in line (12). This is because Polymer Elements are legitimate HTML elements. Note that the name of the Dart class is obtained after converting the first letter of each word separated by - to an uppercase letter, and then removing the -. The Polymer framework provides for synchronization of the model with screen data. In this case, it is the `count` variable that is annotated with `@published` in line (11) to indicate the simple, one-way (model to screen) data binding. Finally, it contains the `increment` method in line (13), which is called at each button click; this will increase the `count` variable by 1. This change will automatically be shown on the web page. In general, the Dart script implements the behavior of the component and can change (model) data. Each time a custom element is instantiated as in line (3) in the `polymer1.html` file, an instance of the Dart class is created and associated with the custom element. Data bindings in the template are bound to fields in that instance.

As a best practice, a web component has two files to separate the HTML markup from the Dart code. In some simple examples, you will see the code embedded in the `<script>` tag in the HTML file, but this is not recommended. When both files have the same name, it is easier to recognize them as parts of the same component.

Developing web applications with web components is a new approach that will let us divide a page in sections and use a web component for each section. If web components become reusable in different contexts, we may have a catalog of web components that would allow us to select and re-use them in a few lines of code. A page can also contain multiple instances of the same component, each behaving independently from each other. A polymer element is like a supercharged custom element, with functionality provided by the Polymer framework. It automatically allows for simple component registration, and uses the Shadow DOM. This means that its markup is hidden in the web page in which it is embedded, thus providing encapsulation by itself. Polymer uses composability of elements as much as possible, to the extent that the framework advocates proclaim that everything is a component in Polymer. Let's now examine data binding a bit closer.

Two-way data binding in Polymer.dart

Model Driven View (MDV) is a set of techniques to help you bind data to your views, in a more direct way than we did in *Chapter 6, Combining HTML5 Forms with Dart*. The idea here is simple:

- We have one or more classes (with properties) in a model
- Our app contains one or more views (implemented as web components) for presenting the model's data (the data binding)

 For code files of this section, refer to `code\chapter_8\ bank_terminal` in the code bundle.

Data binding can be a one-way (model to view) with or without observing (monitoring) changes in the model: this means data from our model (a variable or a method that returns a value) is shown (read-only) on the page and we do this by writing `{{var}}` in the web page and marking the variable `var` in code as: `@observable var`. When its value changes, the altered value is shown in the web page. In general, you can show any Dart expression with the notation `{{ expression }}`, but be careful that the expression doesn't cause any unwanted side effects by changing variables. Use `@published var` when `var` is also an attribute in a tag. Data binding can also be two-way (model to view and view to model): meaning data can be shown, but input from the web page also changes Dart variables. In other words, the data and the web page are then synchronized.

Data binding combined with event listeners allows us to create simple and sophisticated views for our model in a declarative way, thereby reducing the need for manually creating controller objects that do these bindings. They can be exploited fully only as part of web components, that is to say, polymer elements, and that's what we will do in the following projects in this chapter. Let's apply this first to our bank terminal project; we now build a form that also takes an input amount that is deposited on our account, changing the balance on the screen as shown in the following screenshot:

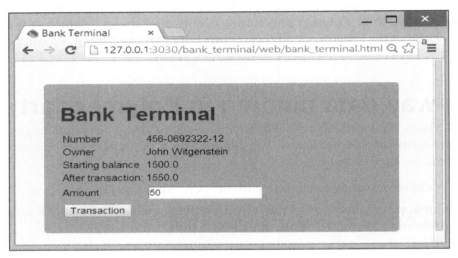

Two-way data binding

The startup page `bank_terminal.html` shows a web component `<bank-app>` through:

```
<h1>Bank Terminal</h1>
<bank-app></bank-app>
```

This web component is linked in with: `<link rel="import" href="bank_app.html">`. Our component uses the following markup in `bank_app.html` file to show the data:

```
<polymer-element name="bank-app">
 <link rel="import" href="bank_account.html">
 <template>
   <bank-account bac="{{bac}}"></bank-account>        (1)
 </template>
 <script type="application/dart" src="bank_app.dart">
  </script>     (2)
</polymer-element>
```

In the template in line (1), a second polymer element named <bank-account> is instantiated. The script bank_app.dart publishes and initializes the BankAccount object bac in lines (3) and (4) respectively:

```
import 'package:polymer/polymer.dart';
import 'package:bank_terminal/bank_terminal.dart';
@CustomTag('bank-app')
class BankApp extends PolymerElement {
  @published BankAccount bac;                                 (3)
  BankApp.created() : super.created()  {   }
  enteredView() {
    super.enteredView();
    var jw = new Person("John Witgenstein");
    bac = new BankAccount(jw, "456-0692322-12", 1500.0);     (4)
  }
}
```

To do this, we have to override the enteredView method of the PolymerElement class, and is called when the element is inserted into the document. The bac object is passed to web component <bank-account> in line (1) in the preceding code. The markup of this component is found in the bank_account.html file:

```
<polymer-element name="bank-account">
<style> // left out
<template>
<table class="auto-style1" on-keypress="{{enter}}">
    <tr>
     <td class="auto-style2">Number</td>
     <td> {{ bac.number }} </td>                             (1)
    </tr>
    <tr>
     <td class="auto-style2">Owner</td>
     <td> {{ bac.owner.name}} </td>                          (2)
     <td></td>
    </tr>
    <tr>
     <td class="auto-style2">Starting balance</td>
     <td> {{bac.balance}}</td>
    </tr>
    <tr>
     <td class="auto-style2"> After transaction:</td>
     <td> {{balance}}</td>                                   (3)
    </tr>
```

```
        <tr>
          <td class="auto-style2">Amount transaction</td>
          <td><input id="amount" type="text"/></td>          (4)
          <td></td>
        </tr>
        <tr>
         <td><button class="btns" on-click="{{transact}}">      (5)
             Transaction</button></td>
        </tr></table></template>
   <script type="application/dart"  src="bank_account.dart"></script>
```

Because the `bac` object is bound to the component, its properties can be shown like `bac.number` in line (1), or even nested properties like in line (2). In line (4), we take in a money amount, which is bound to a variable with the same name in line (13) in the accompanying script `bank_account.dart` (see the following code). A click on the button in line (5) starts the `transact` event handler in line (11), which changes the `balance` in line (12). To show `balance` in line (3), we need to mark it as `@published` in line (9). In lines (6) to (8), we see the required code to define a Polymer web component. Line (10) shows the `BankAccount.created` constructor, which our web component has to override from the `PolymerElement` class:

```
import 'dart:html';
import 'package:polymer/polymer.dart';                        (6)
@CustomTag('bank-account')                                    (7)
class BankAccount extends PolymerElement {                    (8)
  @published var bac;
  @published double balance;                                  (9)
  double amount = 0.0;
  BankAccount.created() : super.created() {  }                (10)
  enteredView() {
    super.enteredView();
    balance = bac.balance;
  }
  transact(Event e, var detail, Node target) {                (11)
    InputElement amountInput =
    shadowRoot.querySelector("#amount");
    if (!checkAmount(amountInput.value)) return;
    bac.transact(amount);
    balance = bac.balance;                                    (12)
  }
```

```
enter(KeyboardEvent  e, var detail, Node target) {
  if (e.keyCode == KeyCode.ENTER) {
    transact(e, detail, target);
  }
}
checkAmount(String in_amount) {
  try {
    amount = double.parse(in_amount);                    (13)
  } on FormatException catch(ex) {
    return false;
  }
  return true;
}
}
```

Creating the polymer_links project

Get the code with: `git clone git://github.com/dzenanr/polymer_links.git`.
We start our discussion with the first spiral in this project: `polymer_links\`
`polymer_links_s01`.

Spiral s01

In this spiral, we just show a web component that contains a list of links of type
`String`, as shown in the following screenshot:

Spiral s01 of polymer_links

The startup HTML page `polymer_links.html` imports the web component with:

```
<link rel="import" href="links.html">
```

The component with name `web-links` is instantiated in the `<body>` tag of the page:

```
<h1>Web Links</h1>
<web-links></web-links>
```

The links.html file contains the UI definition of the component:

```
<polymer-element name="web-links">
  <template>                                                    (1)
    <ul>
      <template repeat="{{webLink in webLinks}}">              (2)
        <li>
          <a href="{{webLink}}">                                (3)
            {{webLink}}
          </a>
        </li>
      </template>
    </ul>
  </template>
  <script type="application/dart" src="links.dart"></script>   (4)
</polymer-element>
```

The outer template in line (1) is required. The template in line (2) uses a repeat statement to iterate over the list webLinks: repeat="{{webLink in webLinks}}". The variable webLink takes on the value of each list item in succession, and is shown through {{webLink }} on the next line. The list is constructed in the links.dart script referenced in line (4):

```
import 'package:polymer/polymer.dart';
@CustomTag('web-links')
class WebLinks extends PolymerElement {
  List webLinks =
    ['http://ondart.me/',
      'https://www.dartlang.org/polymer-dart/'];
  WebLinks.created() : super.created();
}
```

Spiral s02

Now, we base the web component on a model with one simple concept: a web link. This has two attributes: a name and a url. The class Link is defined in lib\links. dart:

```
library links;
class Link {
  String name;
  Uri url;
  Link(this.name, String link) {
    url = Uri.parse(link);
  }
}
```

It is a best practice to put our model in its own library links in a separate lib folder. The Polymer framework is based on the statement: everything is a component. This implies that it is recommended to create a component for the HTML page that starts the application and this is what we do here. We now introduce a web component `<my-app></my-app>` in `polymer_links.html` that encapsulates the user interface and is also imported through a `<link>` tag: `<link rel="import" href="my_app.html">`. We show all our links as a `<web-links>` component in `my_app.html`, so component `<web-links>` is embedded in `<my-app>`:

```
<polymer-element name="my-app">
  <link rel="import" href="web_links.html">
  <template>
    <web-links weblinks="{{links}}"></web-links>        (1)
  </template>
  <script type="application/dart" src="my_app.dart"></script>
</polymer-element>
```

This component in its turn is defined in `web_links.html` and `web_links.dart`.

> Name the definition files of the web component like the component, replacing - with _ . This keeps a more complex project with different components structured.

In the `my_app.dart` file, we find the code for the `<my_app>` component that constructs a links collection named `links`:

```
import 'package:polymer_links/links.dart';
import 'package:polymer/polymer.dart';
@CustomTag('my-app')
class MyApp extends PolymerElement {
  var links = new List<Link>();
  MyApp.created() : super.created() {
    var link1 = new Link('On Dart', 'http://ondart.me/');
    var link2 = new Link('Polymer.dart'
'https://www.dartlang.org/polymer-dart/');
    var link3 = new Link('Books To Read',
  'http://www.goodreads.com/');
    links..add(link1)..add(link2)..add(link3);        (2)
  }
}
```

Our component `<web-links>` is now instantiated through the template in line (1) in the preceding code; it needs a `links` variable, which is made in the `MyApp` constructor in line (2).

The web component in `web_links.html` also uses the repeating template introduced in spiral s01, but now shows the names of the links:

```
<template repeat="{{weblink in weblinks}}">
    <li>
      <a href="{{weblink.url}}">
        {{weblink.name}}
      </a>
    </li>
</template>
```

The `web_links.dart` file now also imports our model from the `links` library and annotates the `weblinks` variable with `@published` in line (3) to show its contents:

```
import 'package:polymer_links/links.dart';
import 'package:polymer/polymer.dart';
@CustomTag('web-links')
class WebLinks extends PolymerElement {
  @published List<Link> weblinks;            (3)
  WebLinks.created() : super.created();
}
```

When you run the preceding code, it looks like the following screenshot:

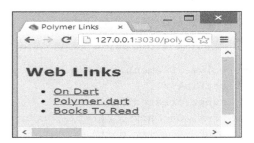

Spiral s02 of polymer_links

Apart from some added style in spiral s03, the `<web-links>` component is identical to that in spiral s02.

Spiral s04

In this spiral, we also provide the possibility to add a web link by the user:

Adding a web link

A new link has to be shown; in order to accomplish this, we have to mark the list with toObservable in my_app.dart file:

```
var links = toObservable(new List<Link>());
```

The definition of the web links component in the web_links.html file now contains additional UI markup in its <template> tag to enable adding links:

```
<div>
    <label for="name">Name</label>
    <input id="name" type="text"/>
    <label for="url">web Link</label>
    <input id="url" type="text"/><br/>
    <button on-click="{{add}}" class="button">Add</button> (1)
    <label id="message"></label>
</div>
<ul> <!-- repeating template --> </ul></template>
<script type="application/dart" src="web_links.dart"></script>
```

The add behavior from line (1) is found in the script web_links.dart:

```
add(Event e, var detail, Node target) {                    (2)
    InputElement name = shadowRoot.querySelector("#name");    (3)
    InputElement url = shadowRoot.querySelector ("#url");
    LabelElement message = shadowRoot.querySelector ("#message");
    var error = false;
    message.text = '';
    if (name.value.trim() == '') {
      message.text = 'name is mandatory; ${message.text}';
      error = true;
    }
```

```
    if (url.value.trim() == '') {
      message.text = 'web link is mandatory; ${message.text}';
      error = true;
    }
    if (!error) {
      var weblink = new Link(name.value, url.value);
      weblinks.add(weblink);                    (4)
    }
  }
```

Notice how in line (1) the add event handler is called in {{ }}, and in line (2) we can see that it has three arguments: the third one is a direct reference to the target element on which the event happened. In lines (3) and the following, we see how to get a reference to the inner markup of a web component. The familiar querySelector method call is now preceded by shadowRoot:

```
shadowRoot.querySelector("#name");
```

Spiral s05

In spiral s05, we add the functionality to store our web links in local storage by adding the code needed to load and save data to the model. The save functionality is implemented in the web_links.dart script of the <web-links> component. In the preceding code after line (4), we now add:

```
  if (!error) {
  // previous code
    save();
}
and this save-method:
save() {
  window.localStorage['polymer_links'] =
  JSON.encode(Model.one.toJson());
}
```

We want to save our data in JSON format. To this end, our model class Link needs to know how to transform itself in a Map (with a toJson method) or to construct itself from a Map (using the Link.fromJson constructor).

```
Map<String, Object> toJson() {
    var linkMap = new Map<String, Object>();
    linkMap['name'] = name;
    linkMap['url'] = url.toString();
    return linkMap;
}
```

```
Link.fromJson(Map<String, Object> linkMap) {
    name = linkMap['name'];
    url = Uri.parse(linkMap['url']);
}
```

Instead of always using `List<Link>`, let's introduce a `Model` class that envelops such a `List` using a singleton design pattern in line (1) (see `lib\links.dart`):

```
class Model {
  var links = new List<Link>();
// singleton design pattern:
    // http://en.wikipedia.org/wiki/Singleton_pattern
  static Model model;
  Model.private();
  static Model get one {                                          (1)
    if (model == null) {
      model = new Model.private();
    }
    return model;
  }
  init() {
    var link1 = new Link('On Dart', 'http://ondart.me/');
    var link2 = new Link('Web UI',
  'http://www.dartlang.org/articles/web-ui/');
    var link3 = new Link('Books To Read',
  'http://www.goodreads.com/');
    Model.one.links
    ..add(link1);
          ..add(link2);
          ..add(link3);
  }
  List<Map<String, Object>> toJson() {
    var linkList = new List<Map<String, Object>>();
    for (Link link in links) {
      linkList.add(link.toJson());                                (2)
    }
    return linkList;
  }
  fromJson(List<Map<String, Object>> linkList) {
    if (!links.isEmpty) {
      throw new Exception('links are not empty');
    }
    for (Map<String, Object> linkMap in linkList) {
      Link link = new Link.fromJson(linkMap);                     (3)
      links.add(link);
    }
  }
}
```

The **Model** class also has toJson and fromJson methods, applying the corresponding methods for Link class while iterating over its internal list of Link objects, see lines (2) and (3) in the preceding code. The constructor MyApp() method in my_app.dart first creates a list in line (4), and then calls the load() method in line (5) to read the data from local storage:

```
MyApp.created() : super.created() {
  toObservable(Model.one.links);              (4)
  load();                                      (5)
}
load() {
  String json = window.localStorage['polymer_links'];
  if (json == null) {
    Model.one.init();                          (6)
  } else {
    Model.one.fromJson(JSON.decode(json));     (7)
  }
}
```

If nothing was stored yet, the Model object is initialized via the init() method in line (6), else it is parsed from local storage in line (7). In line (4), something special happens: We apply the singleton pattern to make sure that we only have one object of Model class ever. The getter one in line (1) in the Model class only constructs an object when model is null, and this object is always returned. Because there is only one model object, we can safely refer to the unique links object of the model to feed links within the web component's Dart code.

Spiral s06

Here the possibility is added to remove links, as shown in the following screenshot:

Removing a web link

A second button is placed inside the `<template>` tag of the `<web-links>` component:

```
<button on-click="{{delete}}" class="button">Remove</button>
```

The `delete` method is implemented in the script of the `web_links.dart` component:

```
delete(Event e, var detail, Node target) {
    InputElement name = shadowRoot.querySelector("#name");
    InputElement url = shadowRoot.querySelector ("#url");
    LabelElement message = shadowRoot.querySelector("#message");
    message.text = '';
    Link link = links.find(name.value);
    if (link == null) {
      message.text = 'web link with this name does not exist';
    } else {
      url.value = link.url.toString();
      if (links.remove(link)) save();              (8)
    }
}
```

It calls in line (8) a `remove` method in the updated `Links` class in `lib\links.dart`. The `Model` class now encapsulates:

```
var links = new Links();
```

Instead of:

```
var links = new List<Link>();
```

The `Links` class now contains:

```
var _list = new List<Link>();
```

The `remove` method goes like this:

```
bool remove(Link link) {
    return _list.remove(link);
}
```

It also has a getter for the private `List _list`:

```
List<Link> get internalList => _list;
```

This is now called in `MyApp.created()` as follows:

```
toObservable(Model.one.links.internalList);
```

Using Polymer for the category links project

On top of the Category Links model that was discussed in *Chapter 4, Modeling Web Applications with Model Concepts and Dartlero* (the model is contained in the `lib` folder), we will now build a typical master-detail screen to present and change its data using web components for displaying, adding, editing, removing, and saving data, as shown in the following screenshot:

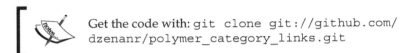

Get the code with: `git clone git://github.com/dzenanr/polymer_category_links.git`

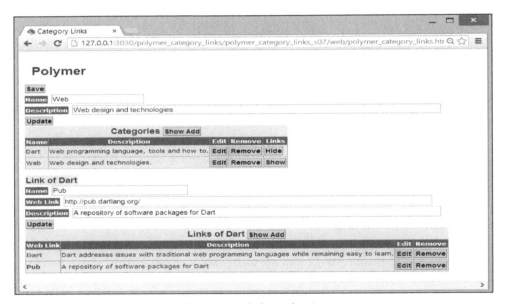

The category_links application

In the final spiral, there are three web components per concept of the model: `table` (for a list), `add` (to add an element to the list), and `edit` (to edit an element of the list); they can be found in the `web\component` folder. In spiral s00, only the Category entity is defined as ConceptEntity together with its collection Categories. The script `test\ categories_entities_test.dart` applies `unittest` on this model. In spiral s01, we build a component for the Category entity: this is the first step towards the upper part of the preceding screenshot. In this spiral, we only show a table with the category data, using a `<category-table>` web component, as shown in the following screenshot:

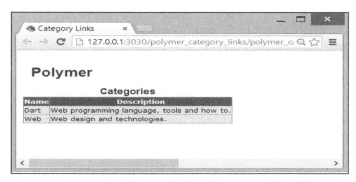

Category_links spiral s01

The `polymer_category_links.html` page exposes a `<polymer-app>` web component defined in the `polymer_app.html` file:

```
<polymer-element name="polymer-app">
<link rel="import"
href="component/category/category_table.html">        (1)
<template>
<category-table categories="{{categories}}">
</category-table>                                       (2)
</template>
<script type="application/dart"
src="polymer_app.dart"></script>
</polymer-element>
```

This contains the `<category-table>` component in line (2) that shows the data from the collection `categories`, which is made and filled with data in line (4) in `polymer_app.dart`:

```dart
import 'package:polymer_category_links/category_links.dart';    (3)
import 'package:polymer/polymer.dart';
@CustomTag('polymer-app')
class PolymerApp extends PolymerElement {
  @observable Categories categories;
  PolymerApp.created() : super.created() {
    var categoryLinksModel = new CategoryLinksModel();
    categoryLinksModel.init();                                  (4)
    categories = categoryLinksModel.categories;
  }
}
```

Line (3) imports the model. The `categories` variable in the `<category-table>` component gets its value from the {{ categories }} polymer expression, where the `categories` object in the expression is the property of the `<polymer-app>`.

In this way, data from the application is passed to the web component. The `<category-table>` component is imported through line (1), and is defined in the `category_table.html` file:

```html
<polymer-element name="category-table">
  <template>
    // <style> markup omitted
    <table>
      <caption class="marker">
        Categories
      </caption>
      <tr>
        <th>Name</th>
        <th>Description</th>
      </tr>
      <tbody template repeat="{{category in
      categories.toList()}}">   (5)
        <tr>
          <td>{{category.code}}</td>
          <td>{{category.description}}</td>
        </tr>
      </tbody>
    </table>
  </template>
  <script type="application/dart" src="category_table.dart"></script>
</polymer-element>
```

The `repeat-template` in line (5) iterates through the `List` to show the categories declared in the `category_table.dart` file:

```dart
import 'package:polymer_category_links/category_links.dart';
import 'package:polymer/polymer.dart';
@CustomTag('category-table')
class CategoryTable extends PolymerElement {
  @published Categories categories;
  CategoryTable.created() : super.created();
}
```

In spirals 02, the application is enriched with the add functionality, as shown in the following screenshot:

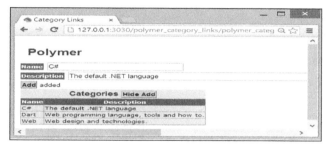

Category_links spiral s02

This is achieved through a `<category-add>` component that is embedded in the `<category-table>` component, and that is only shown when `showAdd` is `true`:

```html
<template if="{{showAdd}}">
    <category-add
      categories="{{categories}}">
    </category-add>
</template>
```

In the **Categories** caption (in the table header), a button is added to toggle the appearance of the add component:

```html
<button id="show-add" on-click="{{show}}">Show Add</button>
```

The button is monitored by the Boolean variable showAdd, marked as observable in the script:

```
@observable bool showAdd = false;
show(Event e, var detail, Node target) {
  ButtonElement addCategory = shadowRoot.querySelector("#show-
  add");
  if (addCategory.text == 'Show Add') {
    showAdd = true;
    addCategory.text = 'Hide Add';
  } else {
    showAdd = false;
    addCategory.text = 'Show Add';
  }
}
```

Now the categories data can change, so we must mark it as observable. This is done in polymer_app.dart through:

```
categories.internalList = toObservable(categories.internalList);
```

This internalList is a property of the ConceptEntities class in the Dartlero model and inherited by the Categories class. It is now shown in category-table through the following code:

```
<tbody template repeat="{{category in
categories.internalList}}">
    <tr>
      <td>{{category.code}}</td>
      <td>{{category.description}}</td>
    </tr>
  </tbody>
```

Our add component defined in the \category_add.html component contains two input text fields and an **Add** button with an add event handler, that checks whether a name is given and that the category is not yet in use. The code property is inherited from ConceptEntity in Dartlero and used as a category name; the inherited add method checks that the code is unique. Here is the code from category_add.dart:

```
add(Event e, var detail, Node target) {
    InputElement code = shadowRoot.querySelector("#code");
    InputElement description = shadowRoot.querySelector
        ("#description");
    Element message = shadowRoot.querySelector("#message");
    var error = false;
    message.text = '';
    if (code.value.trim() == '') {
      message.text = 'category name is mandatory;
                  ${message.text}';
      error = true;
    }
    if (!error) {
      var category = new Category();
      category.code = code.value;
      category.description = description.value;
      if (categories.add(category)) {
        message.text = 'added';
        categories.order();
      } else {
        message.text = 'category name already in use';
      }
    }
}
```

Spiral s03 adds an Edit functionality analogous to Add. This is achieved by a second embedded web component <category-edit>, again shown through a conditional template:

```
<template if="{{showEdit}}">
  <category-edit categories="{{categories}}"
    category="{{category}}">
  </category-edit>
</template>
```

Here, the `categories` and `category` properties of the `category` table component are passed to the `<category edit>` component by using the `{{categories}}` and `{{category }}` expressions. We also add a new button in the table row:

```
<td><button on-click="{{edit}}" category-
code={{category.code}}>Edit</button></td>
```

This button has the following event-handler:

```
edit(Event e, var detail, Element target) {
  String code = target.attributes['category-code'];    (1)
  category = categories.find(code);
  showEdit = true;
  }
```

Notice how we get the category code as the value of an attribute in line (1). The `edit` component is defined in `component\category_edit.html`. It is nearly identical to the `add` component, but the **Name** field is read-only. The following is a snippet of the HTML code:

```
<input readonly="true" value="{{category.code}}"/>
<br/>
<input id="{{category.code}}-description"
  type="text" size="96" value="{{description}}"/>    (2)
```

To be able to change the description, we have to use a `description` variable in line (2), that is marked as `@published` and set to the category description in the `enteredView` method in `category_edit.dart` in line (3):

```
@published String description;
  CategoryEdit.created() : super.created();
  enteredView() {
    super.enteredView();
    description = category.description;    (3)
  }
```

The **Update** button calls the corresponding method in the same script:

```
update(Event e, var detail, Node target) {
  category.description = description;
  categories.order();    (4)
  var polymerApp = querySelector('#polymer-app');
  var categoryTable =
polymerApp.shadowRoot.querySelector('#category-
  table');    (5)
  categoryTable.showEdit = false;    (6)
}
```

The sorting of categories in line (4) is also needed to show the new description. A previously instantiated web component can also be retrieved by `querySelector`. Line (5) uses this to toggle the appearance of the `edit` component in line (6).

Adding local storage

Spiral s04 adds persistency to the browser local storage; our model `Category` class implements the necessary `toJson` and `fromJson` methods. In the body of the `<polymer-app>` component, a **Save** button is added, coupled to a `save()` method in `polymer_app.dart`:

```
save(Event e, var detail, Node target) {
    window.localStorage['polymer_category_links'] =
        JSON.encode(categories.toJson());
}
```

The data is read from local storage in the constructor of the `<polymer-app>` component in line (1) in the following code (see `polymer_app.dart`):

```
PolymerApp.created() : super.created() {
  var categoryLinksModel = new CategoryLinksModel();
  categories = categoryLinksModel.categories;
  String json = window.localStorage['polymer_category_links']; (1)
  if (json == null) {
    categoryLinksModel.init();
  } else {
    categories.fromJson(JSON.decode(json));
  }
  categories.internalList = toObservable(categories.internalList);
}
```

If the data is not in local storage, the `init()` method is called, and the model is populated. Spiral s04 also adds a Remove functionality through a new button in every table row, which invokes the following method in `category_table.dart`:

```
delete(Event e, var detail, Element target) {
    String code = target.attributes['category-code'];
    category = categories.find(code);
    categories.remove(category);
}
```

Now how about viewing the links for each category? This is taken care of in spiral s05, first by adding the `Link` and `Links` classes to our model in `lib\model\link_entities.dart`. Being good Dartlero citizens, they know to construct themselves `fromJson` method and deconstruct `toJson` method, so they are ready for (local storage) persistence. Test programs are also provided in `test\model`. When the app is run, a **Show** button is added to every category row. If this is clicked, a new web component `<link-table>` appears with the links of the selected category shown; this was added to `<category-table>`. This can be seen in the *Category_links spiral s01* screenshot, where the **Web Link** column contains real hyperlinks.

```
<template if="{{showCategoryLinks}}">
    <link-table category="{{category}}"></link-table>      (2)
</template>
```

Here is the code for the **Show** button:

```
<button on-click="{{showLinks}}" category-
code={{category.code}}>Show</button>
```

When clicked, the method `showLinks` from `category_table.dart` is executed:

```
showLinks(Event e, var detail, Element target) {
  String code = target.attributes['category-code'];
  ButtonElement categoryLinks = target;
  if (!showCategoryLinks && categoryLinks.text == 'Show') {
    showCategoryLinks = true;
    category = categories.find(code);
    categoryLinks.text = 'Hide';
  } else if (showCategoryLinks && categoryLinks.text == 'Hide')
   {
    showCategoryLinks = false;
    categoryLinks.text = 'Show';
  }
}
```

This code toggles the appearance of the `<link-table>` component in line (2) in the preceding code, which also passes the `category` variable; the `<link-table>` component gets this value in its `enteredView()` method in `link_table.dart`:

```
class LinkTable extends PolymerElement {
  @published Category category;
  @published Links links;
  @observable bool showAdd = false;
  enteredView() {
    super. enteredView();
    links = category.links;
    links.internalList = toObservable(links.internalList);
  }
```

The links are shown in a repeating template in the `link_table.html` file:

```
<tbody template repeat="{{link in links.internalList}}">
    <tr>
        <td>
            <a href="{{link.url}}">
                {{link.code}}
            </a>
        </td>
        <td>{{link.description}}</td>
    </tr>
</tbody>
```

This web component `<link-table>` also has a **Show Add** button to activate a `<link-add>` component in a conditional template. This is shown when `@observable bool showAdd` becomes true and toggled in the code of the `show` method of the `LinkTable` class.

The `link-add` web component is very similar to `category-add`, so with what we discussed here, you should be able to analyze the code for yourself.

Spiral s06 introduces the edit functionality for links through a new `<link-edit>` component and finally in spiral s07; you can remove links from a category. Now you have now all the knowledge to understand the code in these last spirals completely. Moreover, you are now able to apply the model and build a web components app for every (1-n) relation between data, such as Departments and Employees, or Orders and Order Details. We now look at using web components in a (n-m) or many-to-many relationship.

Applying web components to the project tasks app

(Get the code with: `git clone git://github.com/dzenanr/polymer_project_ tasks.git`)

The model that forms the basis for this app is a typical many-to-many relationship between the two entry concepts Project and Employee: a project has many employees, and an employee works on many projects. The many-to-many relationship between Project and Employee is normalized into two one-to-many relationships by introducing the intermediary Task concept, a Project consists of many Tasks and an Employee has many Tasks:

Project (1-n) Task and Employee (1-n) Task

A Project has a name (its ID), a description, and a Tasks collection. An Employee has an `email` (its ID), a `lastName` and a `firstName` (both required), and a Tasks collection. A Task has a project, an employee, and a description: its ID is composed of the IDs of Project and Employee, so an employee can only have at most one task in a project. The code for this model is based on the Dartlero framework and can be found in the `lib\model` folder. If you want to avoid redundancy, one relationship must be internal and the other one should be external; this is a subjective decision. Let's say that we will start more often with projects, find a project and display its tasks. In that case, the Project (1-n) Task relationship is internal. This means that you will have two hierarchical structures: projects with their tasks and employees only (employees without tasks). In each task, you will have a reference to its employee. The data could be saved as two JSON documents in two different files or in local storage under two different keys. You can see the difference in code by looking at the `toJson` methods, for Project in the `projects.dart` file:

```
Map<String, Object> toJson() {
    Map<String, Object> entityMap = new Map<String, Object>();
    entityMap['code'] = code;
    entityMap['name'] = name;
    entityMap['description'] = description;
    entityMap['tasks'] = tasks.toJson(); // saving tasks
    return entityMap;
}
```

Compared this with the same method for Employee in the `employee.dart` file:

```
Map<String, Object> toJson() {
    Map<String, Object> entityMap = new Map<String, Object>();
    entityMap['code'] = code;
    entityMap['lastName'] = lastName;
    entityMap['firstName'] = firstName;
    entityMap['email'] = email;
    return entityMap;
}
```

(the same is true for the `fromJson` methods).

When you load data, you need to recreate the Employee (1-n) Task relationship in both directions, by using the employee `email` in each task. After the load, all relationships become internal and there are no reference IDs in the model (no employee `email` in every task, only `employee` and `project` properties), which means that the model in main memory is an object model. On start-up, our app instantiates the `<polymer-app>` component in the `polymer_project_tasks.html` file, which fires the `PolymerApp.created()` constructor. Here, the model objects are created and the data is either loaded from local storage; or if data was not saved yet, it is initialized by calling the `tasksModel.init()` method:

```
     static const String EMPLOYEE_TASKS = 'polymer-employee-tasks';
     static const String PROJECT_TASKS = 'polymer-project-tasks';
  PolymerApp.created() : super.created() {
    tasksModel = TasksModel.one();
    employees = tasksModel.employees;
    projects = tasksModel.projects;
    // tasksModel.init()   // comment load to reinit
    load();
    employees.internalList= toObservable(employees.internalList);(1)
    projects.internalList = toObservable(projects.internalList); (2)
  }
  load() {
    loadEmployees();
    loadProjects();
  }
  loadEmployees() {
    String json = window.localStorage[EMPLOYEE_TASKS];
    if (json == null) {
      tasksModel.init();
    } else {
      employees.fromJson(JSON.decode(json));
    }
    employees.order();
  }
  loadProjects() {
    String json = window.localStorage[PROJECT_TASKS];
    if (json != null) {
      projects.fromJson(JSON.decode(json));
    }
    projects.order();
  }
```

Lines (1) and (2) are necessary so that the web components show employee or project updates when a new employee or project is added or removed: the List is observed by toObservable. The web component defined in the polymer_app.html file shows a **Save** button:

```
<button on-click="{{save}}">Save</button>
```

The `save()` method is also contained in the `polymer_app.dart` file and saves the data in local storage:

```
save(Event e, var detail, Node target) {
  saveEmployees();
  saveProjects();
}
saveEmployees() {
  window.localStorage[EMPLOYEE_TASKS] =               JSON.
encode(employees.toJson());
}
saveProjects() {
  window.localStorage[PROJECT_TASKS] =        JSON.encode(projects.
toJson());
}
```

The initial screen shows all **Projects** and all **Employees** as shown in the following screenshot:

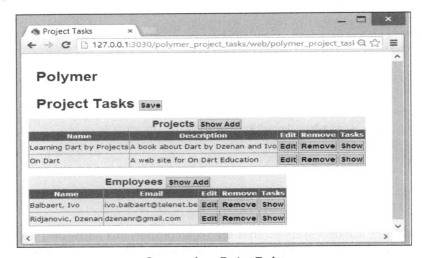

Start-up of app Project Tasks

Here we use two web components: `<project-table>` and `<employee-table>`:

```
<project-table id="project-table"
    projects="{{ projects }}">
</project-table>
<employee-table id="employee-table"
    employees="{{ employees }}">
</employee-table>
```

They are imported through:

```
<link rel="import" href="component/employee/employee_table.html">
<link rel="import" href="component/project/project_table.html">
```

As usual, the code of the components resides in `web\component`. We see that both entities have an add functionality, together with edit, remove, and show tasks. The `<employee-table>` component defined in the `employee_table.html` file is indeed composed of three other components: `<employee-add>`, `<employee-edit>`, and `<task-table>`, again shown in conditional templates:

```
<template if="{{showAdd}}">
  <employee-add employees="{{employees}}"></employee-add>
</template>
<template if="{{showEdit}}">
  <employee-edit employees="{{employees}}"
    employee="{{employee}}"></employee-edit>
</template>
<template if="{{showTasks}}">
  <task-table id="task-table" employee="{{employee}}">
  </task-table>
</template>
```

Controlled by the Boolean variables `showAdd`, `showEdit`, and `showTasks`; these are all marked as `@observable` in the `EmployeeTable` class.

The employees are shown through a repeating template in an HTML table:

```
<tbody template repeat="employee in employees.internalList">
  <tr>
    <td>{{ employee.name }}</td>
    <td>{{ employee.email }}</td>
    <td><button on-click="{{edit}}" code="{{employee.code}}>(2)
        Edit</button></td>
    <td><button on-click="{{delete}}" code="{{employee.code}}>
     Remove</button></td>
    <td><button on-click="{{showEmployeeTasks}}"
    code="{{employee.code}}>Show</button></td>
  </tr>
</tbody>
```

The behavior of the **<employee-table>** component is defined in the **employee_ table.dart** file:

```dart
@CustomTag('employee-table')
class EmployeeTable extends PolymerElement {
  @published Employees employees;
  Employee employee;
  @observable bool showAdd = false;
  @observable bool showEdit = false;
  @observable bool showTasks = false;
  show(Event e, var detail, Node target) {
    ButtonElement showAddButton = $['show-add'];              (3)
    if (showAddButton.text == 'Show Add') {
      showAdd = true;
      showAddButton.text = 'Hide Add';
    } else {
      showAdd = false;
      showAddButton.text = 'Show Add';
    }
  }
  edit(Event e, var detail, Element target) {
    String code = target.attributes['code'];                 (4)
    employee = employees.find(code);
    showEdit = true;
  }
  delete(Event e, var detail, Element target) {
    String code = target.attributes['code'];
    employee = employees.find(code);
    for (var task in employee.tasks) {
      task.project.tasks.remove(task);
    }
    employees.remove(employee);
    showTasks = false;
  }
  showEmployeeTasks(Event e, var detail, Element target) {
    String code = target.attributes['code'];
    ButtonElement tasksButton = target;
    if (!showTasks && tasksButton.text == 'Show') {
      showTasks = true;
      employee = employees.find(code);
      employee.tasks.internalList =
    toObservable(employee.tasks.internalList);
      employee.tasks.order();
      tasksButton.text = 'Hide';
    } else if (showTasks && tasksButton.text == 'Hide') {
      showTasks = false;
      tasksButton.text = 'Show';
    }
  }
}
```

In line (3), we have used $['show-add']$ as an alternative way of writing `querySelector('#show-add')`. It will probably remind you of jQuery, and is included in Polymer. Note how the `edit` event handler (as well as `delete` and `showEmployeeTasks`) gets passed the employee code through line (4), because it is an attribute of the button (see line (2)). If we expand the three subcomponents of the `<employee-table>` component, we get the following screen:

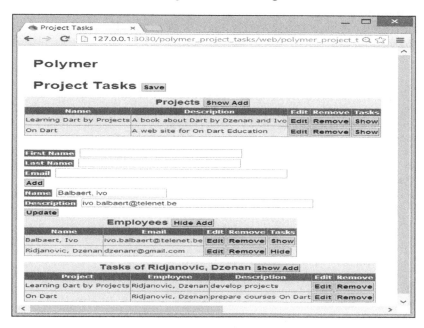

All components of employee activated

The `<employee-add>` component is defined in the `employee_add.html` file:

```
<polymer-element name="employee-add">
  <template>
    <style> // left out </style>
    <br/>
    <label for="first-name">First Name</label>
    <input id="first-name" type="text" size="32"/>
    <br/>
    <label for="last-name">Last Name</label>
    <input id="last-name" type="text" size="32"/>
    <br/>
    <label for="email">Email</label>
    <input id="email" type="text" size="48"/>
    <br/>
```

```
      <button on-click="{{add}}">Add</button>
      <span id="message"></span>
  </template>
  <script type="application/dart"
  src="employee_add.dart"></script>
   </polymer-element>
```

The add method in the employee_add.dart file verifies that all fields are filled in. If so a new Employee object is made and added (only when the employee was new) to the employees collection:

```
class EmployeeAdd extends PolymerElement {
  @published Employees employees;
  add(Event e, var detail, Node target) {
    InputElement firstName = $['first-name'];
    InputElement lastName = $['last-name'];
    InputElement email = $['email'];
    Element message = $['message'];
    var error = false;
    message.text = '';
    if (firstName.value.trim() == '') {
      message.text = 'employee first name is required;
       ${message.text}';
      error = true;
    }
    if (lastName.value.trim() == '') {
      message.text = 'employee last name is required;
      ${message.text}';
      error = true;
    }
    if (email.value.trim() == '') {
      message.text = 'employee email is required;
      ${message.text}';
      error = true;
    }
    if (!error) {
      var employee = new Employee();
      employee.firstName = firstName.value;
      employee.lastName = lastName.value;
      employee.email = email.value;
      if (employees.add(employee)) {
        message.text = 'added';
        employees.order();                                    (1)
      } else {
        message.text = 'employee email already in use';
      }
    }
  }
}
```

The `<employee-table>` component shows the newly added employee because of line (1). The UI of the `<employee-edit>` component is defined in the employee_ edit.html file; update is called in the employee_edit.dart file:

```
class EmployeeEdit extends PolymerElement {
  @published Employees employees;
  @published Employee employee;
  @published String email;
  EmployeeEdit.created() : super.created();
  enteredView() {
    super.enteredView();
    email = employee.email;
  }
  update(Event e, var detail, Node target) {
    employee.email = email;
    employees.order(); // to see a new email in the list
    var polymerApp = querySelector('#polymer-app');
    var employeeTable =
  polymerApp.shadowRoot.querySelector('#employee-
      table');
    employeeTable.showEdit = false;
  }
}
```

Deleting an employee is covered in the `delete` method of the employee_table.dart file. The **Show Tasks** button activates the `<task-table>` component. Its `<template>` definition in the task_table.html file repeats over all the tasks:

```
<tbody template repeat="{{task in tasks.internalList}}">
  <tr>
    <td>{{task.project.name}}</td>
    <td>{{task.employee.name}}</td>
    <td>{{task.description}}</td>
    <td><button on-click="{{edit}}"
  code="{{task.code}}">Edit</button></td>
    <td><button on-click="{{delete}}"
    code="{{task.code}}">Remove</button></td>
  </tr>
</tbody>
```

The browser now shows the name of the employee or project. This component also envelops two other components: tasks can be added through the `<task-add>` component, edited through the `<task-edit>` component, and can also be removed.

Add and remove Task propagations

A new task must be related to one project and one employee. This means that a new task, as one and only one object, must be added to two different collections of tasks, one for the project and the other for the employee. In this application, the internal Project-Task relationship is used to add a task to its project. The external Task-Employee relationship is used to lookup an employee for the new task of the project. In this application, a task cannot be added to an employee.

When a task is removed from project's tasks, it must also be removed from the employee's tasks, and vice versa. When a project is removed, its tasks cannot be accessed anymore. Those tasks must be removed from collections of tasks related to employees found in the project's tasks. Similarly, when an employee is removed, his/her tasks cannot be accessed anymore. Those tasks must be removed from collections of tasks related to projects found in the employee's tasks.

The add and remove propagations of tasks in the model must be reflected in the display of web components. When a task is updated (description only in this application), there is no need for update propagations in the model because there is only one task with the same project and the same employee. However, the same task (with the same project and the same employee) may be displayed in two different web components. When this task is updated, the new description must show up in the display of both web components.

Because it is built in exactly the same way, you should now be able to understand the other web components: `<project-table>`, and its subcomponents `<project-add>` and `<project-edit>`, together with `<task-table>`. Used in the Project context, the task table also shows a `<task-add>` component and a remove functionality. Now, here is the lookup of an employee when adding a task in the `task_add.html` file:

```
<select id="employee-lookup">
    <option template repeat="{{employee in
  employees.internalList}}"> {{employee.code}} </option>
</select>
```

In the `add` event handler, its value is retrieved with the following code:

```
SelectElement employeeLookup = $['employee-lookup'];
String code = employeeLookup.value;
```

Summary

This chapter showed you how easy it is to build web apps that work with data using data-binding and web components in `Polymer.dart`. We did this by exploring three projects: links, category-links, and project-tasks-employee; the last two by building the model starting from the Dartlero framework. Web components through Polymer will revolutionize the way future web apps are built. In the next chapter, we will focus on how to build web apps following the MVC pattern and using the Dartling modeling framework.

9

Modeling More Complex Applications with Dartling

In *Chapter 4, Modeling Web Applications with Model Concepts and Dartlero*, we discussed the importance of modeling the data in your domain before starting your app. We used model concepts to represent the model visually, and showed a simple modeling framework called Dartlero. In this chapter we discuss the full blown domain modeling framework Dartling, which can take the JSON export of model concepts as input to generate code for the model, as well as to generate default app code. We do this by developing the Travel Impressions model and app.

Next, we look at the **Model View Controller (MVC)** design pattern, and why it is a good fit for web applications. This is put into practice by developing a `todomvc` application in spirals. Again, model concepts and Dartling are used to generate the basic application code. So, the following are the topics of this chapter:

- The Dartling domain modeling framework
- Design of the Travel Impressions model in spirals
- Code generation of travel impressions from model
- Initializing the Travel Impressions model with data
- Testing the Travel Impressions model
- What is the MVC pattern, and why is it used in software development
- The TodoMVC app

The Dartling domain modeling framework

Dartling (`https://github.com/dzenanr/dartling`) is a domain model framework for development of complex models with many concepts and relationships. It takes care of a lot of functionality, greatly reducing the amount of code you need to write. A Dartling model is first designed in the graphical tool model concepts, as shown in *Chapter 4*, *Modeling Web Applications with Model Concepts and Dartlero*. A Dartling model consists of **concepts**, concept **attributes**, and concept **neighbors**. Two neighbors make a **relationship** between two concepts. A relationship has two directions; each direction going from one concept to another neighbor concept. Standard **one-to-many**, **many-to-many**, and **is-a** relationships are supported. When both concepts are the same, the relationship is reflexive. When there are two relationships between the same but different concepts, the relationships are twins.

The code for a Dartling model is generated from the JSON representation of a graphical model. The model is initialized with some basic data and tested (model tests are the best way to start learning Dartling). We can also generate a default web application whose purpose is to validate the model by a user in order to discover missing concepts, attributes, and relationships, and improve the existing ones.

A Dartling model has access to actions, action pre and post validations (these are validations of data done before and after actions), error handling, select data views, view update propagations, reaction events, transactions (a transaction is an action that contains other actions), sessions with the history of actions and transactions, so that *undos* and *redos* on the model may be done.

In Dartling, there may be multiple domains and multiple models within domains, which can be used together. A model has **entry points** that are entities. From an entity in one of the entry entities, child entities may be obtained. Data navigation is done by following parent or child neighbors. You can add, remove, update, find, select, and order (sort) data. Actions or transactions may be used to support unrestricted undos and redos in a domain session. The domain allows any object to react to actions (action events) in its models.

To understand what else you can do with Dartling, clone it from Git and examine its API defined in abstract classes with API at the end of their names. The two most important ones are `EntitiesApi` and `EntityApi`; they provide public methods available in Dartling to handle entities.

Dart generics are used to enforce a specific type for a Dartling entity, as shown in the following code snippet:

```dart
abstract class EntitiesApi<E extends EntityApi<E>> implements
Iterable<E> {
  Concept get concept;
  ValidationErrorsApi get errors;
  EntitiesApi<E> get source;

  E firstWhereAttribute(String code, Object attribute);
  E random();
  E singleWhereOid(Oid oid);
  EntityApi singleDownWhereOid(Oid oid);
  E singleWhereCode(String code);
  E singleWhereId(IdApi id);
  E singleWhereAttributeId(String code, Object attribute);

  EntitiesApi<E> copy();
  // sort, but not in place
  EntitiesApi<E> order([int compare(E a, E b)]);
  EntitiesApi<E> selectWhere(bool f(E entity));
  EntitiesApi<E> selectWhereAttribute(String code, Object
attribute);
  EntitiesApi<E> selectWhereParent(String code, EntityApi parent);
  EntitiesApi<E> skipFirst(int n);
  EntitiesApi<E> skipFirstWhile(bool f(E entity));
  EntitiesApi<E> takeFirst(int n);
  EntitiesApi<E> takeFirstWhile(bool f(E entity));
  List<Map<String, Object>> toJson();
  void clear();
  void sort([int compare(E a, E b)]); // in place sort
  bool preAdd(E entity);
  bool add(E entity);
  bool postAdd(E entity);
  bool preRemove(E entity);
  bool remove(E entity);
  bool postRemove(E entity);
}
```

```
abstract class EntityApi<E extends EntityApi<E>> implements Comparable
{
  Concept get concept;
  ValidationErrorsApi get errors;
  Oid get oid;
  IdApi get id;
  String code;
  Object getAttribute(String name);
  bool setAttribute(String name, Object value);
  String getStringFromAttribute(String name);
  bool setStringToAttribute(String name, String string);
  EntityApi getParent(String name);
  bool setParent(String name, EntityApi entity);
  EntitiesApi getChild(String name);
  bool setChild(String name, EntitiesApi entities);

  E copy();
  Map<String, Object> toJson();
}
```

Note that `EntityApi` implements `Comparable`, and `EntitiesApi` implements `Iterable`. Thus, all public members of `Iterable` are available in Dartling entities. There are several Dartling examples at GitHub you can look at (all URLs have the same structure, `https://github.com/dzenanr/`, followed by the name of the project, for example, `https://github.com/dzenanr/art_pen`):

- `art_pen`: This is a drawing tool based on the Logo programming language for children

- `game_parking`: This is a game based on Rush Hour

- dartling_examples: This contains different types of relationships

- `concept_attribute`: This deals with different categories of test data that can be used in the generation of tests

- `travel_impressions`: This is the model we discuss to illustrate Dartling in this chapter

- `dartling_todos`: This is a web application based on TodoMVC with Dartling, action undos, and web components

Schematically, the following sections show how to:

1. Design a graphical model step-by-step:

    ○ **Tool to use**: Model Concepts (`https://github.com/dzenanr/model_concepts`)

    ○ **End result**: Visual model and export to JSON format, `model.json`

2. Generate code for the Dartling model from `model.json`:

    ○ **Tool to use**: dartling_gen (which uses Dartling) (`https://github.com/dzenanr/dartling_gen`)

    ○ The generated app presents data of the model in a web page inherited from the tool, `dartling_default_app` (which uses Dartling, `https://github.com/dzenanr/dartling_default_app`)

3. Initialize the Dartling model with some basic data.

4. Test the model.

If you want to follow new developments in Dartling, consult On Dart Blog (http://dzenanr.github.io/) and On Dart Education (`http://ondart.me/`).

Design of the Travel Impressions model in spirals

(The project can be found at `https://github.com/dzenanr/travel_impressions`.)

We will start the project by designing a domain model in spirals (see the model directory in the project); this is step one in our schema. This new project will allow readers to follow our approach in order to make their development of a first web application with Dartling easier. The project will evolve, but in a way that reflects the usual project progression with Dartling.

The domain of the new project is **Travel**. The principal model of the Travel domain is called **Impressions**. The objective is to create a web application that will allow young travelers to inform their families and friends about their impressions of visited places without losing too much time. With the help from someone in the family or from a friend, their impressions of visited places may be enriched by web links. Even a traveler may send only an e-mail message about impressions of visiting certain places to a friend, and the friend may use the web application to present impressions about visited places, expressed in the message, to other interested people in a more informative and pleasing way. Of course, the traveler can do all of that without help from other people. The first spiral (refer the Travel Impression model figure) starts with the most important concepts from the chosen domain. In our Travel domain, the key concepts are: **Traveler**, **Place**, and **Impression**. In general, a traveler visits many different places and may have an impression (or more than one) for each one. A place is something of interest for a traveler. It may be as general as a city, or as specific as a monument in a city. It may also be a village or a nature spot. The important thing is that a traveler has impressions about visited places to share with family and friends.

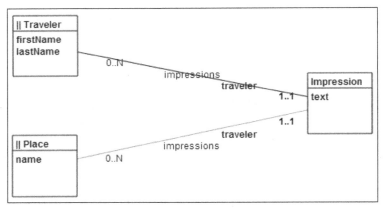

Spiral 1 of the Travel Impressions model

The first cut domain model is created in Model Concepts. There are three concepts and two relationships in the model. Each relationship has two directions. The direction from the Traveler concept to the Impression concept is also a neighbor of the Traveler concept. Thus, the Traveler concept has two attributes and one neighbor (attributes and neighbors are properties). The attributes are `firstName` and `lastName`, and the neighbor is `impressions`. As in Dart, the names of concepts and properties are standardized. Since the concept corresponds to a class, its name starts with a capital letter. An attribute name starts with a small letter, and if a name is composed of several subnames, each subname starts with a capital letter. Spaces, hyphens, or underscores are not used in names. Since a neighbor is a relationship property, its name also starts with a small letter. The meaning of the impression's neighbor for the Traveler concept is expressed in the following way: A traveler may have *0* to *N* impressions. In the opposite direction, an impression has at least one and at most one traveler, so it turns to be exactly one traveler. Similarly, a place may be mentioned in many impressions and an impression is about exactly one place. The Impression concept is an intersection concept between the Traveler and Place concepts. This means that a relationship between the Traveler and Place concepts is many-to-many. A traveler may refer to many places in his or her impressions, and a place may be noted by many travelers. There are two entry concepts that allow a user to navigate through the model's data starting with travelers or places. The two concepts have the entry sign | | in the left section of their title areas.

The relationship between the Traveler and Impression concepts is **internal**. The relationship between the Place and Impression concepts is **external**, which is indicated by a lighter line. A concept with more than one parent must have only one internal relationship. This means that impressions may be saved within their traveler and not within the same place. By introducing internal and external relationships, whose choice is rather subjective, a model may be decomposed into hierarchical submodels by starting with entry concepts and following internal relationships.

What happens if a traveler sends a rather long e-mail message to his family, and if he describes more than one place in the same message? This common situation is introduced in a new spiral of the model with some improvements with respect to the previous spiral. In the spiral approach, each design or development iteration brings more clarifications and more details. If the reasoning behind the spirals is recorded in the documentation of the model, it would be easy for newcomers to get familiar with the model in a step-by-step fashion.

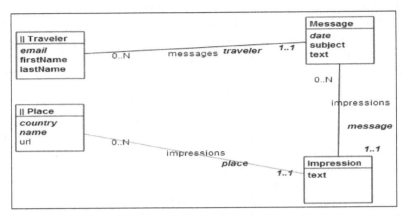

Spiral 2 of the Travel Impressions model

There is a new concept representing a message with impressions of visited places. A traveler may send many messages on his or her trip. A message may contain impressions about several visited places. A traveler would send an e-mail and someone from a circle of family and friends would enter specific impressions about visited places, by extracting portions of the message text. A traveler must have an e-mail attribute (as is the case with names, indicated by bold). A message must have a date when it is sent, a subject of the message, and a full text of the message. An impression's text, country, and name of a place are mandatory. The identifier (ID) of the Traveler concept is its e-mail (indicated by italics). The identifier of the Place concept consists of the country and name attributes. This means that each place name must be unique within its country. An impression is identified by its source message and the place about which the impression is formed (IDs of neighbors). Thus, the identifier of the Impression concept is composed of two neighbors. A message is identified by the traveler that sent the message and by the date when the message was sent. Further analysis leads to the model in the following figure:

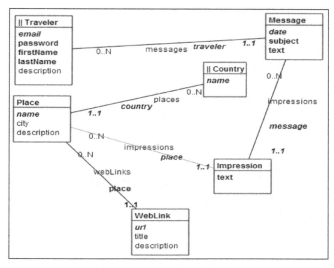

Spiral 3 of the Travel Impressions model

A place must be located in a specific country. Often, a visited place will be in a city. However, there are many interesting places that are not located in cities. A short description may be entered about a new place. Web links that are relevant to the visited place may be added. If we want to allow a traveler's friend to help the traveler by entering some data about his/her trip, the following concept should be added to the model (refer the following figure):

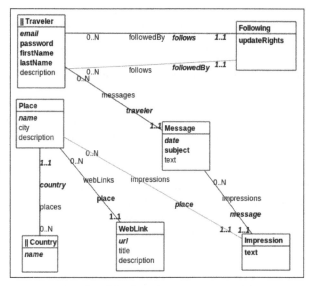

Spiral 4 of the Travel Impressions model

The following concept represents a many-to-many relationship between travelers (real and virtual). In addition, there is a small change in the Message concept. The text attribute is now optional, allowing a traveler with update rights to use text only in the Impression concept. The model could be further extended with more concepts, attributes, and relationships. It is a good practice to spend more time on the model by introducing additional spirals. The new spirals may clarify some issues and provide new ideas. However, it is also a good practice to start programming with a less ambitious model, but with the knowledge of a richer model.

Generating Travel Impressions code from the model

The JSON representation of the last model spiral is generated in the Model Concepts tool and then copied to the `model.json` file that is placed in the empty `travel_impressions` folder of the new app. The project's model code is generated by `dartling_gen`; this is step two in our schema. In the **Run | Manage Launches** of Dart Editor, create a `dartling_gen.dart` command-line launch pointing to the following script in the `dartling_gen` project:

```
bin/dartling_gen.dart
```

In the Script arguments, enter the following argument:

```
--genall projectpath domain model
```

For the `travel_impressions` project, the arguments are as follows:

```
--genall c:/dart/travel_impressions travel impressions
```

The arguments are similar for the project path in Linux: `/home/dart/travel_impressions`.

The `--genall` argument indicates that the complete project will be generated. The `c:/dart/travel_impressions` argument replaces the `projectpath` parameter—a path to the project's folder that contains the `model.json` file. The `travel` argument is the domain name and the `impressions` argument is the model name. By running the `main` function in the `bin/dartling_gen.dart` file, a project, with its domain and model, will be generated in the `project` directory. This project contains the folders `doc`, `lib`, `test` and `web`, as well as a `pubspec.yaml` file, which specifies our project is dependent on Dartling and `dartling_default_app`.

In the generated project, the `lib` folder has the `gen` and `travel` (domain) folders. The `gen` folder also has the `travel` (domain) folder. The `travel` folder, both in `lib` and `gen`, has the `impressions` (model) folder. The `gen` folder keeps the generic code (not to be edited!) that is to be regenerated when the model changes. However, the `travel` subfolder in `lib` contains the specific code that is open for changes. The generic code extends the code in Dartling, and the specific code extends the generic code.

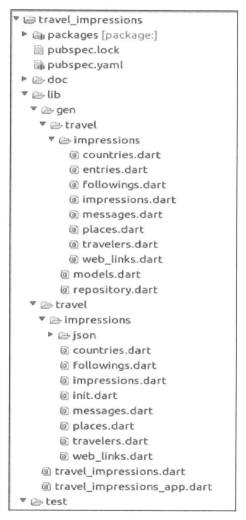

Structure of generated project

But what if the model changes? Then, update the JSON representation of the model in the model.json file. Regenerate only the lib/gen directory, by giving these arguments:

```
--gengen projectpath domain model
```

 The generated code in lib/gen must not be edited by a programmer. The specific code, which is outside of the lib/gen folder, will be changed in the evolution of the application.

If you regenerate the whole project, be sure to have its backup to be able to compare the two versions. If you regenerate only the generic code in the lib/gen folder, you may need to adjust some specific code. When the complete project is generated, the content of the model.json file is reproduced in the lib/travel/impressions/json/model.dart file as the content of its travelImpressionsModelJson variable. This variable, and not the model.json file, is used in the running of the application. In this way, you may experiment with some minor changes in the model (for example, changing essential attributes) without losing the content of the model.json file. However, if you want to keep those changes, you should update the JSON file before the next code generation. After the code is generated, the README.md and travel_impressions_web.html files are usually updated in a minor way to reflect the project in question. To run the application, the web page travel_impressions_web.html (in the folder web/travel/impressions) is selected. If you run the app, it already shows two buttons with text **Show Travelers** and **Show Countries**. When these buttons are pushed, they show a grid with dummy data. The two travel_impressions_web files (.dart and .html) are the only web files, in addition to CSS files, in the project. However, they rely on dartling_default_app. The objective of this application is to validate the model by using its data. The next step is to create that data.

Initializing the Travel Impressions model with Data

After the model is designed (refer the Spiral 4 of the Travel Impression Model figure) and its code is generated, the model is initialized with some basic data starting with its entries. This is done in the lib/travel/impressions/init.dart file.

```
initTravelImpressions(var entries) {
  _initCountries(entries);
  _initTravelers(entries);
}
```

We will start with creating a country and some of its places, together with web links, from the `entries` parameter.

```
_initCountries(var entries) {
  var countries = entries.countries;
  var country = new Country(countries.concept);
  country.code = 'BA';
  country.name = 'Bosnia and Herzegovina';
  countries.add(country);
```

In the Country concept of the graphical model, there is no `code` attribute of the `String` type. The `code` attribute is inherited from Dartling. In a concept, you do not need to use the inherited code attribute. However, if you use it, its values must be unique. Note that a new country is added to the countries' entities. Once the first country is created, its first place may be created.

```
var place = new Place(country.places.concept);
place.name = 'Bascarsija';
place.city = 'Sarajevo';
place.description = 'old town';
place.country = country;
country.places.add(place);
```

After a new place is created, its country is established, and it is added to the country's places. Then, web links for the `Bascarsija` place are created.

```
var webLink = new WebLink(place.webLinks.concept);
webLink.url =
Uri.parse('http://en.wikipedia.org/wiki/Bašaršija');
webLink.title = 'Wikipedia';
webLink.description =
    "Sarajevo's old bazaar and the historical and cultural
      center.";
webLink.place = place;
place.webLinks.add(webLink);

webLink = new WebLink(place.webLinks.concept);
webLink.url =
  Uri.parse('http://en.wikipedia.org/wiki/File: Bašaršija
  _2006.jpg');
webLink.title = 'image';
webLink.place = place;
place.webLinks.add(webLink);
```

Other countries, places, and web links may be created in a similar way. Travelers, with their messages and impressions, are created with their entry into the model.

```
_initTravelers(var entries) {
  var countries = entries.countries;
  var travelers = entries.travelers;

  var traveler = new Traveler(travelers.concept);
  traveler.email = 'dzenan@gmail.com';
  traveler.password = 'dzenan';
  traveler.firstName = 'Dzenan';
  traveler.lastName = 'Ridjanovic';
  traveler.description = 'working hard on Dart projects';
  travelers.add(traveler);

  var message = new Message(traveler.messages.concept);
  message.subject = 'first day in Sarajevo';
  message.traveler = traveler;
  traveler.messages.add(message);

  var country = countries.singleWhereCode('BA');
  var place = country.places.firstWhereAttribute('name',
    'Bascarsija');
  var impression =
      new Impression.withId(message.impressions.concept, place,
        message);
  impression.text = 'as usual, my first meal is "cevapcici"';
  message.impressions.add(impression);
  place.impressions.add(impression);

  place = country.places.firstWhereAttribute('name',
    'Bjelasnica');
  impression =
      new Impression.withId(message.impressions.concept, place,
        message);
  impression.text = 'after "cevapcici", hiking at Bjelasnica is
    calling';
  message.impressions.add(impression);
  place.impressions.add(impression);

  place = country.places.firstWhereAttribute('name', 'Dariva');
  impression =
    new Impression.withId(message.impressions.concept, place,
      message);
  impression.text = 'however, short walk will do';
  message.impressions.add(impression);
  place.impressions.add(impression);
```

The Impression concept has two parents: Message and Place. A place is found within a country. A country's code is unique and the `singleWhereCode` method is used on the country's entry to find the country. A place's name is a part of the identifier (place within country) and the `firstWhereAttribute` method is used on `country. places` to find the place. Once some basic data is created, a default web application (`web/travel/impressions/travel_impressions.html`) may be run to validate the model by navigating from the model's entries and discovering missing concepts, attributes, and relationships. This default application is an example of generic programming based on the meta model of Dartling. Its code is in the `dartling_default_app` project that is imported, based on the pub declaration in the generated `pubspec.yaml` file:

```
name: travel_impressions
author: Your Name
homepage: http://ondart.me/
version: 0.0.1
description: travel_impressions application that uses dartling for its
model.
dependencies:
  browser: any
  dartling:
    git: git://github.com/dzenanr/dartling.git
  dartling_default_app:
    git: git://github.com/dzenanr/dartling_default_app.git
```

This generates the following code in the `web/travel/impressions/travel_impressions_web.dart` file:

```
import "dart:html";
import "package:dartling/dartling.dart";
import "package:dartling_default_app/dartling_default_app.dart";
import "package:travel_impressions/travel_impressions.dart";

initTravelData(TravelRepo travelRepo) {
  var travelModels =
      travelRepo.getDomainModels(TravelRepo.travelDomainCode);
  var travelImpressionsEntries =
    travelModels.getModelEntries(TravelRepo.travelImpressionsModel
      Code);
  initTravelImpressions(travelImpressionsEntries);
  travelImpressionsEntries.display();
  travelImpressionsEntries.displayJson();
}
```

```
showTravelData(TravelRepo travelRepo) {
    var mainView = new View(document, "main");
    mainView.repo = travelRepo;
    new RepoMainSection(mainView);
}

void main() {
    var travelRepo = new TravelRepo();
    initTravelData(travelRepo);
    showTravelData(travelRepo);
}
```

In Dartling, a repository may have many domains and a domain may have many models. However, in a default web application, only one domain and one model are used. After the travel repository is created with the Travel domain and the Impressions model, the model is initialized with some data, and they are shown in a web page of the default application. Data are also displayed in the Dart Editor's console. Note that this is the only code written manually for the time being. The next step is to test the model, and more specific code will be added to the project.

Testing the Travel Impressions model

After the model is designed, generated, and initialized with some data, the model should be tested to validate it further. In addition, writing tests applying the techniques we learned in *Chapter 3, Structuring Code with Classes and Libraries*, is the best way to start learning Dartling. Testing is done in the test/travel/ impressions/travel_impressions_test.dart file. The main function creates a repository based on the JSON definition of the model and passes it to the testTravelData function:

```
testTravelData(TravelRepo travelRepo) {
    testTravelImpressions(travelRepo, TravelRepo.travelDomainCode,
        TravelRepo.travelImpressionsModelCode);
}

void main() {
    var travelRepo = new TravelRepo();
    testTravelData(travelRepo);
}
```

The testTravelImpressions function accepts the repository and names of the domain and the model. In a group of tests, before each test, a setup is done to first obtain the three variables: models, session, and entries. The models (here only one) are obtained from the repository based on the domain's name. A session, with a history of actions and transactions of Dartling, is created by the newSession method of the models object. The entries variable for the only model is obtained from the models object by using the model's name:

```
testTravelImpressions(Repo repo, String domainCode, String modelCode)
{
  var models;
  var session;
  var entries;

  Countries countries;
  Country bosnia;
  Oid darivaOid, oid;
    Travelers travelers;
  group("Testing ${domainCode}.${modelCode}", () {
    setUp((() {
      models = repo.getDomainModels(domainCode);
      session = models.newSession();
      entries = models.getModelEntries(modelCode);
      expect(entries, isNotNull);

      countries = entries.countries;
      travelers = entries.travelers;
      initTravelImpressions(entries);

      var code = 'BA';
      bosnia = countries.singleWhereCode(code);
      darivaOid = bosnia.places.firstWhereAttribute('name',
        'Dariva').oid;
    });
    tearDown((() {
      entries.clear();
    });
    test("Not empty entries test", () {
      expect(!entries.isEmpty, isTrue);
    });
    // code left out
```

The countries and travelers are the entry entities. The `initTravelImpressions` function is called to initiate the model with some basic data. After the initialization, the country Bosnia is found in the `countries` object, based on its unique code. A single place, with the `Dariva` name, is retrieved from the `bosnia` object and its `oid` is kept in the `darivaOid` variable. The `oid` attribute is inherited from Dartling. It is a unique timestamp used as a system identifier in a collection of entities. Each test has an access to all those variables. After a test is run, the entries object is cleared so that the `setUp` function may start from the empty model. The first test is run to show that the entries object is not empty after the setup. A single country is found by the `singleWhereCode` method based on the inherited code attribute. In the Country concept the `code` attribute is used, and in the `countries` object each country must have a unique code.

```
test('Find country by code', () {
  var code = 'BA';
  Country country = countries.singleWhereCode(code);
  expect(country, isNotNull);
  expect(country.name, equals('Bosnia and Herzegovina'));
});
```

A single entity may be found by its user identifier. In the Country concept, the user identifier is the name attribute.

```
test('Find country by id', () {
  Id id = new Id(countries.concept);
  id.setAttribute('name', 'Bosnia and Herzegovina');
  Country country = countries.singleWhereId(id);
  expect(country, isNotNull);
  expect(country.code, equals('BA'));
});
```

If a concept has one attribute identifier (simple identifier), a creation of an ID object may be avoided by using a shortcut method called `singleWhereAttributeId`.

```
test('Find country by name attribute id', () {
  var name = 'Bosnia and Herzegovina';
  Country country = countries.singleWhereAttributeId('name',
    name);
  expect(country, isNotNull);
  expect(country.code, equals('BA'));
});
```

The first entity with an attribute value equal to a value given to the
`firstWhereAttribute` method is obtained. If that attribute is an identifier, methods
that use identifiers perform faster.

```
test('Find country by name attribute', () {
    var name = 'Bosnia and Herzegovina';
    Country country = countries.firstWhereAttribute('name', name);
    expect(country, isNotNull);
    expect(country.code, equals('BA'));
});
```

If an entity is not a member of a collection of entities, a `search` method will
return `null`:

```
test('Find country by name attribute id', () {
    var name = 'Poland';
    Country country = countries.singleWhereAttributeId('name',
        name);
    expect(country, isNull);
});
```

The Place concept has a composite identifier, composed of the country neighbor and
the name attribute. If only the name attribute is used, `singleWhereAttributeId` will
return `null`:

```
test('Find country and (not) place by name id', () {
    var countryName = 'Bosnia and Herzegovina';
    Country country = countries.singleWhereAttributeId('name',
        countryName);
    var placeName = 'Dariva';
    Places places = country.places;
    Place place = places.singleWhereAttributeId('name',
        placeName);
    expect(place, isNull);
});
```

The `name` attribute may be used to find both a country and its place:

```
test('Find country and place by name attribute', () {
    var countryName = 'Bosnia and Herzegovina';
    bosnia = countries.firstWhereAttribute('name', countryName);
    expect(bosnia, isNotNull);
    var placeName = 'Dariva';
    Places places = bosnia.places;
    Place place = places.firstWhereAttribute('name', placeName);
    expect(place, isNotNull);
    expect(place.city, equals('Sarajevo'));
});
```

However, the use of identifiers is recommended for performance reasons.

```
test('Find country and place by id', () {
  var countryName = 'Bosnia and Herzegovina';
  bosnia = countries.singleWhereAttributeId('name', countryName);
  var placeName = 'Dariva';
  Places places = bosnia.places;
  Id id = new Id(bosnia.concept);
  id.setParent('country', bosnia);
  id.setAttribute('name', placeName);
  Place place = places.singleWhereId(id);
  expect(place, isNotNull);
  expect(place.city, equals('Sarajevo'));
});
```

The same results may be obtained by using more elegant method cascades. Note that the bosnia variable is used in order to avoid searching for the country. Besides, in the last line, the place's oid attribute is assigned to the oid variable that will be used in the next test:

```
test('Find country and place by id (method cascades)', () {
  var placeName = 'Dariva';
  Places places = bosnia.places;
  Id id = new Id(bosnia.concept)
    ..setParent('country', bosnia)
    ..setAttribute('name', placeName);
  Place place = places.singleWhereId(id);
  expect(place, isNotNull);
  expect(place.city, equals('Sarajevo'));
  oid = place.oid;
});
```

In the model, the Country concept is an entry. The relationship between the Country and Place concepts is internal. A place may be searched by its oid starting with the countries' entry and following the internal neighbors from the Country concept:

```
test('Find place by oid by searching from countries down',
  {
  Place place = countries.singleDownWhereOid(darivaOid);
  expect(place, isNotNull);
  expect(place.name, equals('Dariva'));
});
```

A specific method that does a job of finding an entity based on an identifier value may be used:

```
test('Find place by a specific method', () {
  var placeName = 'Dariva';
  Place place = bosnia.places.findById(placeName, bosnia);
  expect(place, isNotNull);
  expect(place.city, equals('Sarajevo'));
});
```

The `findById` method is added to the `Places` class in the `lib/travel/impressions/places.dart` file.

```
Place findById(String name, Country country) {
  return singleWhereId(new Id(concept)..setAttribute('name',
    name)..
      setParent('country', country));
}
```

The `city` attribute of the Place concept is not required (not in bold in the Travel Impression model figure) and thus is not an identifier or a part of an identifier (not in italics). All places in the city of Sarajevo may be selected by the `selectWhereAttribute` method. The `select` methods return a new collection of entities:

```
test('Select places in Sarajevo', () {
  Places places = bosnia.places.selectWhereAttribute('city',
    'Sarajevo');
  expect(places.length, greaterThan(0));
    for (var place in places) {
      expect(place.city, equals('Sarajevo'));
      }
});
```

A specific read-only property (with only the get method) may be used in an anonymous function of the `selectWhere` method to select a subset of entities.

```
test('Select places by function', () {
  Places places = bosnia.places.selectWhere((place) =>
    place.old);
  expect(places.length, greaterThan(0));
  for (var place in places) {
    expect(place.description, contains('old')));
    }
});
```

The old property with the `get` method is added to the `Places` class in the `lib/travel/impressions/places.dart` file.

```
bool get old => description.contains('old') ? true : false;
```

The places of the `bosnia` object are sorted by the `city` attribute:

```
test('Sort places by city in Bosnia and Herzegovina', () {
  bosnia.places.sort(
      (place1, place2) => place1.city.compareTo(place2.city));
});
```

A new place is not added because required values for the name attribute and the country neighbor are missing. The corresponding error messages are added to the `errors` property of the `places` object:

```
test('Add place required error', () {
  Places places = bosnia.places;
  var placesCount = places.length;
  var place = new Place(places.concept);
  expect(place, isNotNull);

  var added = places.add(place);
  expect(added, isFalse);
  expect(places.length, equals(placesCount));
  places.errors.display(title:'Add place required error');

  expect(places.errors.length, equals(2));
  expect(places.errors.toList()[0].category,
    equals('required'));
  expect(places.errors.toList()[0].message,
      equals('Place.name attribute is null.'));
  expect(places.errors.toList()[1].category,
    equals('required'));
  expect(places.errors.toList()[1].message,
      equals('Place.country parent is null.'));
});
```

The error messages also appear in the console of the Dart Editor.

If we want to add a place that already exists according to its identifier, the `add` method will not be successful:

```
test('Add place unique error', () {
  Places places = bosnia.places;
  var placesCount = places.length;
  var place = new Place(places.concept);
  expect(place, isNotNull);

  place.name = 'Dariva';
  place.country = bosnia;
  var added = places.add(place);
  expect(added, isFalse);
  expect(places.length, equals(placesCount));

  places.errors.display(title:'Add place unique error');
  expect(places.errors.length, equals(1));
  expect(places.errors.toList()[0].category,
    equals('unique'));
});
```

In Dartling, there are pre- and posthooks for the `add` and `remove` methods. A pre-add hook may be used to validate a specific constraint that is not defined in the model:

```
test('Add place pre validation error', () {
  Places places = bosnia.places;
  var placesCount = places.length;
  var place = new Place(places.concept);
  expect(place, isNotNull);
  place.name =
  'A new place with a name longer than 32 cannot be accepted';
  place.country = bosnia;
  var added = places.add(place);
  expect(added, isFalse);
  expect(places.length, equals(placesCount));
  places.errors.display(title:'Add place pre validation
    error');
  expect(places.errors.length, equals(1));
  expect(places.errors.toList()[0].category, equals('pre'));
});
```

The specific preAdd method is defined in the Places class. The method is called by the add method of Dartling:

```
bool preAdd(Place place) {
  bool validation = super.preAdd(place);
  if (validation) {
    validation = place.name.length <= 32;
    if (!validation) {
      var error = new ValidationError('pre');
      error.message =
        '${concept.codePlural}.preAdd rejects the
          "${place.name}" '
        'name that is longer than 32.';
      errors.add(error);
    }
  }
  return validation;
}
```

Finally, a new place is added:

```
test('Add place', () {
  Places places = bosnia.places;
  var placesCount = places.length;
  var place = new Place(places.concept);
  expect(place, isNotNull);

  place.name = 'Ilidza';
  place.city = 'Sarajevo';
  place.country = bosnia;
  var added = places.add(place);
  expect(added, isTrue);
  expect(places.length, equals(++placesCount));
});
```

The Travel Impressions app is further worked out to show all data that was input: countries and their places, the impressions, and web links associated with each place, or the travelers and their impressions. These screens are not application specific, but use the views, menu bars, and so on provided in the included library dartling_default_app, showing the advantage of starting with a modeling framework.

Defining and using the MVC pattern

Conceptually, there are several basic modules in almost any software. The **model** is a data container and the **user interface** (**UI**) is a way to communicate with the model. A relationship between the model and the UI is bidirectional. Data from the model is displayed to a user, and a user may change the model's data. The model may keep some or all of the data in the main memory and store data in an external storage, such as files or **databases** (**db**). A relationship between the model and the data storage is also bidirectional. The UI has one or many **views** of data, which present data in a format useful to users, and one or many **controllers**, which channel changes in data to the model. For example, a web application, after a user request, retrieves data from a database and displays it in a presentable way. After the user changes the data, the application updates the database. There is a flow of data between the UI and the db. For a simple data model and a simple application, the view is often combined with the model. However, a coupling of those parts produces maintenance problems. One problem is that the UI tends to change more often than the model of the db. Another problem is that an application may have business rules that are more than simple data transmissions. It is important to organize a software application to allow for easy modifications of its parts. There are many design patterns that may help in detailing this software architecture. The most popular one, with a long history of different variations, is the **Model View Controller** (**MVC**) pattern.

MVC (http://en.wikipedia.org/wiki/Model-view-controller) is a design pattern that isolates an application's data from the UI. In MVC, the Model represents data of the application and the business rules used to manipulate the data, the View corresponds to elements of the UI such as text fields, and the Controller manages details involving communication between the model and views.

There may be many views and only one controller or many views and many controllers. A view and its controller may be separate or combined together. A view might have its own model in addition to the model for all views. All those and other variations exist in different versions of MVC that even got some new names such as MVP (`http://en.wikipedia.org/wiki/Model-view-presenter`), MVVM (`http://en.wikipedia.org/wiki/Model_View_ViewModel`), MOVE (`http://cirw.in/blog/time-to-move-on`), and MDV (`http://polymer-project.org/platform/template.html`). There are also many articles about MVC and its variations (`www.mvccentral.net`, `www.infoq.com/ASP-NET-MVC/articles/`). Thus, for a learner, it is not easy to grasp the essence of MVC. The following sentences provide this in a nutshell (refer the MVC pattern figure): a user action triggers a UI event that changes the model's data by invoking data actions in a controller. A view registers with the model to be informed about data changes. When a view is informed about the changes, it reacts by refreshing its display. Implementing this pattern makes our app obey the *Separation of Concerns* design principle (the code of views, controllers, and models are loosely coupled). Thus, the different layers in MVC can be developed independently from each other, so that the code is better maintainable. This is especially important for web applications, where the views are presented in the client's browser, and the data source (which interacts with the model) sits on a server. The model and controller code can be executed on the server (as in traditional web applications) or on the client (as in RIA apps), or distributed.

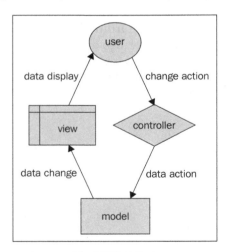

The MVC pattern

It is important to note that the model does not depend on the controller and views. In other words, there are no references to the controller and views in the model (and that is the reason why a view registers with the model to be informed about changes in the data). However, the controller and views depend on the model. In this way, the model may be developed and tested without the views and controllers. In addition, new views of the model may be added easily. Even different applications may use the same model.

The TodoMVC app

We will now show how MVC functions in a Dart version of the famous TodoMVC application (`http://todomvc.com/`), which is used as a standard to compare different web frameworks. This application is developed in spirals in the `dartling_todo_mvc` project and it is built by using the Dartling framework for the model. Download the code from `https://github.com/dzenanr/dartling_todo_mvc_spirals`. In the following screenshot, you see a glimpse of the end result (Spiral 6):

The TodoMVC app

The `todo` items can be added, edited, marked as completed, and deleted; overviews of all tasks, or only the completed or remaining ones can be shown, and the user has undo/redo possibilities after making a mistake. Moreover, it is really useful because the data is stored in local storage (using the JSON format).

Spiral 0 – generating a class model

Spiral 0 does not have any UI; it contains only a simple model with one concept Task and two properties, title and completed. This is designed in Model Concepts with domain name `Todo` and model name `Mvc`, shown in the following figure:

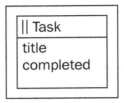

The TodoMVC model

Its JSON representation is exported, and the code is generated by `dartling_gen`. In the generated code (`lib/gen/todo/mvc/tasks.dart`), we find classes that extend Dartling base classes:

```
abstract class TaskGen extends ConceptEntity<Task>
abstract class TasksGen extends Entities<Task>
```

In the `lib/todo` folder, developers may specialize the model:

```
class Task extends TaskGen {
  Task(Concept concept) : super(concept);
}

class Tasks extends TasksGen {
  Tasks(Concept concept) : super(concept);
}
```

The `Task` class describes the Task concept and `Tasks` represents a collection of tasks. There are some basic tests of the model in the `todo_mvc_test.dart` file of the `test` folder. In the `main` function, a repository is constructed and passed to the `testTodoMvc` function together with the domain name and the model name.

```
testTodoData(TodoRepo todoRepo) {
  testTodoMvc(todoRepo, TodoRepo.todoDomainCode,
      TodoRepo.todoMvcModelCode);
}

void main() {
  var todoRepo = new TodoRepo();
  testTodoData(todoRepo);
}
```

The model entries of the `MvcEntries` type are obtained from the `models` object of the repository:

```
var models = repo.getDomainModels(domainCode);
entries = models.getModelEntries(modelCode);
```

The `tasks` variable of the `Tasks` type is the only entry into the model:

```
tasks = entries.tasks;
```

All tests are done on the `tasks` object. The `web` folder contains a default web application of the model.

Spiral 1 – adding todo tasks

In this spiral we start using the MVC pattern; new todos can be entered, and an updated list of todos is displayed. There is a view of todos and a controller to add a new view. A view and a controller are separated into two different classes: the `Todos` view class in the `lib/app` folder and the `TodoApp` control class in the same folder. The web application starts with the `main` function in the `web/dartling_todo_mvc.dart` file:

```
main() {
  var repo = new TodoRepo();
  var domain = repo.getDomainModels('Todo');
  var model = domain.getModelEntries('Mvc');
  new TodoApp(model.tasks);
}
```

The todo application controller accepts the model's tasks while referring to the `todos` view. The `newTodo` element allows a creation of a new task after its title is entered. The new task is added to the tasks entry of the model:

```
class TodoApp {
  TodoApp(Tasks tasks) {
    var todos = new Todos();
    InputElement newTodo = query('#new-todo');
    newTodo.onKeyPress.listen((KeyboardEvent e) {
      if (e.keyCode == KeyCode.ENTER) {
        var title = newTodo.value.trim();
        if (title != '') {
          var task = new Task(tasks.concept);
          task.title = title;
          tasks.add(task);
          todos.add(task);
          newTodo.value = '';
        }
      }
    });
  }
}
```

This new task is also added to the `todos` view of the model:

```
class Todos {
  Element _todoList = query('#todo-list');

  add(Task task) {
    var element = new Element.html('''
      <li>
        <label id='title'>${task.title}</label>
      </li>
    ''');
    _todoList.nodes.add(element);
  }
}
```

In the `add` method, a new todo list item is created and added to nodes of the todo list. The new todo and todo list elements are defined in the `web/dartling_todo_mvc.html` file.

```
<section id="todo-app">
  <header id="header">
    <h1>todos</h1>
    <input id="new-todo" placeholder="What needs to be done?"
autofocus>
  </header>
  <section id="main">
    <ul id="todo-list"></ul>
  </section>
</section>
```

Spiral 1b is an example where a view and a controller are combined within the `Todos` class. By comparing **Spiral 1** and **Spiral 1b**, you may better understand this type of variation in the MVC pattern:

```
class Todos {
  Element _todoList = query('#todo-list');
  Todos(Tasks tasks) {
    InputElement newTodo = query('#new-todo');
    newTodo.onKeyPress.listen((KeyboardEvent e) {
      if (e.keyCode == KeyCode.ENTER) {
        var title = newTodo.value.trim();
        if (title != '') {
```

```
        var task = new Task(tasks.concept);
        task.title = title;
        tasks.add(task);
        _add(task);
        newTodo.value = '';
      }
    }
  });
}

_add(Task task) {
  var element = new Element.html('''
    <li>
      <label id='title'>${task.title}</label>
    </li>
  ''');
  _todoList.nodes.add(element);
}
}
```

The `TodoApp` class becomes a simple application without controller responsibilities:

```
class TodoApp {
  TodoApp(Tasks tasks) {
    new Todos(tasks);
  }
}
```

In **Spiral 2**, the **Spiral 1** will be used as its predecessor. However, in **Spiral 6**, all views will use the form suggested in **Spiral 1b**.

Spiral 2 – showing how many todo tasks left

Todos are loaded (saved) from (to) a local storage. A todo may be completed. A count of todos left is displayed. There is a new `Todo` class in the `lib/app/todo.dart` file to represent a todo in the `Todos` view. It is a task view with its controller to make the task complete. The `SetAttributeAction` class of Dartling is used to update the complete property of the Task concept. The domain session is used by Dartling to memorize actions and provide their history, along the lines of the command pattern: (http://en.wikipedia.org/wiki/Command_pattern).

```
class Todo {
  Task task;
  Element element;
  InputElement _completed;
```

```
Todo(TodoApp todoApp, this.task) {
  DomainSession session = todoApp.session;
  element = new Element.html('''
    <li ${task.completed ? 'class="completed"' : ''}>
      <input class='completed' type='checkbox'
        ${task.completed ? 'checked' : ''}>
      <label id='title'>${task.title}</label>
    </li>
  ''');

  _completed = element.query('.completed');
  _completed.onClick.listen((MouseEvent e) {
    new SetAttributeAction(session, task, 'completed',
        !task.completed).doit();
  });
}

complete(bool completed) {
  _completed.checked = completed;
  if (completed) {
    element.classes.add('completed');
  } else {
    element.classes.remove('completed');
  }
}
}
```

The `Todos` view implements Dartling's `ActionReactionApi` interface in order to react to actions in the model; it is based on the observer pattern (`http://en.wikipedia.org/wiki/Observer_pattern`):

```
class Todos implements ActionReactionApi {
  TodoApp _todoApp;

  List<Todo> _todoList = new List<Todo>();
  Element _todoElements = query('#todo-list');

  Todos(this._todoApp) {
    _todoApp.domain.startActionReaction(this);
  }
```

The view is registered in the constructor to receive information about data changes. The `Todos` view must implement the `react` method to be updated based on actions of the model:

```
react(ActionApi action) {
  if (action is AddAction) {
    add(action.entity);
  } else if (action is SetAttributeAction) {
    _complete(action.entity);
  }
  _todoApp.updateFooter();
  _todoApp.save();
}
```

The `add` method from the previous spiral is replaced with the `doit` method on the new `AddAction` object in the `TodoApp` controller:

```
new AddAction(session, _tasks, task).doit();
```

The session is obtained from the `domain` object that is passed to the constructor of the controller:

```
session = domain.newSession();
```

Changes in the model are saved in a local storage by the `save` method:

```
save() {
  window.localStorage['todos'] = stringify(_tasks.toJson());
}
```

A count of todos left to be completed is displayed by the `updateFooter` method.

Tasks are loaded from a local storage by the following code:

```
String json = window.localStorage['todos'];
if (json != null) {
  _tasks.fromJson(parse(json));
  for (Task task in _tasks) {
    _todos.add(task);
  }
  updateFooter();
}
```

Note that the `todos` view is updated here directly, because the `fromJson` method from Dartling uses the `add` method and not the `AddAction` class.

Spiral 3 – removing a single task and completed tasks

In Dartling, if several actions are done at the same time, they are combined into a transaction. To clear (remove) all completed todos, the following code is used in the controller's constructor.

```
_clearCompleted.onClick.listen((MouseEvent e) {
  var transaction = new Transaction('clear-completed',
    session);
  for (Task task in _tasks.completed) {
    transaction.add(
        new RemoveAction(session, _tasks.completed, task));
  }
  transaction.doit();
});
```

In the `Tasks` class of the model, the completed tasks are selected. This code is added manually, but not typed:

```
Tasks get completed => selectWhere((task) => task.completed);
```

The `react` method in the `Todos` view must now consider both individual actions and transactions:

```
react(ActionApi action) {
  updateTodo(SetAttributeAction action) {
    if (action.property == 'completed') {
      _complete(action.entity);
    }
  }

  if (action is Transaction) {
    for (var transactionAction in action.past.actions) {
      if (transactionAction is SetAttributeAction) {
        updateTodo(transactionAction);
      } else if (transactionAction is RemoveAction) {
        _remove(transactionAction.entity);
      }
    }
  }
```

```
    } else if (action is AddAction) {
      add(action.entity);
    } else if (action is SetAttributeAction) {
      updateTodo(action);
    } else if (action is RemoveAction) {
      _remove(action.entity);
    }

    _todoApp.updateDisplay();
    _todoApp.save();
  }
```

Transaction actions can be found in the past property of the transaction.

Spiral 4 – editing todos (undo and redo)

There is a button for undo and a button for redo in the controller.

```
    Element _undo = querySelector('#undo');
    Element _redo = querySelector('#redo');
```

In the click events, the session.past property is used to make unlimited undos and redos.

```
    _undo.onClick.listen((MouseEvent e) {
      session.past.undo();
    });

    _redo.onClick.listen((MouseEvent e) {
      session.past.redo();
    });
```

The reaction to past actions (and transactions) is defined in the controller by the following code.

```
    class TodoApp implements PastReactionApi {
    // code left out
      session.past.startPastReaction(this);
```

The `PastReactionApi` interface of Dartling provides the following methods, used in the controller, where it is decided whether the undo and redo buttons will be displayed or not.

```
reactCannotUndo() {
  _undo.style.display = 'none';
}


reactCanUndo() {
  _undo.style.display = 'block';
}


reactCanRedo() {
  _redo.style.display = 'block';
}
reactCannotRedo() {
  _redo.style.display = 'none';
}
```

The `react` method in the view must now consider reactions to the undos and redos:

```
react(ActionApi action) {
  updateTodo(SetAttributeAction action) {
    if (action.property == 'completed') {
      _complete(action.entity);
    } else if (action.property == 'title') {
      _retitle(action.entity);
    }
  }

  if (action is Transaction) {
    for (var transactionAction in action.past.actions) {
      if (transactionAction is SetAttributeAction) {
        updateTodo(transactionAction);
      } else if (transactionAction is RemoveAction) {
        if (transactionAction.undone) {
         add(transactionAction.entity);
        } else {
          _remove(transactionAction.entity);
        }
      }
    }
  }
```

```
    } else if (action is AddAction) {
      if (action.undone) {
        _remove(action.entity);
      } else {
        add(action.entity);
      }
    } else if (action is RemoveAction) {
      if (action.undone) {
        add(action.entity);
      } else {
        _remove(action.entity);
      }
    } else if (action is SetAttributeAction) {
      updateTodo(action);
    }

    _todoApp.updateDisplay();
    _todoApp.save();
  }
```

Spiral 5 – displaying completed, remaining, or all todos

Also, a new todo is not accepted if its text is longer than 64 characters. If so, an error message is displayed. In the `Tasks` class of the model, the `preAdd` method is defined. This method is called by the `add` method of Dartling, and if it returns `false`, the add method will be rejected:

```
bool preAdd(Task task) {
  bool validation = super.preAdd(task);
  if (validation) {
    validation = task.title.length <= 64;
    if (!validation) {
      var error = new ValidationError('pre');
      error.message =
          '${concept.codePlural}.preAdd rejects the
          "${task.title}" title, '
          'because it is longer than 64.';
      errors.add(error);
    }
  }
  return validation;
}
```

After the `add` action, the following method is called in the controller to display possible errors:

```
possibleErrors() {
  _errors.innerHtml = '<p>${_tasks.errors.toString()}</p>';
  _tasks.errors.clear();
}
```

The pre and post `add` and `remove` actions in Dartling may be used to define business rules in the model. A creation of a new todo is moved from the `TodoApp` controller to the `Todos` class that becomes a combination of a view and a controller. It is left for the reader to study the `Todos` class and understand how filters are used to show a subset of todos.

Spiral 6 – editing a task

In **Spiral 5**, both `Todo` and `Todos` classes are views with their corresponding controllers. The `TodoApp` class in **Spiral 5** is still a controller. In **Spiral 6**, the events that change the model are moved from the `TodoApp` class to new `Header` and `Footer` classes that represent views with their corresponding controllers. In this way, there are four views (with embedded controllers) in the application: `Todo`, `Todos`, `Header`, and `Footer`. `TodoApp` becomes only the application class that creates views (with embedded controllers), loads and saves data, and updates displays of the header and footer sections of the web page:

```
class TodoApp {
  // code left out
  TodoApp(this.domain) {
    session = domain.newSession();
    MvcEntries model =                          domain.
getModelEntries(TodoRepo.todoMvcModelCode);
    tasks = model.tasks;

    _header = new Header(this);
    _todos = new Todos(this);
    footer = new Footer(this, _todos);

    _load();
  }
// code left out
```

The `Header` class handles undos and redos and the completion of all todos. The `Footer` class displays the remaining number of todos, provides different selections of todos, and clears the completed todos. See the project's code for details.

Summary

This was a deep chapter. We used the domain modeling framework, Dartling, to build an app, from designing the model to generating and testing application code. Then, we discussed the universally applied MVC pattern and used it together with Dartling to build a complete and usable Todo app. In this process, the following advantages of using a domain modeling framework became apparent:

- Once a model is designed, its code is generated, which is a big deal for large models

- Although the code for the model is generated, a programmer may add some specific code that will not be lost if the model is regenerated

- The API of Dartling, for example, for entities, is rich, and it allows handling of identifiers and relationships, which is not done in Dartlero

- The code in the TodoMVC application clearly shows that, after the code is generated, there is not much model programming left to do, allowing a developer to focus on the UI

In the next chapter we'll get an overview of MVC and UI frameworks built by the Dart community.

10

MVC Web and UI Frameworks in Dart – An Overview

In this chapter, we investigate some of the more important UI frameworks that exist in the Dart universe, indicate how and when to use them, and discuss their pros and cons. For instance, we will discuss whether a framework supports responsive design and provides an optimal viewing experience—easy reading and navigation with minimum resizing, panning, and scrolling—across a wide range of devices (from desktop monitors to mobile phones).

Some of them (DQuery and Bootjack) are ports of, or at least are inspired by, famous JavaScript frameworks, such as jQuery or Twitter Bootstrap.

DWT (Dart Web Toolkit) is a port of the Google Web Toolkit.

Some packages built on the (now deprecated) Dart Web UI components library are as follows:

- Dart widgets
- Bee (from Blossom)
- HTML Components

The following libraries heavily use the MVC pattern:

- Rikulo UI (using DQuery and Bootjack)
- Hipster-MVC (no specific UI components)
- PureMVC (no specific UI components)

The others are ports of or built on the Adobe development framework:

- Flash Professional, which is the toolkit for Dart (from Adobe)
- StageXL

Finally, we discuss the porting of Angular.js to Dart using **Angular.dart**.

DQuery

(Developed by *Simon Pai* and *Tom Yeh* from Rikulo, the code for DQuery can be found at https://github.com/rikulo/dquery, and the API reference is at http://api.rikulo.org/dquery/latest/dquery.html.)

Every web developer knows and uses jQuery, the JavaScript library that creates HTML document traversal and manipulation, event handling, animation, and Ajax much simpler than in pure JavaScript. DQuery (in Version 0.5.1 currently) is a strongly typed port to Dart of jQuery, meaning that the externally visible variables are typed, in contrast to jQuery. It remains close to both Dart and jQuery conventions, so it will particularly appeal to developers who are already fluent with jQuery. Dart has some of the features of jQuery, but the event system and element wrapper of the latter still offer additional value, and that's why they have been ported; besides, DQuery uses the ubiquitous $ notation for element queries instead of Dart's query and the queryAll functions. Create a new web application project dquery1 and add dquery: any to the dependencies section in pubspec.yaml to install the package. Also, add the necessary import statement to dquery1.dart:

```
import 'package:dquery/dquery.dart';
```

In the DQuery notation, the template code becomes:

```
$('#sample_text_id')[0]
..text = "Click me!"
..onClick.listen(reverseText);
```

Querying with $, in fact, returns an ElementQuery object—a collection of the elements $elems:

```
ElementQuery $elems = $('#sample_text_id');
```

DQuery also has its own class DQueryEvent to register event listeners, as shown in this code snippet, where the text of the button with the ID btn changes after a click:

```
$('#btn').on('click', (DQueryEvent e) {
 $('#btn')[0].text = "Don't do this!";
});
```

Bootjack

(This is also developed by *Simon Pai* and *Tom Yeh* from Rikulo; the code can be found at `https://github.com/rikulo/bootjack`, and the API reference is at `http://api.rikulo.org/bootjack/latest/bootjack.html`.)

Bootjack is a port of Twitter Bootstrap and is built on DQuery. One of the goals of Bootjack is to ease the use of working with CSS by supplying a great number of style resources, as well as pure CSS components, such as breadcrumbs, pagination, progress bars, thumbnails, labels, and badges. Other Bootstrap UI components require code apart from DOM/CSS, such as alert, button, dropdown, model, and tab; these were converted to be used by Dart. To start using Bootjack, add `bootjack:any` to your `pubspec.yaml`, and let pub install the package. (DQuery is automatically installed because it is a dependent package.) Include the Bootstrap CSS file in your web page:

```
<link rel="stylesheet" href="packages/bootjack/css/bootstrap-
    2.3.1.css">
```

To use Bootjack components, you need to do two things:

1. Attach the right CSS class to your DOM elements, such as `btn btn-info`, `btn dropdown-toggle`, and `nav nav-tabs`.
2. Call a global function, such as `Button.use()` or `Dropdown.use()`, to register its use. With `Bootjack.useDefault()`, all controls are registered.
3. The `bootjack1` project shows the use of many components. DQuery is also imported in `bootjack1.dart`, as shown in the following screenshot.

The `bootjack2` project shows the use of the Scrollspy component to navigate, using a sidebar. (For more info, visit `http://blog.rikulo.org/posts/2013/May/General/bootjack-and-dquery/`.)

Bootjack components

Dart Web Toolkit (DWT)

(Developed by *Sergey Akopkokhyants*, Dart Web Toolkit can be found at
`http://dartwebtoolkit.com/`.)

You have probably heard of **Google Web Toolkit (GWT)** — a framework by Google
to develop web applications in Java and compile them to JavaScript, in many ways
a precursor project to Dart. So it will come as no surprise that this project has been
ported to Dart not only to build Dart web apps, but also to facilitate the migration
from an existing Java web application to Dart, leveraging your existing GWT skills
and themes in DWT. It has a rich set of widgets (for example, button, checkbox,
listbox, textarea, and menus), panels, and utility classes that are compatible with
GWT, and it provides you, at this moment (June 2013, Version 0.3.16), with the most
complete toolbox for Dart UI controls, which can be viewed at `http://akserg.`
`github.io/dart_web_toolkit_showcase/`. Moreover, it has been tested on Chrome
and FireFox. To start using this framework and create a new web application (say
`dwt1`), remove the example code and add the following dependency to the project's
`pubspec.yaml`:

```
dart_web_toolkit: '>=0.3.0'
```

Then run `pub install` (this happens automatically while saving the file). To make
it available to your code add the `import` statement:

```
import 'package:dart_web_toolkit/ui.dart' as ui;
```

Add the following code to `main()` of `dwt1.dart` and run the page:

```
ui.Label label = new ui.Label("Hello from Dart Web Tookit!");
ui.RootLayoutPanel.get().add(label);
```

and a nice label appears with the text.

It will be clear from this and the following example, that in DWT, everything is
constructed from code. Let's now build a more complete example in the `dwt_bank`
project, mimicking our bank application `bank_terminal_s5` from *Chapter 6,
Combining HTML5 Forms with Dart*.

Here, follow the code from `dwt_bank.dart` needed to draw the screen and hook up
the event handling (the rest of the code is identical to that in `bank_terminal_s5`):

```
library bank_terminal;

import 'dart:html';
import 'package:dart_web_toolkit/ui.dart' as ui;        (1)
import 'package:dart_web_toolkit/i18n.dart' as i18n;     (2)
```

```
import 'package:dart_web_toolkit/event.dart' as event;          (3)
import 'dart:convert';

part '../model/bank_account.dart';
part '../model/person.dart';

ui.TextBox number;
ui.Label owner, balance;
ui.IntegerBox amount;
ui.Button btn_deposit, btn_interest;
BankAccount bac;

void main() {
  ui.CaptionPanel panel = new ui.CaptionPanel("BANK APP");   (4)
  panel.getElement().style.border = "3px solid #00c";

  ui.FlexTable layout = new ui.FlexTable();                   (5)
  layout.setCellSpacing(6);
  ui.FlexCellFormatter cellFormatter =
    layout.getFlexCellFormatter();

// Add a title to the form
  layout.setHtml(0, 0, "Enter your account number<br> and
    transaction amount");
// Add some standard form options
  cellFormatter.setColSpan(0, 0, 2);
  cellFormatter.setHorizontalAlignment(0, 0,        i18n.
HasHorizontalAlignment.ALIGN_LEFT);

  layout.setHtml(1, 0, "Number:");
  number = new ui.TextBox();                                 (6)
  number.addValueChangeHandler(new                           (7)
    event.ValueChangeHandlerAdapter((event.ValueChangeEvent event)
    {
    readData();
  }));
  layout.setWidget(1, 1, number);
  layout.setHtml(2, 0, "Owner:");
  owner = new ui.Label("");
  layout.setWidget(2, 1, owner);

  layout.setHtml(3, 0, "Balance:");
  balance = new ui.Label("");
  layout.setWidget(3, 1, balance);
```

```
layout.setHtml(4, 0, "Amount:");
amount = new ui.IntegerBox();
layout.setWidget(4, 1, amount);

btn_deposit = new ui.Button(                                    (8)
    "Deposit - Withdrawal", new
      event.ClickHandlerAdapter((event.ClickEvent event) {
    deposit(event);
    }));

layout.setWidget(5, 0, btn_deposit);
btn_interest = new ui.Button(
    "Add Interest", new event.ClickHandlerAdapter((event.
    ClickEvent event) {
      interest(event);
    }));
layout.setWidget(5, 1, btn_interest);

panel.setContentWidget(layout);
ui.RootLayoutPanel.get().add(panel);
}
```

In lines (1), (2), and (3), the necessary parts from DWT are imported (UI for the controls and event for event handling). We use CaptionPanel in line (4) (this wraps its contents in a border with a caption that appears in the upper-left corner) and FlexTable in line (5) to lay out our labels and controls in cells; these are created starting from line (6). Labels are positioned in a cell indicated by its row and column using the setHtml(row, col, "Text") method and controlled using the setWidget(row, col, widgetName) method. Event handlers are registered through a specialized adapter in a very Java-like syntax in lines (7) or (8); separating both makes them more readable:

```
btn_deposit = new ui.Button("Deposit - Withdrawal"); btn_deposit.
addClickHandler(new event.ClickHandlerAdapter((event.ClickEvent event) {
    deposit(event);
  }));
```

The screenshot is shown as follows:

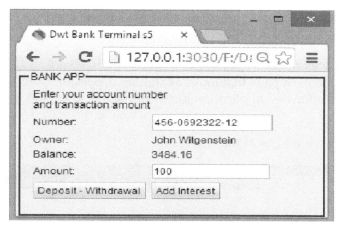

The DWT bank terminal screen

The dartling_dwt_todo_mvc_spirals project

(The code can be cloned from `https://github.com/dzenanr/dartling_dwt_todo_mvc_spirals`.)

To illustrate DWT with a more elaborate and well-known example, here is our `todo-mvc` project from the last chapter, with DWT used for the UI part. We sum what is implemented in each spiral (besides testing the model):

- **Spiral 1**: Add a new todo and display a list of todos
- **Spiral 2**: Load tasks from and save tasks to local storage `ActionReactionApi`
- **Spiral 3**: Undo and redo functionality — `PastReactionApi`
- **Spiral 4**: Complete todo, remove todo, and start using TodoMVC CSS
- **Spiral 5**: Add specific code to `Task` and `Tasks`, enable and disable the `undo` and `redo` buttons, clear completed todos, add count of the remaining todos, continue using TodoMVC CSS
- **Spiral 6**: Add specific code to `Task`, complete all todos, display all remaining or completed todos

- **Spiral 7**: Change the model in the model concepts (`title` is now `id`, `completed` is now `essential`) and generate JSON from the model; generate the code using `test/todo/mvc/todo_mvc_gen.dart`
- **Spiral 8**: Add links to Dartling, DWT, and TodoMVC, edit todo
- **Spiral 9**: Implement standard TodoMVC layout
- **Spiral 10**: Make a page that looks as similar as possible to the page in the standard TodoMVC application; for example, the `undo` and `redo` buttons are gone

The following is a screenshot of the end result:

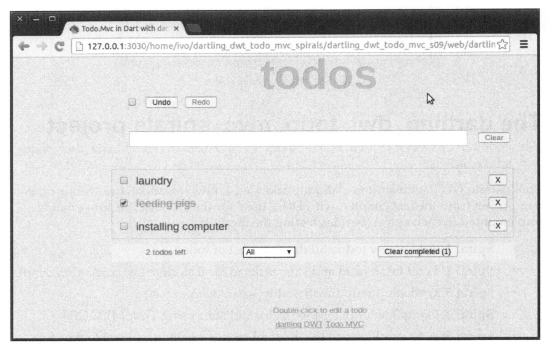

Spiral 9 of DWT_TodoMVC

The DWT-related code is written in `lib/app`. In order to better understand the code, start with Spiral 1 and work your way up. The app is started by instantiating an instance of TodoApp (in `main()` from `web/todo/dartling_dwt_todo_mvc.dart`):

```
new TodoApp(domain);
```

In its constructor (in `lib/app/todo_app.dart`), the layout of the screen is coded: a vertical panel with a header and a footer (code from last spiral, doesn't change much from Spiral 1 to 9):

```
var root = ui.RootPanel.get();
var todoApp = new ui.VerticalPanel();
todoApp.spacing = 8;
root.add(todoApp);
header = new Header(this);
todoApp.add(header);
var todos = new Todos(this);                                    (1)
todoApp.add(todos);
footer = new Footer(this, todos);
todoApp.add(footer);
```

The info text and links at the bottom of the screen are also constructed by a horizontal panel with anchor controls inside a vertical panel:

```
var infoPanel = new ui.VerticalPanel();
infoPanel.addStyleName('info');
todoApp.add(infoPanel);
var todo_edit_info = new ui.Label('Double-click to edit a
   todo');

infoPanel.add(todo_edit_info);
var linkPanel = new ui.HorizontalPanel();
linkPanel.spacing = 4;
infoPanel.add(linkPanel);

var dartling = new ui.Anchor()
   ..text="dartling"
   ..href="https://github.com/dzenanr/dartling";
linkPanel.add(dartling);

var dwt = new ui.Anchor()
   ..text="DWT"
   ..href="http://dartwebtoolkit.com";
linkPanel.add(dwt);
var todoMvc = new ui.Anchor()
   ..text="Todo MVC"
   ..href="http://todomvc.com";
linkPanel.add(todoMvc);
```

In line (1), a `Todos` object is made, which is a vertical panel itself; this happens in `todo.dart` (this code is from Spiral 1):

```
class Todos extends ui.VerticalPanel {
  var _listPanel = new ui.VerticalPanel();

  Todos(Tasks tasks) {
    spacing = 10;
    var newTodo = new ui.TextBox();                              (2)
    newTodo.addKeyPressHandler(new                               (3)
        event.KeyPressHandlerAdapter((event.KeyPressEvent e) {
          if (e.getNativeKeyCode() == event.KeyCodes.KEY_ENTER) {
            var title = newTodo.text.trim();
            if (title != '') {
              var task = new Task(tasks.concept);                (4)
              task.title = title;
              tasks.add(task);
              _add(task);
              newTodo.text = '';
            }
          }
        }));
    add(newTodo);

    _listPanel.spacing = 4;
    add(_listPanel);
  }

  _add(Task task) {
    var title = new ui.Label(task.title);
    _listPanel.add(title);
  }
}
```

In line (2), an input field for a new todo is created, and in line (3) we see the event handler that kicks in when the user enters a todo: a new task is made with this todo, and it is added to the tasks collection; moreover, it is added to the list panel at the bottom. The class `Todos` starts reacting to changes in the model by implementing `ActionReactionApi` in Spiral 2:

```
class Todos extends ui.VerticalPanel implements ActionReactionApi {
  ... }
```

In Spiral 3, a `Header` class is added that inherits from `HorizontalPanel` (see `header.dart`). At this stage, it only comprises the undo/redo buttons; it implements this functionality through `PastReactionApi` from Dartling. The DWT click event handlers are coded in its constructor (lines (5) and (6)):

```
class Header extends ui.HorizontalPanel implements PastReactionApi {
  ui.Button _undo;
  ui.Button _redo;

  Header(TodoApp todoApp) {
    // ...
    _undo = new ui.Button(                                      (5)
        'undo', new event.ClickHandlerAdapter((event.ClickEvent e)
    {
          session.past.undo();
    }));

    _redo = new ui.Button(                                      (6)
        'redo', new event.ClickHandlerAdapter((event.ClickEvent e)
  {
          session.past.redo();
    }));
  }
  // code left out
}
```

In later spirals, the input functionality is moved from the `Todos` class to the `Header` class. In Spiral 4, a `Todo` class is introduced as a horizontal panel that comprises the UI so that the `Todos` class has to now construct only a `Todo` object. In Spiral 5, the `Footer` class also appears as a horizontal panel; it shows the count of todos left, the drop-down box to show all, active or completed todos, and a button to remove the completed todos. In later spirals, `Todo` as well as `Footer` become subclasses of the DWT `Composite` class using the `Grid` class to define their internal layout:

```
class Todo extends ui.Composite {
  ui.CheckBox _completed;
  ui.Label _todo;
  ui.TextBox _todo_retitle;

  Todo(TodoApp todoApp, this.task) {
    // ...
    ui.Grid grid = new ui.Grid(1, 3);
    grid.setCellSpacing(8);
    grid.addStyleName('todo');
    grid.getRowFormatter().setVerticalAlign(
        0, i18n.HasVerticalAlignment.ALIGN_MIDDLE);
```

```
      initWidget(grid);

      _completed = new ui.CheckBox();
      // ...
      grid.setWidget(0, 0, _completed);

      _todo = new ui.Label();
      // ...
      grid.setWidget(0, 1, _todo);

      ui.Button remove = new ui.Button(
        'X', new event.ClickHandlerAdapter((event.ClickEvent e) {
          new RemoveAction(session, tasks, task).doit();
        })
      );
      remove.addStyleName('todo-button');
      grid.setWidget(0, 2, remove);
    }
  }
```

To conclude our discussion, the following are some notes from an experienced GWT developer: `http://blog.hackingthought.com/2013/05/notes-from-my-first-real-dart-web-app.html`.

 If you want make a project allow Dart to work along with GWT, take a look at this video and project packed with tips: `http://architects.dzone.com/articles/dart-google-web-toolkit`.

Dart widgets

(`http://dart-lang.github.io/widget.dart/`, developed by *Kevin Moore*.)

The Dart widgets project by Kevin Moore builds on the Dart web UI and gives us a collection of reusable components and effects. It is a port to Dart's Web UI library from the widely successful **Twitter Bootstrap** project (`http://twitter.github.io/bootstrap/`), which helps web developers build responsive designs for web apps. This means dynamic widgets, such as accordion, alert, carousel, collapse, dropdown, tabs, and more, are reborn as actual web components. To see all of them in action, please refer to `http://dart-lang.github.io/widget.dart/`, where you can find more documentation and examples. The code can be found at `https://github.com/dart-lang/widget.dart`.

This project can also be a source of inspiration for building your own Polymer components.

Bee

(www.blossom.io/bee, developed by *Allan Berger, Nik Graf,* and *Thomas Schranz* from Blossom.)

Blossom is a firm that develops collaboration and organization tools around project management; they have been using the whole web technology stack in the process, including Backbone.js, CoffeeScript, and Python, on the server. Blossom is also a cutting-edge, single-page web application with Google App Engine as the backend. In a recent blog post (April 2013, www.ramen.io/tagged/dartlang), Thomas Schranz discussed why they where switching to Dart: the main reasons were the fragmentation and lack of cohesion in the JavaScript framework offering, and the fact that Dart is designed with performance in mind. Bee (as of writing, Version 0.0.2) is a collection of lightweight and frequently used Dart web components, such as buttons, popovers, overlays, and input fields. It can be installed via pub using bee:any in your pubspec.yaml, and importing the necessary lib files in your app, such as:

```
import 'package:bee/components/loading.dart';
import 'package:bee/components/overlay.dart';
import 'package:bee/components/popover.dart';
import 'package:bee/components/secret.dart';
import 'package:bee/utils/html_helpers.dart';
```

A component, such as a button, is then used as all web components by importing:

```
<link rel="import" href="package:bee/components/button.html">
```

and using the following markup:

```
<x-button value="text on button"></x-button>
```

You can expect a Polymer port of this framework soon.

HTML components

(The code is developed by *Gabor Szabo* and can be downloaded from https://github.com/szgabsz91/html-components.)

This is already an extensive and impressive collection (46 components in the first release August 2013) of very usable web page widgets ranging from input, menu, panel, multimedia to dialog, and even data components such as a datatable, datagrid, tagcloud, tree, and all kinds of list variants. Experiment with the sample application at http://html-components.appspot.com/.

Rikulo UI

(http://rikulo.org/projects/ui has been developed by Potix Corporation; the code is on GitHub https://github.com/rikulo/ui/.)

This is a Dart-based framework using an MVC architecture for web and native mobile applications using HTML5. Already in its 0.6.7 release (June 2013), and also integrating the DQuery and Bootjack projects, it is probably the most elaborate Dart UI framework available today. The apps built with Rikulo not only run in a modern web browser without any plugin, but can also be built as native mobile applications accessing the device's resources transparently through a **Cordova (Phonegap)** integration called Rikulo Gap. Rikulo Gap runs these resources cross-platform (and offline if needed) in iOS, Android, Blackberry, Windows Phone, and others. It has been ported from Cordova to Dart and is a library for accessing the phone's resources; it can be used with any UI framework. Rikulo brings the programming philosophy of Dart to the UI by using a structured UI model. Creating and updating complex layouts can be cumbersome, and this is where Rikulo shines by providing a layout model allowing flexible and precise control. It is based on positioning UI elements using coordinates in relation to their parent, so there is no need to interact with the DOM directly. This means that the UI components are created and embedded in what is called a **view**; so a mix of HTML and Dart code isn't going to work. But if you want to take control over the layout and need more of HTML's and CSS's capabilities, it is still possible because a view also supports HTML markup. Rikulo further defines a **UXL** markup language for defining UI in XML, which compiles the user interface specified in XML into Dart code. Because Rikulo UI starts from a different model, it cannot be integrated easily with the Dart web components. The Rikulo site showcases its framework at http://rikulo.org/examples/; among the examples are a scrollable list and grid view.

To start using it, create a web project rikulo1, add rikulo_ui: any to its pubspec. yaml file, and install the package. Then import the following Dart files, depending on your requirements, to start using its features:

```
import 'package:rikulo_ui/effect.dart';
import 'package:rikulo_ui/event.dart';
import 'package:rikulo_ui/gesture.dart';
import 'package:rikulo_ui/layout.dart';
import 'package:rikulo_ui/message.dart';
import 'package:rikulo_ui/model.dart';
import 'package:rikulo_ui/view.dart';
```

Not all of these files are always needed; the basis is `view.dart` because it contains many UI elements. The website has a tutorial and a very elaborate documentation at `http://docs.rikulo.org/ui/latest/Getting_Started/`. Here, we will indicate the most important concepts and then get on to build our banking screen with Rikulo. The basic building block is the view, which draws something in a rectangular area on the screen and can interact with the user; it is an instance of the class `View` or one of its subclasses. Similar to the DOM tree of element nodes, in Rikulo, a tree of views is constructed from what is often named `rootView`, which is added to the document of the web page. Every view contains the `List<View>` children, so we can have new views with children attached to them through the `addChild` method. These children are positioned in the parent view by specifying their layout type, orientation, and left and top coordinates relative to the parent view. Every view can handle events, and all Rikulo UI controls, such as button, textbox, checkbox, radiobutton, and scrollview are subclasses of `View`.

Because we specify everything through code, the cascading notation is used abundantly. In the project `rikulo1`, we made a simple screen to illustrate these basic techniques:

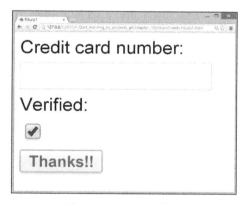

A basic screen with Rikulo

The `main()` method in `rikulo1.dart` contains the code to construct this:

```
var root = new View()
    ..layout.type = "linear"      // specify layout and CSS
    ..layout.orient = "vertical"  // horizontal is default
    ..style.cssText = "font-size: 14px; text-align: center"
    ..addChild(new TextView("Credit card number: "))
    ..addChild(new TextBox())
```

```
..addChild(new TextView("Verified: "))
..addChild(new CheckBox())
..addToDocument();        //make it available to the browser


var hello = new Button("Support our work!")
  ..on.click.listen((event) {    // attach click handler        (1)
    (event.target as Button).text = "Thanks!!";
    event.target.requestLayout();   // redraw screen            (2)
});
  root.addChild(hello);           // attach to root view
```

The Click event handler is registered in line (1) using a mixture of old and new Dart syntax. Whenever a change occurs to the screen, the method requestLayout() must be called, as in line (2), to show this. Every Rikulo web page must include the following link to some basic CSS settings:

```
<link rel="stylesheet" type="text/css"
     href="packages/rikulo_ui/css/default/view.css" />
```

Besides, it adds the following meta tag, if the app is to be run on mobile devices to ensure responsive design (it is ignored in desktop browsers):

```
<meta name="viewport" content="width=device-width, initial-
scale=1.0, maximum-scale=1.0, user-scalable=no" />
```

Let's now rewrite our bank terminal screen in Rikulo; this results in:

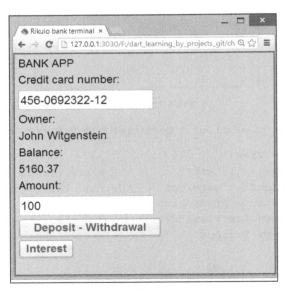

The bank terminal screen with Rikulo

Adding this code to `rikulo_bank.dart` results in a functional screen, and although some layout code must be added, the code is remarkably readable:

```
BankAccount bac;
TextBox number, amount;
TextView owner, balance;
Button btn_deposit, btn_interest;

void main() {
  final View rootView = new View();
  rootView.style.cssText = "border: 1px solid #553; background-color:
lime";
  number = new TextBox();
  owner = new TextView();
  owner.profile.width = "100";
  balance = new TextView();
  amount = new TextBox();
  btn_deposit = new Button("Deposit - Withdrawal");
  btn_deposit.profile.width = "150";
  btn_interest = new Button("Interest");
  number.on.change.listen((event) {
    readData();
    event.target.requestLayout();
  });

  btn_deposit.on.click.listen((event) {
    deposit(event);
    event.target.requestLayout();
  });

  btn_interest.on.click.listen((event) {
    interest(event);
    event.target.requestLayout();
  });

  rootView
    ..layout.text = "type: linear; orient: vertical"
    ..addChild(new TextView("BANK APP"))
    ..addChild(new TextView("Credit card number: "))
    ..addChild(number)
    ..addChild(new TextView("Owner: "))
    ..addChild(owner)
    ..addChild(new TextView("Balance: "))
    ..addChild(balance)
```

```
    ..addChild(new TextView("Amount: "))
    ..addChild(amount)
    ..addChild(btn_deposit)
    ..addChild(btn_interest)
    ..addToDocument();
}
```

Rikulo MVC

For those who like to specify the UI design in an XML format, Rikulo provides the UXL language to declare UI and store it in a .uxl.xml file. The following is a simple example of an input dialog:

```
<Template name="Credit Card">
  <Panel layout="type:linear; orient: vertical; spacing: 8"
     profile="location: center center; width: 180; height: 145">
     Number:   <TextBox id="ccNumber" value="$rememberMe" />
     Owner:    <TextBox id="owner"/>
     <Button text="Verify"/>
  </Panel>
</Template>
```

Through a setup with a build script, these files are compiled to a plain Dart code, which when run, builds the corresponding component tree of the screen. This UXL format is ideally suited for a declarative definition of the View component of the MVC model. It is quite elaborate and contains flow control, data, and event binding. The following are few examples of the same:

For showing a customer name in a textbox:

```
<TextBox value="${customer.firstName}, ${customer.lastName}"/>
```

For running a verify method while pressing the button:

```
<Button text="Verify" on.click="verify"/>
```

To study UXL in detail, visit http://docs.rikulo.org/ui/latest/UXL/ Fundamentals/UXL_Overview.html.

Using UXL, the Rikulo framework easily allows you to build applications that conform to the MVC model explained in *Chapter 9, Modeling More Complex Applications with Dartling*. In the blog on the Rikulo website, you can find a complete explanation of a todo app storing the todo items in the local storage and layered out in separate controllers, models, and views folders: http://blog.rikulo.org/ posts/2012/Dec/General/rikulos-todomvc/.

Clone the code from GitHub: `git clone git://github.com/rikulo/todoMVC`.

Pub contains some MVC frameworks not specifically focused on the UI, which allow you to implement the Model View Controller design pattern described in *Chapter 9, Modeling More Complex Applications with Dartling*. A few among them are mentioned in the next couple of sections:

Hipster-mvc

(Download the code from the GitHub site: `https://github.com/eee-c/hipster-mvc`.)

This framework (now in its Version 0.2.6) is developed by Chris Strom based on Backbone.js. It is used in the development of the Dart comics example in *Dart for Hipsters*, published by *The Pragmatic Programmers* (find the code at `https://github.com/eee-c/dart-comics`). The framework defines a `HipsterModel` class, and your app resource class must inherit from this. The class that represents a collection of your objects must inherit from the `HipsterCollection` class, and the view class from `HipsterView`. To use it, add `hipster_mvc: >=0.2.6` to your app's `pubspec.yaml`. It is a great starting point for a client app that uses the REST pattern to communicate with a server.

Puremvc

(Find the code on GitHub at `https://github.com/PureMVC/puremvc-dart-multicore-framework/wiki`.)

This is conceptually very deeply elaborated but still a lightweight framework and is developed by Cliff Hall from Futurescale. It is extensively documented at `www.puremvc.org` and exists for a whole range of programming languages (such as ActionScript, C#, Java, C++, Python, Ruby, and now Dart as well), allowing its use for a wide variety of platforms (browsers, desktops, mobiles, as well as servers). The Dart version being at 2.0.4, is a port of the Flash/Flex ActionScript3 reference implementation of the MultiCore Version, and it is production-ready. Make it available to your application by adding `puremvc: ">=2.0.4 <3.0.0"` to your `pubspec.yaml` and import it in your app with:

```
import 'package:puremvc/puremvc.dart';
```

Its primary goal is to allow modular programming to follow the MVC pattern by decomposing your app into so-called core actors or cores. Each core is, in fact, a separate PureMVC subsystem that can communicate with other cores in two ways:

- Synchronously through interfaces
- Asynchronously through pipes

PureMVC implements the MVC tiers as the Multiton classes (see http://en.wikipedia.org/wiki/Multiton_pattern), which register and manage communications between the workhorse actors that operate within those tiers; it also provides a handy frontend to the whole system known as **Facade** (http://en.wikipedia.org/wiki/Facade_pattern). Because methods for passing a message vary from platform to platform, PureMVC implements its own internal observer notification system for its actors to communicate with each other. These are not alternatives for events: your application's boundary classes will still interact with the DOM, services, and PureMVC via events. To dig deeper into this framework, analyze the Dart demo from https://github.com/PureMVC/puremvc-dart-demo-reversetext/wiki, which is an elaborate version of the Dart Editor web template that reverses text when you click on it; you can get the code with:

```
git clone git://github.com/PureMVC/puremvc-dart-demo-reversetext .
```

StageXL

(www.stagexl.org developed by Bernhard Pichler)

Adobe with its ActionScript variant of JavaScript and its Flash/Flex developer suite has been a long time contender in the web development world. But Flash isn't such a popular choice for web development anymore, and Dart is quite similar to ActionScript 3. So it comes as no surprise that a solution has been developed to help migrate Flash projects to HTML5 using Dart. The StageXL library (now at Version 0.8.3, formerly known as DartFlash) does exactly that, being highly compatible with the battle-proof Flash API but built with Dart. It is a complete and robust Flash-like engine for Canvas that is built on top of the Dart programming language using the familiar Flash class hierarchy, with classes such as DisplayObject, MovieClip, Stage, and Sprite. Working with sound is made simple with the Flash Sound API; a number of visual effect filters are provided, and an easy-to-use animation framework called Juggler also comes with it.

StageXL is intended for Flash/ActionScript developers who want to migrate their projects as well as their skills to HTML5. The library's site is up to date and provides extensive documentation, examples, and tutorials at `http://stagexl.org/docs/wiki-articles.html`. To start using it, add the following dependency to your `pubspec.yaml` file: `stagexl: any`; add the following `import` statement to your Dart code:

```
import 'package:stagexl/stagexl.dart';
```

Flash Professional CC – toolkit for Dart

(Download the software from `http://toolkitfordart.github.io/`, where you can also find the documentation.)

Flash Professional (`http://www.adobe.com/products/flash.html`) is Adobe's most popular authoring tool for creating vector graphics, animations, games, and rich Internet applications for the Web. Previously, its content was exported to the SWF file format, which could be viewed only with the Flash Player plugin. But at Google I/O 2013, Adobe announced their new and open-sourced toolkit for Dart, a plugin for Flash Professional CC that allows developers to export their animations and games to Dart code, HTML5, and the StageXL library. This feature allows Flash web designers and animators to use the tool they love (Flash Pro) and at the same time, create content for the modern Web by publishing their content to the Dart language and HTML5 APIs.

Most of the animation and drawing functionality of Flash Pro is supported in the toolkit for Dart, such as bitmaps, shapes, movie clips, simple buttons, text fields, filters, masks, and embedded audio. Dart code is generated for stage items, symbols, images and sounds. The developer has to write Dart code for the interactive parts of the content. The toolkit also uses the Dart StageXL library for the Flash runtime. You can find it as an export panel in Flash Professional CC: its output is a functional Dart project, partly being auto-generated code, and you can add your business logic in other code files.

Angular.dart

(See www.angularjs.org, the Dart project is on https://github.com/angular/angular.dart)

Angular.js (or Angular for short) is a popular open source JavaScript framework, maintained by Google, for developing single-page applications. Its goal is to make browser-based apps with MVC capabilities in an effort to make both development and testing easier. It accomplishes this by using declarative programming for building UI and wiring software components. It uses a templating system with a number of so called directives (starting with ng-) to specify customizable and reusable HTML tags and expressions that moderate the behavior of certain elements; for example, ng-repeat for instantiating an element for each item from a collection, or ng-model for 2-way data binding:

```
<input type="text" ng-model="lastName" placeholder="Your name">
```

The $scope service detects changes to the model and modifies HTML expressions in the view via a controller. Likewise, any alterations to the view are reflected in the model. In June 2013, the Angular team was expanded to announce and work on a Dart-optimized port of their framework using the same templates but a separate implementation: large parts of Angular functionality—components such as $compiler and $scope, basic directives such as ngBind and ngRepeat—have already been ported over to Dart, and can be used today. Other critical Angular parts such as Dependency Injection and routes are being ported now. Karma, the Angular test runner, already works with Dart. An important project in development within Google uses the Dart version of Angular. So developers can choose to use Angular either with Dart or with JavaScript. At this moment, Angular is not yet published on pub, but it soon will; for now it has to be used as a local package by adding the dependency:

```
angular:
path: ../..
```

and importing the package in code as follows:

```
import 'package:angular/angular.dart';
```

Check out the hello angular example at https://github.com/jbdeboer/dart-seed.

Summary

We surveyed the available Dart UI frameworks in this chapter. Based on your previous web technology experience (be it JavaScript, GWT, or Adobe Flash), you already have some definite choices. For example, there are some beautiful MVC frameworks or a framework built on Flash. This is a field that is very much in evolution, so if you are evaluating UI frameworks, a search in pub (`pub.dartlang.org`) will certainly be worthwhile. Also, expect to see more and more libraries based on the Polymer project, discussed in *Chapter 8, Developing Business Applications with Polymer Web Components*, when you read this. In the next chapter, we will learn how to store data on the client with IndexedDB and then send it in the JSON format to a Dart web server.

11

Local Data and Client-Server Communication

Data goes around in applications, but, eventually, new and modified data has to be stored; this can be done on the client or server. In the previous chapters, we used local storage (also called web storage) in the browser. Here, we will investigate a better client-side storage mechanism called **IndexedDB** and a layer called **Lawndart** that automatically chooses the best local storage mechanism available on the client. Most of the time, the data needs to be available to many people, so it needs to be stored centrally on a server. We will see how to communicate data between client and server with JSON, and, in the next chapter, how to store this data in a database on the server side. Then, we'll see that Dart can be used for both sides of a client-server app. To do this, we need to learn how Dart works with asynchronous calls using **Futures**, and how it can run as a web server. The following are the topics for this chapter:

- What are the options for browser storage?
- Asynchronous calls and Futures
- How to use IndexedDB with Dart
- Using Lawndart
- A Dart web server
- Using JSON web services

The options for browser storage

Using client-side data storage reduces bandwidth traffic, decreases network response times (latency), increases UI performance, and, best of all, allows your application to run offline. The local storage mechanism that we've used until now is a very simple key/value store and does have good cross-browser coverage. However, it can only store strings and is a blocking (synchronous) API; this means that it can temporarily stop your web page from responding while it is doing its job. This can be bad for performance when your app wants to store or read large amounts of data, such as images. Moreover, it has a space limit of 5 Mb (this varies with browsers); you can't detect when you are nearing this limit and you can't ask for more space! These properties make it only as useful as a temporary data storage tool — better than cookies, but not suited for reliable, database kind of storage.

On the other hand, IndexedDB is the future of offline, local object storage for your web app. It has all the advantages of local storage, but no size limit. It is a full-fledged database; but, being essentially an indexed object store, it belongs to the family of NoSQL databases (similar to MongoDB and CouchDB on the server). It is on the track to becoming an official standard and does have Chrome, Firefox, and Internet Explorer (a version greater than or similar to 10) implementations. Using indexes, it provides a far better search performance than web storage, but programming it is more complex. (The equivalent of relational database storage in the browser also exists and is called Web SQL DB; however, its specification is no longer maintained and Firefox and Internet Explorer do not support it. That's why we won't discuss it here.) IndexedDB works in a non-blocking way for our app, and before we dive into how to use it, we explore Dart's mechanism for programming non-blocking codes called Futures.

Asynchronous calls and Futures

How should our app handle a situation where it needs a service that can take some time to return its result, for example, when we have to fetch or store data, read a large file, or need a response from a web service. Obviously, the app can't wait for this to end and the result to arrive (the so called **synchronous** way), because this would freeze the screen (and the app) and frustrate users. A responsive web app must be able to call this service and, immediately, continue with what it was doing. Only when the result returns should it react and call some function on the response data. This is called working in an **asynchronous**, non-blocking way, and most of the methods in dart:io for server-side Dart apps work in this way. Developers with a Java or C# background would immediately think of starting another thread to do the additional work, but Dart can't do this; it has to compile to JavaScript, so Dart also works in a single-threaded model that is tightly controlled by the browser's event loop.

On the Web (client as well as server), the code has to execute as asynchronously as possible in order not to block the browser from serving its user or a server process from serving its many thousands of client requests. The JavaScript world has long solved this issue using **callbacks**; this is a function that is "called" when the result of the first function call returns ("backs"). In the following code snippet, the first function that returns the result is `doStuff` and `handle` is registered as a callback that works on the result; when an error occurs (`onError`), `handleError` is invoked:

```
doStuff((result) {
  handle(result);
}, onError: (e) {
  handleError(e);
});
```

The same mechanism can be used in Dart, but here we have a more elegant way to handle this with objects appropriately called Futures. Now, we define `doStuff` to return a Future; this is a value (which could be an error) that is not yet available when `doStuff` is called, but that will be available sometime in the future, after `doStuff` has asynchronously executed (indicated using the keyword `then`). The same code snippet written using Futures is much more readable:

```
doStuff()
  .then( (result) => handle(result) )
  .catchError( (e) => handleError(e) );
```

The `doStuff` method returns a `Future` object, so it could have been written as:

```
Future fut1 = doStuff();
fut1.then( (result) => handle(result) )
    .catchError( (e) => handleError(e) );
```

But the first or even the following shorter way is idiomatically used:

```
doStuff()
  .then(handle)
  .catchError(handleError);
```

Then, it registers the callback `handle` and `catchError` calls `handleError` when an error occurs and stops the error from propagating. It could be considered the asynchronous version of a try/catch construct (there is also a `.whenComplete` handler that is always executed and corresponds with finally). The advantage becomes even more clear when callbacks are nested to enforce the execution order, because, in the JavaScript way, this results in ugly and difficult-to-read code (sometimes referred to as callback hell). Suppose a computation `doStuff2` has to occur between `doStuff` and `handle`, the first snippet becomes much less readable:

```
doStuff((result){
doStuff2((result){
handle((result) {
        });
    }, onError: (e) {
    handleError(e);
    });
}, onError: (e) {
    handleError(e);
    });
```

But, the version using Futures remains very simple:

```
doStuff()
    .then(doStuff2)
    .then(handle)
    .catchError(handleError);
```

Through this chaining syntax, it looks like synchronous code, but it is purely asynchronous code executing; catchError catches any errors that occur in the chain of Futures. As a simple, but working, example, suppose an app future1 needs to show or process a large file bigfile.txt and we don't want to wait until this I/O is completely done:

```
import 'dart:io';                               (1)
import 'dart:async';                            (2)

main() {
    var file = new File('bigfile.txt');         (3)
    file.readAsString()                         (4)
        .then( (text) => print(text) )          (5)
        .catchError( (e) => print(e) );         (6)
    // do other things while file is read in
    ...                                         (7)
}
```

To work with files and directories, dart:io is needed in line (1); the Future functionality comes from dart:async (line (2)). In line (3), a File object is created, and, in line (4), the action to read the file in is started asynchronously; but, the program immediately continues executing lines (7) and beyond. When the file is completely read through, line (5) prints its contents; should an error e (for example, a non-existing file) have occurred, this is printed in line (6). You can even leave out the intermediary variables and write:

```
      file.readAsString()
        .then(print)
    .catchError(print);
```

 You can find more info in the following article:
https://www.dartlang.org/articles/futures-and-error-handling/

Using IndexedDB with Dart

We will learn how to work with IndexedDB and JSON web services through the `indexed_db_spirals` project (https://github.com/dzenanr/indexed_db_spirals), which is a `todo` app like the ones we've built in previous chapters, but that stores its data in IndexedDB. Get a copy of the code with a git clone: https://github.com/dzenanr/indexed_db_spirals.git.

Spiral s00

In this spiral, todo tasks can be entered, and they are stored in IndexedDB; the following is a screenshot:

The Tasks screen of Spiral s00

Our model class is called `Task`, and lives in `model.dart`; with `toDb` and `fromDb`, it can transform an object to or make an object from a map:

```
class Task {
  String title;
```

```dart
bool completed = false;
DateTime updated = new DateTime.now();
var key;

Task(this.title);

Task.fromDb(this.key, Map value) :
  title = value['title'],
  updated = DateTime.parse(value['updated']),
  completed = value['completed'] == 'true' {
}

Map toDb() {
  return {
    'title': title,
    'completed': completed.toString(),
    'updated': updated.toString()
  };
}
}
```

Besides `Task`, the model also contains the class `TasksStore`, which contains `List<Task>` and interacts with IndexedDB. In order to do this, we need to import the `dart:indexed_db` library to `model.dart`, which provides the Dart API to use IndexedDB:

```dart
import 'dart:indexed_db';
```

The web page is `view.html` and references `view.dart`; this contains all UI code setup from the `main()` entry point:

```dart
import 'dart:html';
import 'model.dart';

Element taskElements;
TasksStore tasksStore;

main() {
  taskElements = querySelector('#task-list');
  tasksStore = new TasksStore();
  tasksStore.open().then((_) {                        (1)
    loadElements(tasksStore.tasks);
  });
```

```
    InputElement newTask = querySelector('#new-task');
    newTask.onKeyPress.listen((KeyboardEvent e) {
      if (e.keyCode == KeyCode.ENTER) {
        var title = newTask.value.trim();
        if (title != '') {
          tasksStore.add(title).then((task) {                    (2)
            addElement(task);
          });
          newTask.value = '';
        }
      }
    });

    ButtonElement clear = querySelector('#clear-tasks');
    clear.onClick.listen((MouseEvent e) {
      tasksStore.clear().then((_) {                              (3)
        clearElements();
      });
    });
  }
Element newElement(Task task) {
  return new Element.html('''
    <li>
      ${task.title}
    </li>
  ''');
}

addElement(Task task) {
  var taskElement = newElement(task);
  taskElements.nodes.add(taskElement);
}

loadElements(List tasks) {
  for (Task task in tasks) {
    addElement(task);
  }
}

clearElements() {
  taskElements.nodes.clear();
}
}
```

All interactions with IndexedDB are asynchronous and return Futures; that's why we use `then` in lines (1) to (3), respectively, when opening a database and adding a task or removing all tasks. The callback functions `loadElements`, `addElement`, and `clearElements` update the screen after the database has been changed (the code is straightforward; see `view.dart`). In line (1), we see that, for the parameter of the `then` callback function, (_) is written; this means that there is one parameter, but that we don't need it, so we don't name it. What happens now in line (1) in the preceding code with the `open()` call on `TaskStore`? You can imagine that we need to open the database or create it the first time the page is requested. This is done with a call to `window.indexedDB.open` in line (4) in `model.dart`:

```
class TasksStore {
  static const String TASKS_STORE = 'tasksStore';
  final List<Task> tasks = new List();
  Database _db;

  Future open() {
    return window.indexedDB.open('tasksDb00',          (4)
        version: 1,
        onUpgradeNeeded: _initDb)                      (5)
      .then(_loadDb);                                  (6)
  }
// code left out
```

The `open()` method takes three parameters: the first two are listed in alphabetical order by the name of the database and the third, by version number. When the app is first started on a client, a database with that name and Version 1 is created; every subsequent time, it is simply opened. At creation, the third parameter `onUpgradeNeeded` kicks in to fire an upgrade event, which calls `_initDb` in line (5). You can upgrade a database to a higher version by opening it with a new version number and then an upgrade event takes place and the previous version of the database doesn't exist anymore. Our database `tasksDb00` needs one or more object stores; these can only be created during an upgrade event. Here, in `_initDb`, we get a reference to the database object in line (7) and, in line (8), we create an object store (that can contain data records) named `TasksStore`; the value of the constant is `TASKS_STORE`:

```
void _initDb(VersionChangeEvent e) {
  var db = (e.target as Request).result;              (7)
  var objectStore = db.createObjectStore(TASKS_STORE  (8)
    autoIncrement: true);
}
```

The `autoIncrement` property, when true, lets the database generate unique primary keys for you. In a later spiral, we will also create an index to enhance query speed. A database can contain multiple object stores if needed, and our app can have access to multiple databases at once. After initialization, the `then` callback in line (6) kicks in, calling `_loadDb`:

```
Future _loadDb(Database db) {
    _db = db;
    var trans = db.transaction(TASKS_STORE, 'readonly');          (9)
    var store = trans.objectStore(TASKS_STORE);
    var cursors = store.openCursor(autoAdvance:                    (10)
        true).asBroadcastStream();
    cursors.listen((cursor) {                                      (11)
        var task = new Task.fromDb(cursor.key, cursor.value);
        tasks.add(task);
    });

    return cursors.length.then((_) {                              (12)
        return tasks.length;
    });
}
```

In order to make sure that it is reliable, every operation on the database happens within a transaction, so that transaction is created in line (9) and attached to the object store (this is also required for reads; the second argument can be readonly, readwrite, or versionchange). Database transactions take time, so the results are always provided via Futures. Getting records from a database is mostly done using a Cursor object, which is created here in line (10) with the openCursor method on the object store. The cursors object indicates the current position in the object store and returns the records one by one through a Stream object automatically because of the autoAdvance parameter (otherwise, use the `next()` method). For each record that returns, a listen event fires the code defined in line (11). Here, the database values cursor.key and cursor.value are given to the named Task constructor fromDb, so a new task is created and added to the list. A BroadcastStream method also returns the length of the cursor as a final event in line (12), which is also the length of the tasks collection. When a task is added, the add method on the store is called in line (2):

```
Future<Task> add(String title) {
    var task = new Task(title);
    var taskMap = task.toDb();                                     (13)
```

```
var transaction = _db.transaction(TASKS_STORE, 'readwrite');
var objectStore = transaction.objectStore(TASKS_STORE);

objectStore.add(taskMap).then((addedKey) {                    (14)
  task.key = addedKey;
});

return transaction.completed.then((_) {                       (15)
  tasks.add(task);
  return task;
});
}
```

The class `Task` has a `toDb` method called in line (13) to transform the `Task` object into a map. A read/write transaction is created and the `add` method is called on the store in line (14) with the task data. This also returns a Future, resulting in the key generated by the database (`addedKey`), which is also stored in the task object. When the transaction completes in line (15), the task is added to the collection and returned as the Future's result, which is then used in `view.dart` to update the view. Removing all objects from the store is easy; calling `clear` on the store in line (3) executes:

```
Future clear() {
    var transaction = _db.transaction(TASKS_STORE, 'readwrite');
    transaction.objectStore(TASKS_STORE).clear();
    return transaction.completed.then((_) {
      tasks.clear();
    });
}
```

This results in the clearing of the tasks collection and then the updating of the view. To see the data in your IndexedDB database at any moment, navigate to **Chrome View | Developer | Developer Tools**, and then choose **Resources** from the tabs along the top of the window:

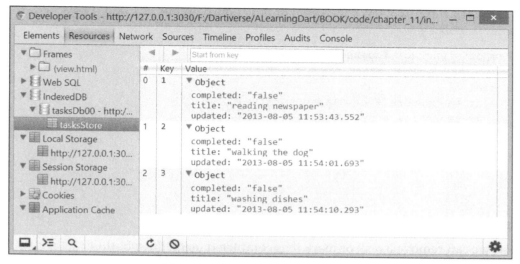

Viewing IndexedDb with developer tools

Spiral s01

No new functionality is added here, but the startup web page is renamed to `app.html` and the layout is improved through CSS. Furthermore, the methods are made private where possible and the app architecture is refactored to MVC by introducing a library in line (1); all of the UI code is moved from `view.dart` to the class `TasksView` in `lib/view/view.dart`, and the model code to `lib/model/model.dart`. Both are now contained in the library file `lib/indexed_db.dart`:

```dart
library indexed_db;                                        (1)

import 'dart:async';
import 'dart:html';
import 'dart:indexed_db';

part 'model/model.dart';
part 'view/view.dart';
```

The main Dart file `app.dart` imports our new library in line (2) and uses a `TasksView` object:

```
import 'package:indexed_db/indexed_db.dart';                    (2)

main() {
  var tasksStore = new TasksStore();
  var tasksView = new TasksView(tasksStore);
  tasksStore.open().then((_) {
    tasksView.loadElements(tasksStore.tasks);
  });
}
```

Spiral s02

Now, we can remove a task or mark it as completed using the x button:

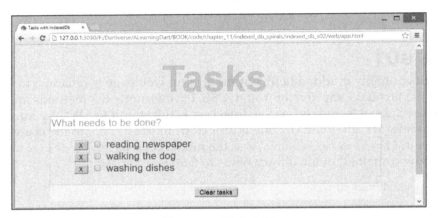

The screen of Spiral s02

To accomplish this, the `newElement` method is expanded a bit to draw the checkbox and remove button:

```
Element _newElement(Task task) {
    return new Element.html('''
        <li>
          <button class='task-button remove-task'>X</button>
          <input class='task-completed' type='checkbox'
            ${task.completed ? 'checked' : ''}>
          <label class='task-title'>${task.title}</label>
        </li>
    ''');
}
```

In `_addElement`, a click event handler on the `x` button is added, which removes the task from the object store:

```
tasksStore.remove(task).then((_) {
    _taskElements.nodes.remove(taskElement);
    _updateFooter();
});
```

The click event handler then calls the `remove` method in the class `TasksStore` to delete it in the object store:

```
Future remove(Task task) {
    var transaction = _db.transaction(TASKS_STORE, 'readwrite');
    transaction.objectStore(TASKS_STORE).delete(task.key);
    return transaction.completed.then((_) {
      task.key = null;
      tasks.remove(task);
    });
}
```

Clicking the checkbox to signal a task as complete invokes an update on the object store:

```
taskElement.querySelector('.task-completed').onClick.
listen((MouseEvent e) {
    task.completed = !task.completed;
    task.updated = new DateTime.now();
    tasksStore.update(task);
});

The update method transforms the Task object to a map and calls the
put method on the object store:
Future update(Task task) {
    var taskMap = task.toDb();
    var transaction = _db.transaction(TASKS_STORE, 'readwrite');
    transaction.objectStore(TASKS_STORE).put(taskMap, task.key);
    return transaction.completed;
}
```

Spiral s03

The new elements in this spiral are: a checkbox above the textbox to mark all tasks as completed, the number of active (incomplete) tasks is shown at the bottom, and a button to clear (remove) all completed tasks (their number is indicated in parentheses) is added. The active and completed tasks are returned by getters in the class `TasksStore`, for instance:

```
List<Task> get activeTasks {
    var active = new List<Task>();
    for (var task in tasks) {
      if (!task.completed) {
        active.add(task);
      }
    }
    return active;
}
```

In _initDb, we create a new database by changing the name and creating a unique index on the title by calling createIndex on the object store:

```
store.createIndex(TITLE_INDEX, 'title', unique: true);
```

The click handler for the "complete all tasks" button calls the following method:

```
Future completeTasks() {
    Future future;
    for (var task in tasks) {
      if (!task.completed) {
        task.completed = true;
        task.updated = new DateTime.now();
        future = update(task);
      }
    }
    return future;
}
```

In fact, this will only return the future of the last update. In this example, it will be the last one that completes, but it would be more correct to return a future that completes when all updates are complete. We'll make improvements in spirals s06 and s07.

All kinds of detailed screen updates are now assembled in _updateDisplay() in view.dart.

Spiral s04

Now, it has become a fully functional todo application with nice links to all active and completed task lists, the possibility of editing the task's title, and persisting the data in IndexedDB, as shown in the following screenshot:

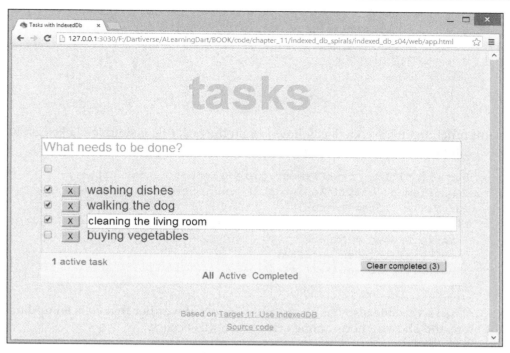

The screen of Spiral s04

The following code changes are worth discussing. In the previous spiral, a unique index on the title was created, but no error message was shown when a duplicate task was entered; the double task was simply not added and the IndexedDB error was ignored. Now, we do better using the `catchError` method in line (1) and changing the `Keypress` event handler of the input field to:

```
InputElement newTask = querySelector('#new-task');
newTask.onKeyPress.listen((KeyboardEvent e) {
  if (e.keyCode == KeyCode.ENTER) {
    var title = newTask.value.trim();
    if (title != '') {
      _tasksStore.add(title)
        .then((task) {
          _addElement(task);
          newTask.value = '';
          _updateFilter();
        })
```

```
          .catchError((e) {  // IndexedDB error unique index     (1)
              newTask.value = '${title} : title not unique';
              newTask.select();
          });
        }
      }
  });
```

The edit functionality is coded as follows when the task title is double-clicked on in line (2), and a textbox editTitle is shown in line (3) and selected:

```
Element title = taskElement.querySelector('.task-title');
InputElement editTitle = taskElement.querySelector('.edit-title');
editTitle.hidden = true;
title.onDoubleClick.listen((MouseEvent e) {                       (2)
  title.hidden = true;
  editTitle.hidden = false;                                       (3)
  editTitle.select();
});
```

The editTitle variable also has an onKeyPress event handler that calls an update on the store and shows a non-unique error when this occurs.

The model now has a find method based on querying the index in line along with get in line (4):

```
Future<Task> find(String title) {
    var trans = _db.transaction(TASKS_STORE, 'readonly');
    var store = trans.objectStore(TASKS_STORE);
    var index = store.index(TITLE_INDEX);
    var future = index.get(title);                                (4)
    return future
      .then((taskMap) {
        var task = new Task.fromDbWoutKey(taskMap);
        return task;
      });
  }
```

This is used in the _showActive and _showCompleted methods of the view:

```
_showCompleted() {
  _setSelectedFilter(_completedElements);
  for (LIElement element in _taskElements.children) {
    Element titleLabel = element.querySelector('.task-title');
    String title = titleLabel.text;
    _tasksStore.find(title)
```

```
     .then((task) {
       element.hidden = !task.completed;                          (5)
     })
     .catchError((e) {});
   }
 }
```

In line (5), we see that the task in the list is hidden when it is not yet completed.

Spiral s05

In this spiral, the UI and functionality remain the same, but the model is reorganized. The model code, which contains the class `Task` and a collection class `Tasks` (with methods, such as `sort`, `contains`, `find`, `add`, `remove`, and `display0` in `lib/model/model.dart`), is cleanly decoupled from the data access code: the classes `TasksDb` and `TasksStore` in `lib/model/idb.dart`. This makes it easier to change or enhance the model code or to use another data source by switching to a different data access layer, which is what we do in **Spiral s05_1**.

Using Lawndart

IndexedDB doesn't (yet) work on all browsers. What if you don't know what browser your clients will use? Can we still provide universal offline key-value storage? The solution is Lawndart (https://github.com/sethladd/lawndart), a pub package that you can import in your app, which has been developed by Seth Ladd as a Dart reworking of Lawnchair. Lawndart presents an asynchronous, but consistent, interface to local storage, IndexedDb, and Web SQL. Your app simply works with an instance of the class `Store` and the factory constructor will try IndexedDB, Web SQL, and then, finally, local storage. This is implemented in **Spiral s05_1**; the only change with **Spiral s05** is that IndexedDB (`idb.dart`) is replaced with Lawndart (`lawndart.dart`). For example, the `load` method is now written as:

```
Future load() {
    Stream dataStream = _store.all();
    return dataStream.forEach((taskMap) {
      var task = new Task.fromDb(taskMap);
      tasks.add(task);
    });
}
```

Study lawndart.dart to see how the interface code changes.

A Dart web server

The Dart VM can also run as a server application on the command line or as a background job. When creating the application, choose the command-line application template. Most of Dart's server functionality lives in the dart:io library, which cannot be used in writing browser Dart apps; in the same way, dart:html cannot be used on the server. The class HttpServer is used to write Dart servers; a server listens on a particular host and port for incoming requests and provides event handlers (so-called request handlers) that are triggered when a request with incoming data from a client is received. The latter is described by the class HttpRequest, which is an asynchronous API provided by the browser (formerly known as Ajax) and has properties, such as method, path, query parameters, and InputStream with the data. The server responds by writing to the OutputStream of an HttpResponse object. The following is the code of the project webserver, where you can easily see all parts interacting:

```
import 'dart:io';

main() {
  print('simple web server');
  HttpServer.bind('127.0.0.1', 8080).then((server) {
    print('server will start listening');
    server.listen((HttpRequest request) {
      print('server listened');
      request.response.write('Learn Dart by Projects, develop in
        Spirals!');
      request.response.close();
    });
  });
}
```

Firstly, start the server from the editor or on the command line with dart webserver. dart. Then, start (any) browser with the URL http://localhost:8080 to see the response text appear on the client; the print output appears in the server console.

Using JSON web services

In this section, we code a web server that communicates with our clients and runs the todo app; the todo data is sent to and from the web server in the JSON string format. **Spiral s06** consists of a server and a client part. To run it, first start the server (lib/server/server.dart) in Dart Editor or from the console; it runs when you see in the server.dart tab in Dart Editor: **Listening for GET and POST on http://127.0.0.1:8080**.

(If it does not run, navigate to **Run | Manage Launches**.) Then start one or more clients (web/app.html) in Dartium. Locally, the client still saves the data in IndexedDB. Our screen has two new buttons:

- **To server**: The client converts the the data to the JSON format and sends it to the server, where the data is stored in the main memory (post data to server)

- **From server**: An another client (on a different machine) can request the server data to update its local database (get data from server)

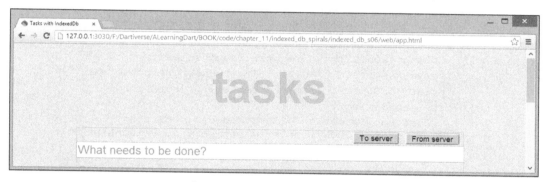

Server communication in Spiral s06

The following is the client code (from lib/view/view.dart) for **To server** (posting data):

```
ButtonElement toServer = querySelector('#to-server');
    toServer.onClick.listen((MouseEvent e) {
        var request = new HttpRequest();                          (1)
        request.onReadyStateChange.listen((_) {                   (2)
            if (request.readyState == HttpRequest.DONE &&
                request.status == 200) {
                // Data saved OK on server.
                serverResponse = 'Server: ' + request.responseText;
            } else if (request.readyState == HttpRequest.DONE &&
                request.status == 0) {
                // Status is 0...most likely the server isn't running.
                serverResponse = 'No server';
            }
        });

        var url = 'http://127.0.0.1:8080';
        request.open('POST', url);                                (3)
        request.send(_tasksStore.tasks.toJsonString());           (4)
    });
```

In line (1), a new client request is made; from line (3), we see that the method is POST; and in line (4), the data from the tasks collection is sent to the server. Then, the client listens to a possible server response (the status and responseText) in the onReadyStateChange event. HttpStatus 200 indicates that everything went fine. The code for "from server" (getting data) is shown as follows:

```
ButtonElement fromServer = querySelector('#from-server');
    fromServer.onClick.listen((MouseEvent e) {
      var request = new HttpRequest();
      request.onReadyStateChange.listen((_) {
        if (request.readyState == HttpRequest.DONE &&
            request.status == 200) {
          String jsonString = request.responseText;          (5)
          serverResponse = 'Server: ' + request.responseText;
          print('JSON text from the server: ${jsonString}');
          if (jsonString != '') {
            List<Map> jsonList = JSON.decode(jsonString);      (6)
              print('JSON list from the server: ${jsonList}');
            _tasksStore.loadFromJson(jsonList)                (7)
              .then((_) {
                var tasks = _tasksStore.tasks;
                _clearElements();
                loadElements(tasks);
              })
              .catchError((e) {
                print('error in loading data into IndexedDB from
                  JSON list');
              });
          }
        } else if (request.readyState == HttpRequest.DONE &&
            request.status == 0) {
          serverResponse = 'No server';
        }
      });

      var url = 'http://127.0.0.1:8080';
      request.open('GET', url);                               (8)
      request.send('update-me');
    });
```

In line (8), we see that this is a GET request; the response from the server containing the data is stored in jsonString in line (5), decoded in List<Map> in line (6), and added to IndexedDB through the loadFromJson method (line (7)). Of course, the print statements are only needed as a way to log what takes place and what can be left out. We will improve on this code in **Spiral s07**.

But, what happens on the server? The server is started up through the following code:

```dart
import 'dart:io';
import 'dart:convert';

const String HOST = "127.0.0.1"; // or: "localhost"
const int PORT = 8080;
List<Map> jsonList;

void main() {
  start();
}

start() {
  HttpServer.bind(HOST, PORT).then((server) {
    server.listen((HttpRequest request) {
      switch (request.method) {                              (1)
        case 'GET':
          handleGet(request);
          break;
        case 'POST':
          handlePost(request);
          break;
        case 'OPTIONS':
          handleOptions(request);
          break;
        default: defaultHandler(request);
      }
    },
    onError: print);                                         (2)
  })
    .catchError(print)
    .whenComplete(() => print('Listening for GET and POST on
      http://$HOST:$PORT'));
}
```

In line (1), in the `listen` handler, we now match the method of the request. Notice in line (2), the `onError` handler, which is, in fact, the second optional parameter of the `listen` method (`onError: print` could also be written as `onError: (e) => print(e)` to see an error in trying to start the server on port `80`, and then you get `SocketException`). Everything between lines (1) and (2) is the (anonymous) `onData` handler of `listen`.

In the "To Server" situation, handlePost is executed:

```
void handlePost(HttpRequest request) {
  print('${request.method}: ${request.uri.path}');
  request.listen((List<int> buffer) {                          (3)
    var jsonString = new String.fromCharCodes(buffer);
    jsonList = JSON.decode.(jsonString);                       (4)
    print('JSON list in POST: ${jsonList}');                   (5)
  },
  onError: print);
}
```

Here, in the listen handler, the client data is loaded in the buffer in line (3) and then decoded to the List<Map> jsonList variable on the server storing the data in memory (line (4)), and the server prints to its console in line (5):

```
POST: /
JSON list in POST: [{title: washing dishes, completed: true, updated:
2013-08-08 15:40:51.999}, {title: walking the dog, completed: true,
updated: 2013-08-08 10:30:47.794}, {title: cleaning the kitchen,
completed: false, updated: 2013-08-08 15:21:44.626}, {title: buying
vegetables, completed: false, updated: 2013-08-08 10:32:20.707}]
```

In the "From Server" situation, handleGet is executed:

```
void handleGet(HttpRequest request) {
  HttpResponse res = request.response;                         (6)
  print('${request.method}: ${request.uri.path}');
  addCorsHeaders(res);                                         (7)
  res.headers.contentType =
      new ContentType("application", "json", charset: 'utf-8');(8)
  if (jsonList != null) {
    String jsonString = JSON.encode(jsonList);                 (9)
    print('JSON list in GET: ${jsonList}');
    res.write(jsonString);                                     (10)
  }
  res.close();                                                 (11)
}
```

Here, the response is prepared from line (6) onward; line (8) sets the content type of the server response to the JSON text. In line (9), the server variable jsonList is encoded to a JSON string and written into the response stream in line (10), which is then closed in line (11). The server prints out:

```
GET: /
```

```
JSON list in GET: [{title: washing dishes, completed: true, updated:
2013-08-08 15:40:51.999}, {title: walking the dog, completed: true,
updated: 2013-08-08 10:30:47.794}, {title: cleaning the kitchen,
completed: false, updated: 2013-08-08 15:21:44.626}, {title: buying
vegetables, completed: false, updated: 2013-08-08 10:32:20.707}]
```

and the client then prints out:

```
JSON list from the server: ... same list as above ...
```

In line `(7)`, the method `addCorsHeaders` adds the following so-called **CORS (Cross Origin Resource Sharing)** headers to the response:

```
void addCorsHeaders(HttpResponse response) {
  response.headers.add('Access-Control-Allow-Origin', '*, ');
  response.headers.add('Access-Control-Allow-Methods', 'POST,
    OPTIONS');
  response.headers.add('Access-Control-Allow-Headers', 'Origin, X-
    Requested-With, Content-Type, Accept');
}
```

In order to prevent cross-site scripting attacks, browser vendors have added a **same-origin policy** to their browsers. If your web page comes from a server at URL domain1, you can only send requests to the same domain1. If the server sends CORS headers back in the response, the client can also send requests to other servers. In general, it is not safe to use CORS headers. However, for development purposes, it is useful to allow them so that you can run apps from Dart Editor that uses 3030 by default for its internal server.

Spiral s07

But wait! Something is not yet right; the data of a new client overwrites on the server the data from a previous client, so we have to implement some form of data integration:

- **To server** (POST) adds local tasks without conflicting titles to data on the server
- **From server** (GET) removes tasks with conflicting titles from local data and adds tasks without conflicting titles to local data

In `handlePost`, on the server (`bin/server.dart`), we now call `_integrateDataFro`
`mClient(jsonList)`, which contains the algorithm for the merging of tasks:

```
_integrateDataFromClient(List<Map> jsonList) {
  var clientTasks = new Tasks.fromJson(jsonList);
  var serverTasks = tasks;
  var serverTaskList = serverTasks.toList();
  for (var serverTask in serverTaskList) {
    if (!clientTasks.contains(serverTask.title)) {
      serverTasks.remove(serverTask);
    }
  }
  for (var clientTask in clientTasks) {
    if (serverTasks.contains(clientTask.title)) {
      var serverTask = serverTasks.find(clientTask.title);
      if (serverTask.updated.millisecondsSinceEpoch <
          clientTask.updated.millisecondsSinceEpoch) {
        serverTask.completed = clientTask.completed;
        serverTask.updated = clientTask.updated;
      }
    } else {
      serverTasks.add(clientTask);
    }
  }
}
```

This means that the server now has to know about the model (class `Task`/`Tasks`) to
realize that we now share the model between client and server by making it into a
library (`lib/shared_model.dart`):

```
library shared_model;
import 'dart:convert';
part 'model/model.dart';
```

and importing this in `server.dart` and `idb_client.dart`:

```
import 'package:client_server/shared_model.dart';
```

First, start the server and then two or more clients, for example, the first in Dartium
and the second in Chrome or another browser (run as JavaScript) (see `doc/use.txt`)
and juggle a few tasks between them!

The code for "From server" (getting data) in `lib\view\view.dart` is improved using a Future in `HttpRequest` in line `(1)`:

```
fromServer.onClick.listen((MouseEvent e) {
    HttpRequest.getString('http://127.0.0.1:8080')
      .then((result) {                                        (1)
        String jsonString = result;
        serverResponse = 'Server: ' + result;
        print('JSON text from the server: ${jsonString}');
        if (jsonString != '') {
          List<Map> jsonList = JSON.decode(jsonString);
          print('JSON list from the server: ${jsonList}');
          _tasksStore.loadDataFromServer(jsonList)
            .then((_) {
              var tasks = _tasksStore.tasks;
              _clearElements();
              loadElements(tasks);
            })
            .catchError((e) {
              print('error in loading data into IndexedDB from
                JSON list');
            });
        }
      });
});
```

Also, as an improvement to the `completeTasks` method in **Spiral s03,** we have now this `complete` method that now guarantees that it will wait until all update tasks are finished using `Future.wait` on a list `futureList` of all the following tasks:

```
Future complete() {
    var futureList = new List<Future>();
    for (var task in tasks) {
      if (!task.completed) {
        task.completed = true;
        task.updated = new DateTime.now();
        futureList.add(update(task));
      }
    }
    return Future.wait(futureList);
}
```

Summary

In this chapter, you got acquainted with using Futures in order to call methods asynchronously. We discussed the pros and cons of browser storage mechanisms and used the best mechanism (IndexedDB) extensively in a complete reworking of our `todo` app. We also looked at Lawndart for when you want to program against a uniform local storage interface. Then, we started with Dart on the server: how to write a web server and how to communicate between clients and the server. With it, we rewrote our app into a real client-server app, and stored data locally on the clients and in the memory on the server.

However, any system failure can have server memory loss as a result and, most probably, we do want to have more persistent central data storage; this is the topic of the following chapter.

12
Data-driven Web Applications with MySQL and MongoDB

Data is usually stored on a server in a database; in order to do that, our Dart app needs a middle layer called a **database driver**. We'll review which drivers are already available and then see how you can store and access your data on the server with MySQL and MongoDB. These are two of the most popular databases: MySQL is a typical relational database, and MongoDB is a NoSQL database (according to the following link, http://db-engines.com/en/ranking, MySQL is second in popularity after Oracle, and MongoDB occupies the sixth place). The following are the topics covered in this chapter:

- Database drivers for Dart
- Storing the todo data in MySQL
- Dartlero tasks: a many-to-many model in MySQL and JSON
- MongoDB: a NoSQL database
- Using the mongo_dart driver to store the todo data in MongoDB

Database drivers for Dart

The amazing Dart community has already provided a whole spectrum of drivers (**(P)** means published in the pub repository, pub.dartlang.org).

For the relational databases we have:

- **MySQL**: An actively developed connector called SQLJocky (P) by *James Ots*; we will use this driver in the next section (https://github.com/jamesots/sqljocky)

- **PostgreSQL**: A driver called `postgresql` (P) by Greg Lowe (`https://github.com/xxgreg/postgresql`)

- **SQLite**: A native extension library called `Dart-sqlite` by Sam McCall (`https://github.com/sam-mccall/dart-sqlite/`)

- **ODBC-driver**: A library called `dart-odbc` (P) by Juan Mellado; this allows connections to any database vendor (Oracle, MySQL, PostgreSQL, SQLServer, and so on) with legacy ODBC drivers (`http://code.google.com/p/dart-odbc/`)

For the NoSQL databases, the choice is even greater:

- **MongoDB**: This is a driver called `mongo_dart` (P) by Vadim Tsushko, Ted Sander, and Paul Evans; we'll use it in this chapter (`https://github.com/vadimtsushko/mongo_dart`). Another client by Vadim Tsushko is an object document mapper tool called **Objectory**, which can be used on the client as well as the server (`https://github.com/vadimtsushko/objectory`).

- **CouchDB**: This is a driver called `couchclient` (P) by Henri Chen. Another driver called `wilt` (P) is created by S. Hamblett (`https://github.com/shamblett/wilt`).

- **Redis**: This is a driver called `redis-dart` by Adam Singer (`https://github.com/financeCoding/redis-dart`). Another Redis client called `DartRedisClient` (P) is created by Dartist (`https://github.com/dartist/redis_client`).

- **Riak**: This is a driver called `riak-dart` (P) by Istvan Soos and Ian Jones (`https://code.google.com/p/riak-dart/`).

- **RethinkDB**: This is a driver called `rethinkdb` (P) by Dave Bettin (`https://github.com/dbettin/rethinkdb`).

- **HashMap**: This is a driver called `dart-dirty` (P) by Chris Strom, a dirt simple NoSQL DB that is a persistent, server-side HashMap (`https://github.com/eee-c/dart-dirty`).

There also exists an **Object Relational Mapper (ORM)** framework:

- Dorm: This framework is created by Frank Pepermans. It provides an ORM mapping on the client, and the goal is to hook it up with existing server-side ORM solutions (Hibernate, Entity Framework, and so on) (`https://github.com/frankpepermans/dorm`).

Storing todo data in MySQL

Building further on **Spiral s07** from the previous chapter, we will now add the functionality to store our data on the server in a MySQL database. The project is named `todo_mysql` and the code can be obtained from `https://github.com/dzenanr/todo_mysql`.

It contains three subprojects: one for the client, which is the same as the client portion of `client_server_db_s07` in the project `indexed_db_spirals` from *Chapter 11, Local Data and Client-Server Communication*, and two server projects, both with MySQL. The server projects are equivalent in functionality: `todo_server_mysql` uses MySQL directly and `todo_server_dartling_mysql` is built with a task model in Dartling, to show how the database is updated by reacting to changes in the model. Both the server projects need to talk to MySQL, so they have the dependency `sqljocky: any` in their `pubspec.yaml`, to import the MySQL driver. But, of course, we also need the database software, so download and install the MySQL Community Server installer from `http://dev.mysql.com/downloads/mysql/`. This is straightforward, but in case you need any help with the installation, visit `http://dev.mysql.com/doc/refman/5.7/en/installing.html`.

Be sure that the MySQL server process (`mysqld`) is started before going further. Then start the MySQL Workbench tool (contained in the download) and create a new empty database (schema) with the name `todo`. We need only one table, `task`, which you can easily drag-and-drop using this tool; you can also run the Dart script from `test/mysql_test.dart` to create and populate the table with some initial data (recommended to avoid errors in a creation of the table).

```
You can now run the app as follows; run the server first:
todo_server_mysql/bin/server.dart
```

Alternatively, you can run the following in the Dart Editor:

```
todo_server_dartling_mysql/bin/server.dart
```

When you run, the output you see in the `server.dart` tab in Dart Editor is as follows: **Server at** `http://127.0.0.1:8080`.

If it does not run, navigate to **Run | Manage Launches** (put a path to the project folder; for example, `d:\todo_mysql\todo_server_mysql` in the working directory field in **Run | Manage Launches** in order to have access to the `connection.options` file). Run the first client in Dartium (`todo_client_idb/web/app.html`), and the second client as JavaScript (`todo_client_idb/web/app.html`) in Chrome.

Use the client app in Dartium to add, update, or remove a task. The screen hasn't changed since the screenshot showing the screen in **Spiral s04** and the server communication in **Spiral s06** (*Chapter 11, Local Data and Client-Server Communication*). Send it by pushing the **To Server** button where it is stored in the database; check this by viewing the task table data in MySQL Workbench. The second client can then retrieve this data using the **From Server** button. Experiment with the data by adding other clients; remember, that all the clients also store the data locally in IndexedDB.

How do we go about storing our data in MySQL? We'll first examine the `todo_server_mysql` project. The code that interacts with `sqljocky` sits in `lib/model/mysql.dart` and contains the classes `TodoDb` and `TaskTable`. The model, together with the data access layer, is contained in `library todo_server_mysql`, which is imported in `bin/server.dart`.

The code starts executing with the `main()` function in `server.dart`: a `todoDb` object is made on which (asynchronously) the open method is called, a connection is made with MySQL, and the task data is loaded in `taskTable`, and finally the webserver is started:

```
void main() {
  var todoDb = new TodoDb();
  todoDb.open().then((_) {
    taskTable = todoDb.taskTable;
    start();    // start webserver
  });
}
```

In order to connect to a MySQL server and database, we need a minimal set of configuration settings that our app needs to read: a username, password, database, hostname, and a port number. These are stored as the `key=value` pairs in the file `connection.options`:

```
# connection.options defines how to connect to a MySQL db
user=root
password=xyz # fill in your own password
port=3306
db=todo
host=localhost
```

The `connection.options` file sits right beneath the `project` directory. In order to have access to it from our app, or any file with a `main` method that you run, we need to navigate to **Run** | Manage Launches from the **Dart Editor** menu, and put a path to the project folder (`todo_mysql`) in the working directory field. The quickest way to do this is to run it first; it will fail because it doesn't find the file, but then you have a readymade **Manage Launch** window for inserting the right path.

To read the contents of such a file in Dart, create an object of the class `OptionsFile`, passing it the filename (see line (1) in the following code). This class comes from the `options_file` package by *James Ots*, available from pub; in order to use it, we must include the following in our library file:

```
import 'package:options_file/options_file.dart';
```

Line (3) and onwards, the `getString` or `getInt` method is used, which, given the key name, provides the value. Here is how it is done in the `TodoDb` class from `lib/model/mysql.dart`:

```
class TodoDb {
  TaskTable _taskTable;
  TaskTable get taskTable => _taskTable;

  Future open() {
    var pool = getPool(new OptionsFile('connection.options'));  (1)
    _taskTable = new TaskTable(pool);
    return _taskTable.load();
  }

  ConnectionPool getPool(OptionsFile options) {                 (2)
    String user = options.getString('user');                   (3)
    String password = options.getString('password');
    int port = options.getInt('port', 3306);
    String db = options.getString('db');
    String host = options.getString('host', 'localhost');
    return new ConnectionPool(                                  (4)
      host: host, port: port, user: user, password: password,
        db: db);
  }
}
```

With these values, the method `getPool` (starting in line (2)) builds a `ConnectionPool` object in line (4), which knows everything needed to connect to the MySQL database. This is returned from this method and assigned to the variable `pool` in line (1). On the next line, a `TaskTable` object is constructed on which the `load` method is called. When the server starts, it loads data from MySQL to the model in the main memory. When the model changes, the database is updated. Our code continues executing in the class `TaskTable`:

```
class TaskTable {
  final ConnectionPool _pool;
  Tasks _tasks;

  TaskTable(this._pool) {
    _tasks = new Tasks.withTable(this);
  }

  Tasks get tasks => _tasks;
  bool get isEmpty => tasks.length == 0;

  Future load() {                                          (1)
    Completer completer = new Completer();                 (2)
    _pool.query(                                           (3)
      'select t.title, t.completed, t.updated '
      'from task t '
    ).then((rows) {                                        (4)
      var taskMap;
      rows.listen((row) {                                  (5)
        taskMap = {
          'title'    : '${row[0]}',                        (6)
          'completed': '${row[1]}',
          'updated'  : '${row[2]}'
        };
        var task = new Task.fromDb(taskMap);               (7)
        tasks.load(task);
      },
        onError: (e) => print('data loading error: $e'),   (8)
        onDone: () {
          completer.complete();                            (9)
          print('all tasks loaded');
        }
      );
    });
    return completer.future;                               (10)
  }
}
```

The load method in line (1) executes asynchronously, so it returns a Future (so do all methods accessing the database). But we also see, here in line (1), the use of an intermediate instance of the class Completer from the dart:async library.

When the asynchronous code becomes more complex, the use of a `Completer` method helps write more maintainable and readable code. Using the `Completer` method, you can explicitly indicate when the Future value will be available by calling the `complete` method as in line (9) in the `onDone` handler. This signals the Future that the asynchronous operation has been completed. At the end of the `load` method, the Future value is returned in line (10) as `completer.future`. The code of the load method can seem daunting at first sight; let's analyze it step-by-step with the help of the many built-in functions in the editor (another visual theme from **Tools | Preferences** can also be useful). MySQL is a relational database, so at some point, our code will have to construct the SQL statements to be sent to the database for execution. In line (3), the `query` method (defined in `sqljocky`) is called on the pool object with a SQL string as the parameter; the following is the signature taken from the pop-up window when the cursor hovers over query:

```
Future<Results> query(String sql)
```

As we expected, query returns a Future; so, a `then` clause has to follow in line (4). The following is the signature:

```
Future then( onValue(Results) -> dynamic, { onError(Object) ->
    dynamic})
```

From this we see that it has an `onValue` handler to process the results and an optional `onError` handler. In our code, we have an anonymous `onValue` handler that runs all the way down to stop just before line (10):

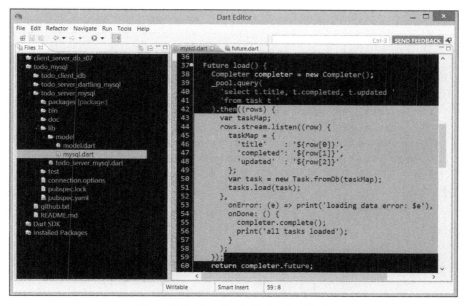

The onValue handler in the load method

The retrieved rows come in like a stream; the `stream` getter has a `listen` method to subscribe to this stream with the signature:

```
StreamSubscription<Row> listen( onData(Row) -> void, {
  onError(dynamic) ->  void, onDone() -> void, bool  cancelOnError}
 )
```

It has an `onData` handler that is called for every row that comes in, and the optional `onError` and `onDone` handlers. The `onData` handler is again an anonymous method and stretches from line (4) just up to line (8). Here, the data is extracted using an indexing operator `row[i]`. With string interpolation, we construct a literal map `taskMap` from which a `Task` object is made and added to the tasks collection; so, all the task data is in the server memory. Then, we see `onError`, which prints possible errors, and `onDone`, which signals the completion of the `async` operation in line (9). The value of the Future is returned in line (10).

The `_integrateDataFromClient` method in `bin/server.dart` updates the data in the server memory and the database (we'll see this shortly):

```
_integrateDataFromClient(List<Map> jsonList) {
  var clientTasks = new Tasks.fromJson(jsonList);
  var serverTasks = taskTable.tasks;
  var serverTaskList = serverTasks.toList();
  for (var serverTask in serverTaskList) {
    if (!clientTasks.contains(serverTask.title)) {
      serverTasks.remove(serverTask);                          (1)
    }
  }

  for (var clientTask in clientTasks) {
    if (serverTasks.contains(clientTask.title)) {
      var serverTask = serverTasks.find(clientTask.title);
      if (serverTask.updated.millisecondsSinceEpoch <
          clientTask.updated.millisecondsSinceEpoch) {
        serverTask.completed = clientTask.completed;
        serverTask.updated = clientTask.updated;
      }
    } else {
      serverTasks.add(clientTask);                             (2)
    }
  }
}
```

The remove and add methods in lines (1) and (2) are found in model.dart (use **Open Declaration** from the context menu), and in turn they call the delete and insert methods from mysql.dart. The update method gets called in the completed and updated setters in model.dart. Let us look a bit deeper at these methods, for example, the insert method:

```
Future<Task> insert(Task task) {
    var completer = new Completer();
    var taskMap = task.toDb();
    _pool.prepare(                                          (1)
      'insert into task (title, completed, updated) values (?, ?,
        ?)'
    ).then((query) {
      print("prepared query insert into task");
      var params = new List();                              (2)
      params.add(taskMap['title']);
      params.add(taskMap['completed']);
      params.add(taskMap['updated']);
      return query.execute(params);                         (3)
    }).then((_) {
      print("executed query insert into task");
      completer.complete();                                 (4)
    }).catchError(print);                                   (5)
    return completer.future;
}
```

Here, we see that the SQL of the query is first prepared in line (1) (a sort of parse step in the database), which returns a Future. In the returned result, the task data is inserted in the ? placeholders using a list that contains the parameter values. This list is constructed in line (2) and the subsequent lines. Then, the execute method is called on the query in line (3), again returning a Future. The async operation is marked as completed in line (4). Note, the error handling in line (5); always include this while dealing with the database access. Now, you'll be able to understand the update and delete methods by yourself, as shown in the following code:

```
Future<Task> update(Task task) {
    var completer = new Completer();
    var taskMap = task.toDb();
    _pool.prepare(
      'update task set completed = ?, updated = ? where title = ?'
      ).then((query) {
```

```
          print("prepared query update task");
          var params = new List();
          params.add(taskMap['completed']);
          params.add(taskMap['updated']);
          params.add(taskMap['title']);
          return query.execute(params);
      }).then((_) {
        print("executed query update task");
        completer.complete();
      }).catchError(print);
      return completer.future;
  }


  Future<Task> delete(Task task) {
    var completer = new Completer();
    var taskMap = task.toDb();
    _pool.prepare(
      'delete from task where title = ?'
    ).then((query) {
      print("prepared query delete from task");
                var params = new List();
        params.add(taskMap['title']);
      return query.execute(params);
    }).then((_) {
      print("executed query delete from task");
      completer.complete();
    }).catchError(print);
    return completer.future;
  }
}
```

You have now seen a complete data access layer to a relational database in action!

The second project todo_server_dartling_mysql builds upon the dartling_ todo_mvc_spirals project in *Chapter 9, Modeling More Complex Applications with Dartling*. Dartling was used to model tasks and generate a code basis; so the lib/ gen code is the same. The data access code lives in lib/persistence/mysql.dart. With Dartling, a model is not dependent on MySQL — the model does not call insert, update, and delete methods (with the SQL code). The TodoDb class, in its constructor, starts listening to the actions of the Dartling model:

```
domain.startActionReaction(this);
```

In the react method, the `TodoDb` class reacts to actions in the Dartling model.

```
react(ActionApi action) {
  if (action is AddAction) {
    taskTable.insert((action as AddAction).entity);
  } else if (action is RemoveAction) {
    taskTable.delete((action as RemoveAction).entity);
  } else if (action is SetAttributeAction) {
    taskTable.update((action as SetAttributeAction).entity);
  }
}
```

In this way, one may use more than one database with Dartling without updating the model code. The `_integrateDataFromClient` method now works with the model's actions (such as `AddAction` and `RemoveAction`):

```
_integrateDataFromClient(List<Map> jsonList) {
  var clientTasks = new Tasks.fromJson(db.tasks.concept, jsonList);
  var serverTaskList = db.tasks.toList();
  for (var serverTask in serverTaskList) {
    var clientTask =
        clientTasks.singleWhereAttributeId('title',
          serverTask.title);
    if (clientTask == null) {
      new RemoveAction(db.session, db.tasks, serverTask).doit();
    }
  }
  for (var clientTask in clientTasks) {
    var serverTask =
        db.tasks.singleWhereAttributeId('title',
          clientTask.title);
    if (serverTask != null) {
      if (serverTask.updated.millisecondsSinceEpoch <
          clientTask.updated.millisecondsSinceEpoch) {
        new SetAttributeAction(
          db.session, serverTask, 'completed',
            clientTask.completed).doit();
      }
    } else {
      new AddAction(db.session, db.tasks, clientTask).doit();
    }
  }
}
```

To experiment with this version, first run the `bin/server.dart` server, and then one or more clients from `todo_client_idb`.

Dartlero tasks – a many-to-many model in MySQL

A one-table project is quite unrealistic; let us now revisit the `dartlero_project_tasks` application in *Chapter 8, Developing Business Applications with Polymer Web Components*. This has a many-to-many relationship between the concepts Project and Employee, Task being the intermediate concept; data is stored only in the browser's local storage. In the `dartlero_tasks` project (code can be cloned from `https://github.com/dzenanr/dartlero_tasks`), we have the same model built on Dartlero, but the data can be stored on the server either in the JSON format or in a MySQL database. The startup script for both the options is `bin/dartlero_tasks.dart`. The model and the data access layer are defined in `library dartlero_tasks lib/model/darlero_tasks.dart`.

The JSON storage

If you want to use the JSON file storage, you have to create a command-line launch for the `bin/dartlero_tasks.dart` script. In **Run | Manage Launches** of Dart Editor, enter two script arguments (`--dir` and `path`), for example:

```
--dir C:/Users/"username"/git/dartlero/dartlero_tasks/json_data
  (on Windows)
--dir /home/username/git/dartlero/dartlero_tasks/json_data (on
  Linux)
```

By running the `main` function in the `bin/dartlero_tasks.dart` file, a model, with two entry points, will be initialized and saved in the given directory. For each entry concept, a file with the concept name and the `.json` extension will be created. The next time the program is run, data from the two files will be loaded. View the data in the JSON documents with a text editor, or use a JSON pretty printer. Let's dig into the code; first, let's examine `bin/dartlero_tasks.dart`:

```
import 'package:dartlero_tasks/dartlero_tasks.dart';           (1)

void main(List<String> arguments) {
  var model = TasksModel.one();

  try {
    if (arguments.length == 2 && (arguments s[0] == '--dir')) {
      model.persistence = 'json';
```

```
          model.jsonDirPath = args[1];
          if (!model.loadFromJson()) {                        (3)
            model.init();
            model.saveToJson();
          }
          model.display();
        }
      } else if (arguments s.length == 1 && (arguments s[0] == '--mysql'))
    {
            // code for MySQL storage
      } else {
        print('No arguments: consult README');
      }
    } catch (e) {
      print('consult README: $e');
    }
  }
```

The arguments are passed to main as a List<String> property with the same name, on an object from this class, constructed in line (3). The loadFromJson method from lib/model/model.dart reads in the JSON files with:

```
    File employeesFile = getFile(employeesFilePath);
    // ... code left out
    String employeesFileText = readTextFromFile(employeesFile);
```

The getFile and readTextFromFile variables are defined in lib/model/file_persistence.dart; this file contains all the methods from the project that directly use dart:io:

```
part of dartlero_tasks;

Directory getDir(String path) {
  var dir = new Directory(path);
  if (dir.existsSync()) {
    print('directory ${path} exists already');
  } else {
    dir.createSync();
    print('directory created: ${path}');
  }
  return dir;
}
```

```
File getFile(String path) {
  File file = new File(path);
  if (file.existsSync()) {
    print('file ${path} exists already');
  } else {
    file.createSync();
    print('file created: ${path}');
  }
  return file;
}

addTextToFile(File file, String text) {
  IOSink writeSink = file.openWrite();
  writeSink.write(text);
  writeSink.close();
}

String readTextFromFile(File file) {
  return file.readAsStringSync();
}
```

The methods in dart:io work asynchronously by default; for example, the create, exists, open, read, and write methods all return a Future. These should be used in the real production apps. To simplify the code in our case, we used their synchronous counterparts, createSync and existsSync, for the directory, reading the entire content of the file as a string with readAsStringSync. Writing the files is done when the model saves itself with the saveToJson method in model.dart. This calls addTextToFile, and here we see that openWrite is called on the file object, returning an object of the class IOSink, a helper class that is used to write to a file. It contains a buffer, which must be closed explicitly when the writing is completed. Take some time to explore the API for dart:io, especially the file methods and properties. (http://api.dartlang.org/docs/releases/latest/dart_io.html)

MySQL storage

For using the MySQL storage, use the script argument --mysql in **Run | Manage Launches** of Dart Editor. There is no need to create a new database (the default database test will be used), but do not forget to start the MySQL server. Before running a Dart file with main, put a path to the project folder dartlero_tasks in the working directory field in **Run | Manage Launches**, in order to have access to the connection.options file.

Run `example/mysql/example.dart` to drop and create all the tables; the following output appears (every script produces some output to monitor its execution):

```
opening connection
connection open
running example
dropping tables
dropped tables
creating tables
executing queries
created tables
prepared query 1
executed query 1
prepared query 2
executed query 2
prepared query 3
executed query 3
querying
got results
bye
```

In the following screenshot, you see the `project` table contents in SQL Workbench after execution:

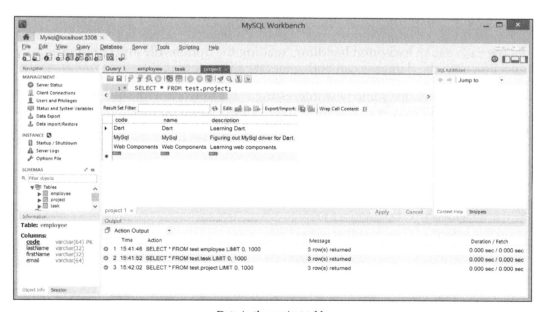

Data in the project table

The following is the `main` method:

```
void main() {
  try {
    OptionsFile options = new OptionsFile('connection.options');
    String user = options.getString('user');
    String password = options.getString('password');
    int port = options.getInt('port', 3306);
    String db = options.getString('db');
    String host = options.getString('host', 'localhost');
    // create a connection
    print('opening connection');
    var pool = new ConnectionPool(host: host, port: port, user:
      user, password: password, db: db);
    print('connection open');
    // create an example class
    var example = new Example(pool);
    // run the example
    print('running example');
    example.run().then((_) {
      // finally, close the connection
      print('bye');
      pool.close();
    });
  } catch(e) {
    print('consult README: $e');
  }
}
```

Note the `try/catch` exception handling; reading the options file and opening a connection with the database can both generate an exception.

The script itself contains some new interesting ways to work with sqljocky. It reads the options file and makes a `ConnectionPool` object based on this info. It then makes an example object and calls run on it:

```
Future run() {
    var completer = new Completer();
    dropTables()
      .then((_) => createTables())
      .then((_) => addData())
      .then((_) => readData())
      .then((_) => completer.complete())
      .catchError( (e) => print(e) );
    return completer.future;
}
```

This is a good example of how methods that return a Future can be chained in a succession of the `then` calls. This produces elegant and readable code. The `dropTables` method uses a `TableDropper` object to drop a list of tables:

```
Future dropTables() {
    print("dropping tables");
    var dropper = new TableDropper(pool, ['task', 'employee',
        'project']);
    return dropper.dropTables();
}
```

The `createTables` Future uses a `QueryRunner` object. Its `executeQueries` method can execute a list of SQL statements:

```
Future createTables() {
    print("creating tables");
    var querier = new QueryRunner(pool,
        [
            'create table employee (code varchar(64) not null, '
            'lastName varchar(32) not null, '
            'firstName varchar(32) not null, '
            'email varchar(64) not null, '
            'primary key (code))',

            'create table project (code varchar(64) not null, '
            'name varchar(64) not null, '
            'description varchar(256), '
            'primary key (code))',

            'create table task (code varchar(128) not null, '
            'projectCode varchar(64), '
            'employeeCode varchar(64), '
            'description varchar(256), '
            'primary key (code), '
            'foreign key (projectCode) references project (code), '
            'foreign key (employeeCode) references employee (code))'
        ]);
    print("executing queries");
    return querier.executeQueries();
}
```

The `addData` Future shows how a prepared SQL statement with parameters (as before each `?` is a parameter that needs a value) can be given a list of `Lists`, where each inner list contains all the parameter values for one statement. The `executeMulti` method on the query executes the statements in succession:

```
Future addData() {
    var completer = new Completer();
    pool.prepare(
        "insert into employee (code, lastName, firstName, email)
         values (?, ?, ?, ?)"
      ).then((query) {
    print("prepared query 1");
    var parameters = [
        ["dzenanr@gmail.com", "Ridjanovic", "Dzenan",
         "dzenanr@gmail.com"],
        ["timur.ridjanovic@gmail.com", "Ridjanovic", "Timur",
         "timur.ridjanovic@gmail.com"],
        ["ma.seyer@gmail.com", "Seyer", "Marc-Antoine",
         "ma.seyer@gmail.com"]
      ];
    return query.executeMulti(parameters);
  }).then((results) {
    print("executed query 1");
    // code left out
```

The other scripts in the `example/mysql` folder use the same techniques to populate each table separately.

The project also contains test scripts exercising the Dart `unittest`; for example, `test/mysql/employee_test.dart` for employee data; the following is the main code:

```
main() {
  try {
    var pool = getPool(new OptionsFile('connection.options'));
    dropTables(pool)
      .then((_) => createTable(pool))
      .then((_) => initData(pool))
      .then((_) => testProjects(pool));
  } catch(e) {
    print('consult README: $e');
  }
}
```

The testing output is:

```
PASS: Testing employees Select all employees
PASS: Testing employees Select Ridjanovic employees
PASS: Testing employees Select all employees, then select Ridjanovic
employees
```

```
All 3 tests passed.
unittest-suite-success
selected all employees
count: 1 - code: dzenanr@gmail.com, last name: Ridjanovic, first name:
Dzenan, email: dzenanra@gmil.com
 // other data.
```

The following is the code of the `testing` method:

```
testEmployees(ConnectionPool pool) {
    group("Testing employees", () {
    test("Select all employees", () {
        var count = 0
        pool.query(
            'select e.code, e.lastName, e.firstName, e.email '
            'from employee e '
        ).then((rows) {
          print("selected all employees");
          rows.stream.listen((row) {
              count++;
            print(
                'count: $count - '
                'code: ${row[0]}, '
                'last name: ${row[1]}, '
                'first name: ${row[2]}, '
                'email: ${row[3]}'
            );
          }).onDone(() => expect(count, equals(3)));
        });
    });

    test("Select Ridjanovic employees", () {
      pool.query(
          'select e.code, e.lastName, e.firstName, e.email '
          'from employee e '
          'where e.lastName = "Ridjanovic" '
      ).then((rows) {
        print("selected Ridjanovic employees");
        rows.stream.listen((row) {
            expect(row[1], equals('Ridjanovic'));
          print(
              'code: ${row[0]}, '
              'last name: ${row[1]}, '
              'first name: ${row[2]}, '
```

```
                        'email: ${row[3]}'
                    );
                });
            });
        });

        test("Select all employees, then select Ridjanovic employees",
    () {
            var futures = new List<Future>();                        (1)
            var completer = new Completer();
            futures.add(completer.future);                           (2)
                var count = 0;
            pool.query(
                'select e.code, e.lastName, e.firstName, e.email '
                'from employee e '
            ).then((rows) {
              print("selected all employees");
              rows.stream.listen((row) {
                count++;
                print(
                        'count: $count - '
                    'code: ${row[0]}, '
                    'last name: ${row[1]}, '
                    'first name: ${row[2]}, '
                    'email: ${row[3]}'
                );
                 }).onDone(() {
                    expect(count, equals(3));
                    completer.complete();
                });
            });

            Future.wait(futures).then((futures) {                    (3)
              pool.query(
                  'select e.code, e.lastName, e.firstName, e.email '
                  'from employee e '
                  'where e.lastName = "Ridjanovic" '
              ).then((rows) {
                print("selected Ridjanovic employees");
                rows.stream.listen((row) {
```

```
        expect(row[1], equals('Ridjanovic'));
      print(
        'code: ${row[0]}, '
        'last name: ${row[1]}, '
        'first name: ${row[2]}, '
        'email: ${row[3]}'
      );
    });
  });
 });
});
});
}
```

In the test ("Select all employees, then select Ridjanovic employees"), we see how we can wait for the execution of the code until all Futures contained in a list have terminated. In line (1), List<Future> is defined, and in line (2), a Future object is added to the list. In line (3), the static method wait is called on Future: it waits until all the methods in its List argument (here only one) have returned their Future value. Run test/mysql/project_test.dart to test the projects table:

```
dropping tables
creating project table
initializing project data
prepared query insert into project
executed query insert into project
unittest-suite-wait-for-done
PASS: Select all projects

All 1 tests passed.
unittest-suite-success
selected all projects
count: 1 - code: Dart, name: Dart, description: Learning Dart.
count: 2 - code: MySql, name: MySql, description: Figuring out MySql
driver for Dart.
count: 3 - code: Web Components, name: Web Components, description:
Learning web components.
```

MongoDB – a NoSQL database

Many NoSQL databases exist in the market today, but MongoDB, by the company with the same name (http://www.mongodb.org/), is the most popular among them. An important distinction between relational and NoSQL databases is that NoSQL databases are **schema-less**; this means you don't have to define the tables before inserting data. This in itself, of course, adds a lot to the flexibility and agility in the use of these databases; for example, adding a new field no longer means that you have to alter the table and run the SQL update commands. As there are no SQL queries to be used here, all the data retrieval happens via standard **CRUD** calls (create, read, update, and delete). In MongoDB, this is known as insert, find, update, and remove. MongoDB presents itself as an open source, distributed, document-oriented database: each data record is actually a document. A table is called a collection in MongoDB. Documents are stored in a JSON-like format called **Binary JSON (BSON)**. BSON documents are objects that contain an ordered list of saved elements; each element comprises a field name, and a value, which is of a specific type. BSON is designed to be more efficient than JSON, both in storage space and reading speed, adding to the performance for which MongoDB is known. In a MongoDB database, you can query data not only through keys and secondary keys, but also with ranges and regular expressions; indexes can be applied to pretty much everything, such as 2D and 3D spatial data; there's absolutely no limitation.

To guarantee high availability, a master-slave replication (so-called **replica-sets**) is built. For Big Data applications, support for spreading data across multiple servers (so-called **auto-sharding**) is a key feature, making MongoDB a very scalable solution. Install the latest production release for your system from http://www.mongodb.org/downloads.

This is easy; for details refer http://docs.mongodb.org/manual/installation/.

A number of binaries are installed in the bin map; amongst them are mongod, which is the server (or daemon) process, and mongo, which is a command-line client. The following is a good tutorial to get started: http://docs.mongodb.org/manual/tutorial/getting-started/. Start the mongod server process (for example, from c:\mongodb\bin on Windows) before going further. If all is well, you should see an output similar to the following on the console:

```
Fri Aug 23 10:57:19.256 [initandlisten] MongoDB starting : pid=1568
port=27017 db
path=\data\db\ 64-bit host=predator
Fri Aug 23 10:57:19.258 [initandlisten] db version v2.4.5
```

To close the MongoDB server safely, issue a *Ctrl + C* in the console. Before using a Dart driver, let's get acquainted a bit with the Mongo shell, which works with JavaScript, and communicates directly with MongoDB. Open a console window and start the command: `mongo`. The following output appears, telling us that we are using the default database test and showing us a prompt:

```
MongoDB shell version: 2.4.5
connecting to: test
>
```

Suppose we want to save stock data; for example, GOOG (the symbol), Google Inc. (the company's name), and its current rating 13. We will call our database invest. Switch to that database with `use invest`, which returns `switched to db invest`. At this point, the database doesn't really exist as it doesn't contain any data. In MongoDB, data is stored in collections, allowing you to separate documents if required. Let's create a document and store it as a new collection named `stocks`:

```
db.stocks.save({symbol:"GOOG",name:"Google Inc.",rating:13});
```

Save some other data as follows:

Symbol	Company	Current rating
MSFT	Microsoft Technologies	7
KOG	Kodiak Oil & Gas Corp	11
AAPL	Apple Inc	11
CSCO	Cisco Systems	12

Our collection now contains five documents; retrieve them with `db.stocks.find()`:

```
{"_id" : ObjectId("521df951abd1215f4673c8ed"), "symbol" : "GOOG",
  "name" : "Google Inc.", "rating" : 13 }
{ "_id" : ObjectId("521df997abd1215f4673c8ee"), "symbol" : "MSFT",
  "name" : "Microsoft Technologies", "rating" : 7 }
{ "_id" : ObjectId("521df9caabd1215f4673c8ef"), "symbol" : "KOG",
  "name" : "Kodiak Oil & Gas Corp", "rating" : 10 }
// 2 other documents left out
```

The `_id` attribute is a unique identifier generated by MongoDB, and will be different in your result. Documents can be way more complex than these, storing various data types including strings, integers, floats, dates, arrays, and other objects. Suppose we only want to see the stocks with a rating greater than 11; the query gives us GOOG and CSCO:

```
db.stocks.find({rating:{$gt:11}});
```

For example, sorting on the symbol is also easy:

```
db.stocks.find().sort({symbol: 0});
```

Add `.count()` at the end of any find command that will give the number of documents found. If Microsoft's new CEO comes along and the company's rating rises to 12, how do we change that in our database via the shell? First, we must get a variable reference to the document we want to change:

```
var ms= db.stocks.findOne({symbol: "MSFT"});
```

Then, make the change as you would in the code:

```
ms.rating = 12;
```

Then, save the change with:

```
db.stocks.save(ms);
```

Verify with `find()` that the change is stored. You can create an index in the symbol field with:

```
db.stocks.ensureIndex({symbol: 1});
```

To create a backup, issue the `mongodump` command. To explore the shell and its commands further, visit the MongoDB website.

The Mongo shell showing the stocks collection

Using the mongo_dart driver to store the todo data in MongoDB

MongoDB drivers exist for a whole range of programming languages, including Dart. We will use `mongo_dart` in our app, which is a server-side driver implemented purely in Dart. Simply add `mongo_dart: any` to your app's `pubspec.yaml`, and issue pub install. In the code, write:

```
import 'package:mongo_dart/mongo_dart.dart';
```

`todo_mongodb` is a version of `todo_server_dartling_mysql`, but now use MongoDB as a persistent data source (clone the project from `https://github.com/dzenanr/todo_mongodb`). It contains a client app `todo_client_idb`, identical to the one in the previous section, which stores data in `IndexedDB`. The server part `todo_server_dartling_mongodb` can be started by running `bin/server.dart`; you should see in the editor or the console:

```
Server at http://127.0.0.1:8080;
```

If you see the following exception, it means that the mongod server has not yet been started:

```
SocketException: Connection failed (OS Error: No connection could be
made because the target machine actively refused it., errno = 10061),
address = 127.0.0.1, port = 27017.
```

Run a Dartium client (`todo_client_idb/web/app.html`) from the editor and a JavaScript client in Chrome or another browser. Fill in some tasks if you see nothing to do and click the **To Server** button. The mongod console outputs that it has created a data file with index, and that it has inserted a number of rows:

```
Fri Aug 23 11:19:55.839 [FileAllocator] allocating new datafile \data\
db\todo.1,
filling with zeroes...
Fri Aug 23 11:19:55.842 [conn1] build index todo.tasks { _id: 1 }
Fri Aug 23 11:19:55.844 [conn1] build index done.  scanned 0 total
records. 0.002
  secs
Fri Aug 23 11:19:55.846 [conn1] insert todo.tasks ninserted:1
keyUpdates:0 locks(
micros) w:412870 412ms
Fri Aug 23 11:19:56.466 [FileAllocator] done allocating datafile \
data\db\todo.1,
  size: 128MB,  took 0.625 secs
```

Synchronize the other clients by clicking their **From Server** button. To verify that the data is actually in MongoDB, open a Mongo shell by typing mongo in a console and issuing the commands to retrieve the documents from the tasks collection in the todo database:

```
> use todo
```

The output will be as follows:

```
switched to db todo
```

The command to retrieve the documents is as follows:

```
> db.tasks.find()
```

The output will be as follows:

```
{ "_id" : ObjectId("5217293b479e4132cdecef0e"), "title" :
"administration", "comp
leted" : false, "updated" : ISODate("2013-08-16T09:14:50.569Z") }  ...
```

Running test/mongodb_test.dart is an alternative to create and populate the database todo with a tasks collection. From the structure of our app, we can deduce that the data access code resides in lib/persistence/mongodb.dart, which contains the classes TodoDb and TaskCollection. Let us now see how our Dart code reaches out to MongoDB. In the main method of the server script, we see:

```
void main() {
  db = new TodoDb();                    (1)
  db.open().then((_) {                  (2)
    start();
  });
}
```

Line (1) calls the constructor from TodoDb, and in line (2), the database is opened. The following is the code from the TodoDb class:

```
class TodoDb implements ActionReactionApi {
  static const String DEFAULT_URI = 'mongodb://127.0.0.1/';
  static const String DB_NAME = 'todo';

  TodoModels domain;
  DomainSession session;
  MvcEntries model;
  Tasks tasks;
```

```
    Db db;

    TaskCollection taskCollection;

    TodoDb() {                                              (3)
      var repo = new TodoRepo();
      domain = repo.getDomainModels('Todo');
      domain.startActionReaction(this);
      session = domain.newSession();
      model = domain.getModelEntries('Mvc');
      tasks = model.tasks;
    }

    Future open() {
      Completer completer = new Completer();
      db = new Db('${DEFAULT_URI}${DB_NAME}');             (4)
      db.open().then((_) {                                  (5)
        taskCollection = new TaskCollection(this);          (6)
        taskCollection.load().then((_) {                    (7)
          completer.complete();
        });
      }).catchError(print);
      return completer.future;
    }

    close() {
      db.close();
    }

    react(ActionApi action) {
      if (action is AddAction) {
        taskCollection.insert((action as AddAction).entity);
      } else if (action is RemoveAction) {
        taskCollection.delete((action as RemoveAction).entity);
      } else if (action is SetAttributeAction) {
        taskCollection.update((action as      SetAttributeAction).
  entity);
      }
    }
  }
```

The constructor starting in line (3) does everything necessary to start up the Dartling model. The `open` method creates a new MongoDB database in line (4) (with the substituted value):

```
db = new Db('mongodb://127.0.0.1/todo );
```

The `Db` class comes from `mongo_dart`; it has an `open` method called in line (5). From the `then` keyword, we see that it returns a Future as expected. As dictated by Dartling, any change in the app's data calls react to update the model and the database, as `TodoDb` listens to actions in the model through the line:

```
domain.startActionReaction(this));
```

When an action happens, all listeners are informed about that action in the `react` method for listeners. The `TaskCollection` class, whose object is constructed in line (6), is the closest we will get to MongoDB in this project, again, using Futures throughout. The code is as follows:

```
 class TaskCollection {
static const String COLLECTION_NAME = 'tasks';
TodoDb todo;
DbCollection dbTasks;

TaskCollection(this.todo) {
  dbTasks = todo.db.collection(COLLECTION_NAME);            (8)
}

Future load() {                                            (9)
  Completer completer = new Completer();
  dbTasks.find().toList().then((taskList) {
    taskList.forEach((taskMap) {
      var task = new Task.fromDb(todo.tasks.concept, taskMap);
      todo.tasks.add(task);
    });
    completer.complete();
  }).catchError(print);
  return completer.future;
}
```

```
Future<Task> insert(Task task) {
  var completer = new Completer();
  var taskMap = task.toDb();
  dbTasks.insert(taskMap).then((_) {
    print('inserted task: ${task.title}');
    completer.complete();
  }).catchError(print);
  return completer.future;
}

Future<Task> delete(Task task) {
  var completer = new Completer();
  var taskMap = task.toDb();
  dbTasks.remove(taskMap).then((_) {
    print('removed task: ${task.title}');
    completer.complete();
  }).catchError(print);
  return completer.future;
}

Future<Task> update(Task task) {
  var completer = new Completer();
  var taskMap = task.toDb();
  dbTasks.update({"title": taskMap['title']}, taskMap).then((_){
    print('updated task: ${task.title}');
    completer.complete();
  }).catchError(print);
  return completer.future;
  }
}
```

It contains a `DbCollection` object (also defined in `mongo_dart`) named `dbTasks`, which mirrors the tasks collection in the database through the assignment in line (8) of the constructor. In line (9), its `load` method (called in the previous code snippet in line (7)) calls `find()` on `dbTasks`. When the results return, a new Task object is made for each document, found, and added to the tasks collection. The `insert`, `delete`, and `update` methods respectively call insert, remove, and update on the `DbCollection` object `dbTasks`. Notice the exceptional handling clause that will signal any error:

```
.catchError(print);
```

When a server starts, all data from a database are loaded into the model in the main memory. When the model changes, these changes are propagated immediately to the database through actions/reactions. In this approach, a database system is used only minimally: all searches for the data are done in the main memory without using the slower database system. With Dartling, a model is not dependent on MongoDB—the model does not call the `insert`, `update`, and `remove` methods. The use of (only a few methods of) the `mongo_dart` driver shields us from using and knowing the slightly more elaborate MongoDB commands in our Dart code. The complete API reference of the driver can be found at `http://vadimtsushko.github.io/mongo_dart/` `mongo_dart/Db.html`.

Again, we clearly see the advantages of using a modeling framework and a well-structured library; our data access code in lib/persistence was all we needed to adapt while changing from the MySQL version to the MongoDB version!

Summary

This chapter gave you the tools necessary for writing the client-server Dart applications that store their data in the server databases. You learned how to work with files, storing data in the JSON format. We also stored our data in a typical relational database (MySQL), using the `sqljocky` driver for Dart. Then, we gave you an intro into the document database system MongoDB, and showed you how to use it from a Dart app with the `mongo_dart` connector.

This brings us to the end of our Dart journey in this book. We hope you've enjoyed it as much as we enjoyed developing the code and writing the text for it. You now have the tools to develop all sorts of apps using Dart. Join the Dart community and start using your coding talents! Perhaps we'll meet again in the Dartiverse.

Index

Memory class 177
memory game
  about 174, 175
  board, drawing 175-177
  cells, coloring 179, 180
  cells, drawing 177, 178
  finishing touches 187, 188
  images, using 189-191
  logic 186, 187
  rules, implementing 182-185
metaprogramming 72
methods 49
model
  about 98
  concepts 99
  domain model 101
  drawing 102, 103
  exporting 104
  graphical design tool 99, 100
  Travel Impressions code,
      generating from 252-254
  validation 160
  working 101, 102
model_concepts.dart 100
Model View Controller (MVC)
    design pattern
  about 243
  defining 267-269
mongo_dart driver 362
  using, to store todo data 357-361
MongoDB
  about 333, 334
  todo data storing, mongo_dart
      driver used 357
mongodump command 356
mouseDown event handler 186
Multiton classes
  URL 302
MVP 268
MVVM 268
MySQL
  about 333
  todo, storing 335-343
MySQL Community Server installer
  URL, for installing 335

N

name conflicts
  resolving 83, 84
namedArguments property 71
named constructor 64
Name input field 156
newElement method 318
newEntity method 108
nextInt method 180
NoSQL database 354-356
noSuchMethod() method 71
notEmpty method 159

O

Object Relational Mapper
    (ORM) framework 334
ODBC-driver 334
onBlur event handler 159
onChange event handler 29, 159
onChange handler 159
onData handler 340
onDone handler 340
onMouseDown event handler 183
onProgramming method 113
openCursor method 315
operator overloading 63
operators 37, 38
Outline tab 17

P

packages 19
page elements
  style, manipulating 130, 131
parameters 50, 51
periodic method 131
polymer
  local storage, adding 229-231
  using, for category links project 222-228
Polymer.dart
  Two-way data binding 209-212
  web components with 205
polymer_links project
  creating 213
  Spiral s01 213, 214

About Packt Publishing

Packt, pronounced 'packed', published its first book "*Mastering phpMyAdmin for Effective MySQL Management*" in April 2004 and subsequently continued to specialize in publishing highly focused books on specific technologies and solutions.

Our books and publications share the experiences of your fellow IT professionals in adapting and customizing today's systems, applications, and frameworks. Our solution based books give you the knowledge and power to customize the software and technologies you're using to get the job done. Packt books are more specific and less general than the IT books you have seen in the past. Our unique business model allows us to bring you more focused information, giving you more of what you need to know, and less of what you don't.

Packt is a modern, yet unique publishing company, which focuses on producing quality, cutting-edge books for communities of developers, administrators, and newbies alike. For more information, please visit our website: www.packtpub.com.

Writing for Packt

We welcome all inquiries from people who are interested in authoring. Book proposals should be sent to author@packtpub.com. If your book idea is still at an early stage and you would like to discuss it first before writing a formal book proposal, contact us; one of our commissioning editors will get in touch with you.

We're not just looking for published authors; if you have strong technical skills but no writing experience, our experienced editors can help you develop a writing career, or simply get some additional reward for your expertise.

Learning Kendo UI Web Development

ISBN: 978-1-84969-434-6   Paperback: 288 pages

An easy-to-follow practical tutorial to add exciting features to your web pages without being a JavaScript expert

1. Learn from clear and specific examples on how to utilize the full range of the Kendo UI tool set for the web

2. Add powerful tools to your website supported by a familiar and trusted name in innovative technology

3. Learn how to add amazing features with clear examples and make your website more interactive without being a JavaScript expert

HTML5 Web Application Development By Example

ISBN: 978-1-84969-594-7   Paperback: 276 pages

Learn how to build rich, interactive web applications from the ground up using HTML5, CSS3, and jQuery

1. Packed with example applications that show you how to create rich, interactive applications, and games

2. Shows you how to use the most popular and widely supported features of HTML5

3. Full of tips and tricks for writing more efficient and robust code while avoiding some of the pitfalls inherent to JavaScript

Please check **www.PacktPub.com** for information on our titles

PUBLISHING

Easy Web Development
with Wavemaker

A practical, hands-on guide for amateur developers to
design, develop, and deploy web and mobile applications
using WaveMaker

Edward Callahan

PACKT Open source *

Easy Web Development with WaveMaker

ISBN: 978-1-78216-178-3   Paperback: 306 pages

A practical, hands-on guide for amateur developers
to design, develop, and deploy web and mobile
applications using WaveMaker

1. Develop and deploy custom, data-driven,
   and rich AJAX web and mobile applications
   with minimal coding using the drag-and-drop
   WaveMaker Studio

2. Use the graphical WaveMaker Studio IDE to
   quickly assemble web applications and learn
   to understand the project's artefacts

3. Customize the generated application and
   enhance it further with custom services
   and classes using Java and JavaScript

HTML5 for Flash Developers

Leverage your Flash skill set and learn to create content
using a wide range of HTML5 web development features

Matt Fisher

PACKT

HTML5 for Flash Developers

ISBN: 978-1-84969-332-5   Paperback: 322 pages

Leverage your Flash skill set and learn to create
content using a wide range of HTML5 web
development features

1. Discover and utilize the wide range of
   technologies available in the HTML5 stack

2. Develop HTML5 applications with external
   libraries and frameworks

3. Prepare and integrate external HTML5
   compliant media assets into your projects

Please check **www.PacktPub.com** for information on our titles

CPSIA information can be obtained at www.ICGtesting.com
Printed in the USA
BVOW09s0014050914

365427BV00006B/137/P